MOUNTAINS OF THE MIND

A History of a Fascination

Robert Macfarlane

GRANTA

Granta Publications, 12 Addison Avenue, London W11 4QR

First published in Great Britain by Granta Books, 2003
First paperback edition published by Granta Books, 2004
This paperback edition published by Granta Books, 2017

A CIP catalogue record for this book
is available from the British Library.

3 5 7 9 10 8 6 4

ISBN 978 1 78378 450 9

Typeset by M Rules

Printed and bound by CPI Group (UK) Ltd, Croydon, CR0 4YY

MOUNTAINS
OF THE MIND

'If you have ever wondered why people climb mountains, then here is your answer. Part history, part personal observation, this is a fascinating study of our (sometimes fatal) obsession with height. A brilliant book, beautifully written' Fergus Fleming

'Traditionally, words are not supposed to be able to capture what goes on above the snowline, but Robert Macfarlane's subtle, personal, many-sided cultural history of mountaineering proves tradition gloriously wrong' Francis Spufford

'A seriously good book; with learning worn lightly it leads us, sure-footed, from the time when mountains and glaciers were places of horror, abode of witches and dragons, to the Enlightenment, the cult of the sublime, through to the almost imperial and nationalist competition to colonise wild places and tame their impertinent mysteries' *Spectator*

'A beguiling mix of memoir and cultural essay ... Macfarlane puts an audacious new route up the familiar rock-face. Not many would attempt a move from George Mallory to Roland Barthes without falling flat on their faces, but he manages it with some style. It is fine writing like this, rather than the urge to plant flags on summits, which will continue to draw the followers of Eric Shipton to the mountains' *Independent*

'Macfarlane writes beautifully and has found that most crucial thing, a distinctive voice' Sara Wheeler

'This is the sort of book that restores confidence in the travel genre. Erudite, full of information you didn't know you wanted to know, and charged with the author's singular passion for his subject' Robyn Davidson

'Robert Macfarlane is for me the perfect mountain guide through blue crevasse fields, ice walls, prayer flags, Sherpas and Shangri Las. He's been up there, and come back down through the foothills to offer us his thoughtful and gracio͟u͟ t is that no one can eve

Also by Robert Macfarlane

The Wild Places
The Old Ways: A Journey on Foot
Holloway (with Dan Richards and Stanley Donwood)
Landmarks
The Lost Words (with Jackie Morris)

To my grandparents

O the mind, mind has mountains . . .

GERARD MANLEY HOPKINS, *c.* 1880

Contents

1

Possession

I thought of the resistless passion which drives men to undertake terrific scrambles. No example can deter them . . . a peak can exercise the same irresistible power of attraction as an abyss.

THÉOPHILE GAUTIER, 1868

I was a twelve-year-old in my grandparents' house in the Scottish Highlands when I first came across one of the great stories of mountaineering: *The Fight for Everest*, an account of the 1924 British expedition during which George Mallory and Andrew Irvine disappeared near the summit of Everest.

We were staying in the house for the summer. My brother and I were allowed to go anywhere except into the room at the end of the hallway, which was my grandfather's study. We played hide and seek, and I often hid in the big wardrobe in our bedroom. It smelt strongly of camphor, and there was a clutter of shoes on the floor of the wardrobe which made it difficult to stand up in. My grandmother's fur coat hung in it, too, sheathed in thin clear plastic to keep the moths away. It was strange to put a hand out to touch the soft fur and feel the smooth plastic instead.

The best room in the house was the conservatory, which my grandparents called the Sun Room. Its floor was paved with grey flagstones, always cold underfoot, and two of its walls were giant windows. On one of the windows my grandparents had stuck a black card cut-out in the shape of a hawk. It was supposed to scare away small birds but they regularly flew into the windows and killed themselves, thinking that the glass was air.

Even though it was summer, the inside of the house was filled with the cold mineral air of the Highlands, and every surface was always chilly to the touch. When we ate dinner, the chunky silver pieces of cutlery which came out of the dresser were cold in our hands. At night, when we went to bed, the sheets were icy. I would wriggle as far down the bed as I could go, and hold the top sheet down over my head to create an airlock. Then I would breathe as deeply as I could until I had warmed up the bed.

There were books everywhere in the house. My grandfather had not tried to organize them and so very different books found themselves neighbours. On a small shelf in the dining room *Mr Crabtree Goes Fishing*, *The Hobbit* and *The Fireside Omnibus of Detective Stories* shared space with two leather-bound volumes of J. S. Mill's *System of Logic*. There were several books about Russia whose titles I did not properly understand, and dozens about exploration and mountaineering.

One night, unable to sleep, I came downstairs for something to read. Against one side of the hallway was a long pile of books lying stacked on their sides. Almost at random, I pulled a big green volume out from halfway down the pile, like a brick from a wall, and carried it to the Sun Room. In the bright moonlight, I sat on one of the wide stone window-ledges and started to read *The Fight for Everest*.

I already knew some of the details from my grandfather, who had told me the story of the expedition. But the book, with its long descriptions, its twenty-four black-and-white photographs and its fold-out maps bearing unfamiliar place names – the Far East Rongbuk glacier, the Dzongpen of Shekar, the Lhakpa La – was far more potent than his account. As I read, I was carried out of myself and to the Himalaya. The images rushed over me. I could see the gravel plains of Tibet scrolling away to distant white peaks; Everest itself like a dark pyramid; the oxygen bottles the climbers wore on their backs and which made them look like scuba-divers; the massive ice-walls on the North Col which they scaled using ropes and ladders, like medieval warriors besieging a city; and, finally, the black T of sleeping-bags which was laid out on the snow at Camp VI to tell the climbers at the lower camps, who were staring up at the mountain's higher slopes through telescopes, that Mallory and Irvine had disappeared.

One passage of the book excited me more than any other. It was the description by Noel Odell, the expedition's geologist, of his last sighting of Mallory and Irvine:

> There was a sudden clearing of the atmosphere above me, and I saw the whole summit ridge and final peak of Everest unveiled. I noticed far away on a snow slope leading up to what seemed to me to be the last step but one from the base of the final pyramid, a tiny object moving and approaching the rock step. A second object followed, and then the first climbed to the top of the step. As I stood intently watching this dramatic appearance, the scene became enveloped in cloud . . .

Over and over I read that passage, and I wanted nothing more than to be one of those two tiny dots, fighting for survival in the thin air.

❄

That was it – I was sold on adventure. In one of the reading binges which only the expanses of childhood time permit, I plundered my grandfather's library and by the end of that summer I had read a dozen or so of the most famous real-life exploration stories from the mountains and the poles, including Apsley Cherry-Garrard's tale of Antarctic endurance, *The Worst Journey in the World,* John Hunt's *The Ascent of Everest* and Edward Whymper's bloody account of his *Scrambles amongst the Alps.*

The childish imagination has more trust in the transparency of a story than the adult imagination: a readier faith that things happened the way they are said to have done. It is more powerful in its capacity for sympathy, too, and as I read those books I lived intensely with and through the explorers. I spent evenings with them in their tents, thawing pemmican hoosh over a seal-blubber stove as the wind skirled outside. I sledge-hauled through thigh-deep polar snow. I bumped over sastrugi, tumbled down gullies, clambered up arêtes and strode along ridges. From the summits of mountains I surveyed the world as though it were a map. Ten times or more I nearly died.

I was fascinated by the hardships these men – for they were almost all men – faced and endured. At the poles there was cold intense enough to freeze brandy solid, to freeze dogs' tongues to their coats if they tried to lick them, and to freeze men's beards to their jackets if they looked down. Woollen clothing stiffened to the rigidity of sheet metal, and had to be beaten with hammers to make it bend. At night the explorers melted their way inch by agonizing inch into their reindeer-hair sleeping-bags, which the cold had hardened into icy scabbards. In the mountains there were the cornices that overhung cliff-edges like horizontal waves, the invisible attacks of altitude, and avalanches and blizzards which could whitewash the world in an instant.

Except for Hillary and Tensing's successful ascent of Everest in 1953, and Ernest Shackleton's salvation of his entire crew in 1916 –

Worsley's miraculous navigation, the little *James Caird* steering its impeccable line across 800 miles of stormy southern ocean, Shackleton remaining imperturbable while above him Europe fractured like pack-ice – almost all of these stories resulted in death or mutilation of some sort. I liked these grisly details. In some of the polar stories barely a page went by without the loss of a crew member or a body part. Occasionally crew member meant body part. Scurvy ravaged the explorers as well, destabilizing the flesh so that it fell from bones like wet biscuit. One man was so badly afflicted that blood seeped from pores all over his body.

There was also something about the setting of these stories, the stages on which they took place, which stirred me profoundly. I was attracted by the bleakness of the places these men got to – the parsimony of the landscapes of mountain and pole, with their austere, Manichean colour scheme of black and white. The human values in the stories were polarized, too. Bravery and cowardice, rest and exertion, danger and safety, right and wrong: the unforgiving nature of the environment sorted everything into these neat binaries. I wanted my life to be this clear in its lines, this simple in its priorities.

I came to love them, these men: the polar explorers with their sledges, their songs and their soft spot for penguins; and the mountaineers with their pipes, their insouciance and their unfeasible stamina. I loved how inconsistent their rough appearance – their indestructible tweed breetches, their bristling mutton-chops and moustaches, the silk and the bear grease with which they insulated themselves against the cold – seemed to be with their almost fastidious sensitivity to the beauties of the landscapes they moved in. Then there was the combination of aristocratic finickiness (the sixty tins of quail in *foie gras*, the bow-ties and the vintage Montebello champagne that were carried on the 1924 Everest expedition, for example) with enormous hardihood. And their acceptance that a violent death was, if not probable, certainly very possible.

They seemed to me then the ideal travellers: unfazed by adversity and unassuming in person. I longed to be like them. I longed in particular for the thermostat of little Birdie Bowers, Scott's right-hand man, who, during the voyage south on the *Terra Nova*, washed on deck every morning in a bucket of sea water, and who was able to sleep – to *sleep* – in temperatures down to –30°C.

Above all, I was drawn to those men who travelled to climb the high peaks of the Greater Ranges. So many of them died. I learned the roll-call by heart: Mallory and Irvine on Everest, Mummery on Nanga Parbat, Donkin and Fox on Koshtan-Tau . . . The list went on and on, through the ranks of the less familiar. The imaginative light the mountaineers cast over me was like that cast by the polar expeditions – the beauty and danger of the landscape, the immensities of space, the utter uselessness of it all – but with high altitudes in place of high latitudes. To be sure these people had their faults. They were beset by the sins of their age: racism, sexism and an unflagging snobbery. And mingled with their bravery was an acute selfishness. But I didn't notice these traits at the time. All I saw was impossibly brave men stepping out into the brilliant light of the unknown.

The book which undoubtedly made the deepest impression on me was Maurice Herzog's *Annapurna*, dictated by Herzog from a hospital bed in 1951. He couldn't write it himself because he had no fingers left. Herzog was the leader of a team of French mountaineers which, in the spring of 1950, travelled to the Nepal Himalaya with the aim of being the first group to summit one of the world's fourteen 8,000-metre peaks.

After an arduous month of reconnaissance, and with time running out before the arrival of the monsoon, the French team made their way into the heart of the Annapurna range, a lost world of ice and rock locked off by a ring of the highest mountains on earth. 'We were in a savage and desolate cirque of mountains never before seen by man,' wrote Herzog.

> No animal or plant could exist here. In the pure morning light this absence of all life, this utter destitution of nature, seemed only to intensify our own strength. How could we expect anyone else to understand the peculiar exhilaration that we drew from this barrenness, when man's natural tendency is to turn towards everything in nature that is rich and generous?

Gradually, the team moved up the mountain, establishing successively higher camps. The altitude, the extreme cold and the load-bearing began to take their toll. But as Herzog grew physically weaker, so his conviction strengthened that the summit was attainable. Eventually, on 3 June, he and a climber called Louis Lachenal left Camp V, the highest camp, in a bid for the top of Annapurna.

This final stage of the mountain involved the ascent of a long, curving ramp of ice the team had nicknamed the Sickle glacier, and then of a steep band of rock which protected the summit itself. Aside from this band, the route offered nothing serious in the way of technical obstacles and, keen to save weight, Lachenal and Herzog left their rope behind them.

The weather was immaculate when they departed Camp V, with a pristine sky. Clear skies bring the lowest temperatures, though, and the air was so cold that both men felt their feet freezing inside their boots as they climbed higher. Quite soon it became apparent that they would have to turn back or run the risk of severe frostbite. They carried on.

In his account of the climb, Herzog describes becoming progressively more detached from what was happening to him. The clarity and thinness of the air, the crystalline beauty of the mountains and the strange painlessness of frostbite conspired to send him into a state of numbed serenity, which made him insensitive to his worsening injuries:

> There was something unusual in the way I saw Lachenal and everything around us. I smiled to myself at the paltriness of our efforts. But all sense of exertion was gone, as though there were no longer any gravity. This diaphanous landscape, this quintessence of purity – these were not the mountains I knew; they were the mountains of my dreams.

Still in this trance – still immune to pain – he and Lachenal forced a way through the final rock band, and reached the summit:

> I felt my feet freezing, but paid little attention. The highest mountain to be climbed by man lay under our feet! The names of our predecessors on these heights chased each other through my mind: Mummery, Mallory and Irvine, Bauer, Welzenbach, Tilman, Shipton. How many of them were dead – how many had found on these mountains what, to them, was the finest end of all . . . I knew the end was near, but it was the end that all mountaineers wish for – an end in keeping with their ruling passion. I was consciously grateful to the mountains for being so beautiful for me that day, and as awed by their silence as if I had been in church. I was in no pain, and had no worry.

The pain and the worry came later. While descending the rock-band, Herzog dropped his gloves and, by the time he reached Camp IV, he was barely able to walk. Both his feet and his hands were severely frostbitten. During the desperate retreat down steep ground to Base Camp, he fell and smashed several bones in his already devastated feet. When he was forced to abseil, the ropes ripped away the flesh of his hands in thick strips.

Once the terrain became less precipitous, it was possible for Herzog to be carried, and he was portaged off the mountain first by piggy-back, then in a basket, then on a sledge and finally on a stretcher. During the retreat, his feet and hands were wrapped and bagged in plastic to save them from further harm. When they reached camp each night, Oudot, the expedition doctor, injected novocaine, spartocamphor and penicillin into Herzog's femoral and brachial arteries, pushing the long needle in through the left and right flanks of his groin, and the bends of his elbows: an experience so painful that Herzog begged for death in preference. By the time he was off the mountain, Herzog's feet had turned black and brown; by the time they reached the safety of Gorakpur, Oudot had amputated almost all of his toes and fingers.

I read *Annapurna* three times that summer. It was obvious to me that Herzog had chosen wisely in going for the top, despite the subsequent costs. For what, he and I were agreed, were toes and fingers compared to having stood on those few square yards of snow? If he had died it would still have been worth it. This was the lesson I took away from Herzog's book: that the finest end of all was to be had on a mountain-top – from death in valleys preserve me, O Lord.

Twelve years after I first read *Annapurna* – twelve years during which I had spent most of my holidays in the mountains – running my finger along the spines in a second-hand bookshop in Scotland, I came across another copy. That night I sat up late and read it through again, and again fell under its spell. Soon afterwards, I booked flights and a climbing partner – an Army friend of mine called Toby Till – for a week in the Alps.

We arrived in Zermatt in early June, hoping to climb the Matterhorn before the summer crowds clogged it up. But the mountain was still thickly armoured with ice: too dangerous for us to attempt. So we drove round to the next valley, where the thaw was supposed to be a little more advanced. Our plan was to camp high overnight, and then the following morning ascend a mountain called the Lagginhorn by its easy south-east ridge. At 4,010 metres, I reflected briefly, the Lagginhorn was almost exactly half the height of Annapurna.

It snowed that night, and I lay awake listening to the heavy flakes falling on to the flysheet of our tent. They clumped together to make dark continents of shadow on the fabric, until the drifts became too heavy for the slope of the tent and slid with a soft hiss down to the ground. In the small hours the snow stopped, but when we unzipped the tent door at 6 a.m. there was an ominous yellowish storm light drizzling through the clouds. We set off apprehensively towards the ridge.

Once we were on it, the ridge turned out to be harder than it looked from below. The difficulty came from the old, rotten snow which was cloaking the ridge to a depth of several feet, together with six inches of fresh fall lying on top of it, uncompacted and sticky. Rotten snow is either granular, like sugar, or forms a crunchy matrix of longer, thinner crystals which have been hollowed out and separated from one another. Either way, it is unstable.

Instead of picking our way cleanly from rock to rock, we had to clamber along the snow, never sure if there was a rock beneath each foot placement, or air. There was no path broken to guide us, either: evidently nobody had been up the ridge since the previous summer. And it was cold, too, violently cold. Where my nose ran, the liquid froze to my face in plump trails. The wind made my eyes water, and the eyelashes on my right eye froze together. I had to separate them by pulling my eyelids apart.

After two hours of work we were nearing the summit, but the angle of the ridge was becoming more severe and our progress had become even slower. I could feel the cold chilling me deep inside. My brain, too, felt slower, more slurred, as though the temperature had congealed my thought processes, turned them viscous. We could have turned back, of course. We carried on.

The final fifty feet of the mountain were very steep indeed, and deep in old, unsound snow. I stopped and assessed the situation. It looked as though the mountain could shuck all the snow off at any moment, like shrugging off a coat. Now and again little avalanches scurried past me. I heard the clatter of a rock-fall on the east face of the mountain.

I was jammed into the snow with the toes of my boots, the slope rearing up in front of my face. I tilted my head right backwards and looked up to the skyline. Clouds were hurtling over the summit, and for a moment it felt as though the mountain was toppling slowly on to me.

I turned back and called down to Toby, twenty feet below me, 'Do we go on? I don't like the look of this stuff at all. I reckon the whole lot could go at any time.'

Below Toby, the slope narrowed down to a chute which funnelled out over the precipices on the south face of the ridge. If I slipped, or the snow gave way, I'd slide past Toby, pull him off, and we'd free-fall hundreds of feet down to the glacier.

'Of course we do, Rob, of course we do,' Toby called up.

'Right.'

I had only one ice-axe with me, but the slope was severe enough to need two. Some improvisation was necessary. I transferred the axe to my left hand and made the fingers of my right hand as rigid as possible. I would try to stab them into the snow, using them as an axe-head to give myself purchase. Nervously, I started to climb.

The snow held, the ad hoc axe worked, and suddenly we were there, on a summit the size of a kitchen table, clasping the iron-piping cross which peeked out of the thick snow on the summit, terrified and elated at once. To every side of us the mountain fell away. It felt as though we were balanced on the pinnacle of the Eiffel Tower. The clouds had cleared and a glossy white light had replaced the murk of the early morning. I spotted the yellow dot of our tent thousands of feet below. Seen from this height, the glacier which we had crossed the previous day to reach the base of the ridge resolved itself into a pattern of shallow pale billows. I could see dozens of tiny meltwater lakes which had formed in the hollows between the billows, winking at me like shields in the sun. Their blueness was startling. To our west, the light of the rising sun poured down the mountain faces of the Mischabel range. The wind was fierce, drumming against the skin of my cheeks until it was numb, and pushing coldly through the gaps in my clothing.

I looked down at my hands. I had been wearing thin gloves all the way up and, from jabbing them into the ice slope, three fingertips on the right-hand glove had been ripped off. I couldn't feel those fingers. In fact, I realized with a strange lack of alarm, I couldn't feel the hand at all. I held it up close to my streaming eyes. The fingertips which were exposed to the freezing air had turned a waxy yellow colour and become translucent, like old cheese.

I didn't have any spare gloves. But there wasn't time to worry about it anyway, because the rotten snow which had just about tolerated our weight during the ascent would already be melting in the morning sun. We needed to get down as fast as possible.

We moved quickly and efficiently during the descent, until we reached what looked like our final obstacle. It was a snow bridge, a thin, sagging ridge of snow maybe thirty feet long suspended between two rock pinnacles – like a sheet pegged up at either end. It was far too sharp and fragile to walk along the top of, and there was no way to climb down and round it. We'd have to climb out along its side, as we had done on the way up, with even less guarantee that the whole structure wouldn't collapse and send us plummeting down to the glacier.

Toby began to kick himself a little bucket seat in the soft snow.

'I take it from your behaviour that you'd like me to go first?' I asked.

'Yes, please, that'd be grand.'

I edged out along the near-vertical side of the ridge, kicking my feet into its side, the rope bowing horizontally between me and Toby. Where I kicked my feet in, the snow slid away like wet sugar, with a hiss. Here I am, I thought, standing on a more or less vertical wall of slushy snow, edging crabwise across its face, with frostnip in three fingers and only one axe. I cursed Maurice Herzog. Then I glanced down.

Between my legs I could see a whole lot of nothing. I kicked another crampon in, and a big slab of rotten snow lurched off from beneath my foot and cart-wheeled away towards the glacier, disintegrating as it went. I hung there, my arms raised above me, watching the snow tumble. A tingling began in my buttocks and then scampered to my groin and my thighs, and soon my whole midriff was encased in a humming, jostling swarm of fear. The space felt vast and malevolently active, as though it were inhaling me; pulling me off into its emptiness.

One axe only – why did I bring only one? Again, I used my right hand, the hand with the waxy fingers, to stab into the snow. The fingers didn't hurt, which helped. And so I carried on, keeping up a rhythm. Kick, kick, stab, stab, swear. Kick, kick, stab, stab, swear.

We made it, of course – I wouldn't be writing this otherwise – and as we sledged down the remaining slopes to our tent on our rucksacks, we whooped with joy and relief at having got the summit and made it back.

Sitting on a boulder outside the tent two hours later, I stared at my fingers with a fatigued disinterest. It had turned into a bright day, warm and windless, and the landscape was illuminated with the exact, egalitarian sunlight of high places. Sound carried precisely through the thin air, and I could hear the clanking and talking of climbers descending the Weissmies, half a mile or so away. My right hand didn't particularly feel like part of me. But, I was vaguely relieved to notice, only the pads of three fingers were affected, and those not to any serious depth. When I tapped them against the rock they made a hard, hollow sound, like wood knocking on metal. I got out my penknife and started to whittle at them. On the flat grey rock between my knees grew a pile of little iotas of skin. Eventually, when I had whittled down to pink skin, and my fingers had started to hurt at each scrape of the knife, I cremated the pyre of shavings in the orange flame of a lighter. They went with a crackle and the scent of charred flesh.

Three centuries ago, risking one's life to climb a mountain would have been considered tantamount to lunacy. The notion barely existed, indeed, that wild landscape might hold any sort of appeal. To the orthodox seventeenth- and early eighteenth-century imagination, natural scenery was appreciated largely for the extent to which it spoke of agricultural fecundity. Meadows, orchards, grazing fields, the rich sillion of crop lands – these were the ideal components of a landscape. Tamed landscapes, in other words, were attractive: landscapes which had had a human order imposed upon them by the plough, the hedgerow and the ditch. As late as 1791 William Gilpin noted that 'the generality of people' found wilderness dislikeable. 'There are few,' he continued, 'who do not prefer the busy scenes of cultivation to the greatest of nature's rough productions.' Mountains, nature's roughest productions, were not only agriculturally intractable, they were also aesthetically repellent: it was felt that their irregular and gargantuan outlines upset the natural spirit-level of the mind. The politer inhabitants of the seventeenth century referred to mountains disapprovingly as 'deserts'; they were also castigated as 'boils' on the earth's complexion, 'warts', 'wens', 'excrescences' and even, with their labial ridges and vaginal valleys, 'Nature's *pudenda*'.

Moreover, mountains were dangerous places to be. It was believed that avalanches could be triggered by stimuli as light as a cough, the foot of a beetle, or the brush of a bird's wing as it swooped low across a loaded snow-slope. You might fall between the blue jaws of a crevasse, to be regurgitated years later by the glacier, pulped and rigid. Or you might encounter a god, demi-god or monster angry at having their territory trespassed upon – for mountains were conventionally the habitat of the supernatural and the hostile. In his famous *Travels*, John Mandeville described the tribe of Assassins who lived high among the peaks of the Elbruz range, presided over by the mysterious 'Old Man of the Mountains'. In Thomas More's *Utopia* the Zapoletes – a 'hideous, savage and fierce' race – are reputed to dwell 'in the high mountains'. True, mountains had in the past provided refuge for beleaguered peoples – it was to the mountains that Lot and his daughters fled when they were driven out of Zoar, for instance – but for the most part they were a form of landscape to be avoided. Go around mountains by all means, it was thought, along their flanks or between them if absolutely necessary – as many merchants, soldiers, pilgrims and missionaries had to – but certainly not up them.

During the second half of the 1700s, however, people started for the first time to travel to mountains out of a spirit other than necessity, and a coherent sense began to develop of the splendour of mountainous landscape. The summit of Mont Blanc was reached in 1786, and mountaineering proper came into existence in the middle of the 1800s, induced by a commitment to science (in the sport's adolescence, no respectable mountaineer would scale a peak without at the very least boiling a thermometer on the summit) but very definitely born of beauty. The complex aesthetics of ice, sunlight, rock, height, angles and air – what John Ruskin called the 'endless perspicuity of space; the unfatigued veracity of eternal light' – were to the later nineteenth-century mind unquestionably marvellous. Mountains began to exert a considerable and often fatal power of attraction on the human mind. 'The effect of this strange Matterhorn upon the imagination is indeed so great,' Ruskin could claim proudly of his favourite mountain in 1862, 'that even the gravest philosophers cannot resist it.' Three years later the Matterhorn was climbed for the first time; four of the successful summitteers fell to their deaths during the descent.

By the end of the century the Alpine peaks had all been climbed – mostly by the British – and almost all the Alpine passes mapped. The so-called Golden Age of mountaineering had come to an end. Europe was considered by many to be *passé*, and mountaineers began to turn their attention to the Greater Ranges, where they exposed themselves to extreme hardship and even greater risks in their bids to reach the summits of Caucasian, Andean and Himalayan mountains – Ushba, Popocatépetl, Nanga Parbat, Chimborazo, or Kazbek, where Vulcan was said to have chained and bolted Prometheus to the rock.

The imaginative potency of these greater peaks around the turn of the nineteenth century was formidable, and they frequently became objects of obsession within the minds of their individual admirers. Kanchenjunga, the 8,000-metre peak visible in good weather from the white-roofed hill-station of Darjeeling, enthralled decades of sahibs and memsahibs escaping the lowland heat of the Indian summer. 'Clear and clean against the intense blue sky the snowy summit of Kinchinjunga,' intoned Francis Younghusband, the Great

Gamer who led the British attack on Tibet in 1904, 'ethereal as spirit, white and pure in the sunshine . . . We are uplifted.' An avid public followed the fortunes of Martin Conway's bold 1892 expedition to Gasherbrum in the Karakorum via dispatches to *The Times* of London. And Everest, the highest and most potent of them all, came to enchant the British *entière*, who considered it very much their mountain. Among the enchanted was George Mallory, whose death on its shoulder in 1924 shocked the nation. A newspaper obituary for Mallory and Irvine drew admiring attention to the 'close link of minds between the people at home and the assailants themselves'.

Today, the emotions and attitudes which impelled the early mountaineers still prosper in the Western imagination: indeed if anything they are more unshiftably ensconced there. Mountain-worship is a given to millions of people. The vertical, the ferocious, the icy – all these are now automatically venerated forms of landscape, images of which permeate an urbanized Western culture increasingly hungry for even second-hand experiences of wildness and wilderness. Mountain-going has been one of the fastest growing leisure activities of the past twenty years. An estimated 10 million Americans go mountaineering annually, and 50 million go hiking. Some 4 million people in Britain consider themselves to be hill-walkers of one stripe or another. Global sales of outdoor products and services are reckoned at $10 billion annually, and growing.

What makes mountain-going peculiar among leisure activities is that it demands of some of its participants that they die. In seven murderous weeks in the Alps in the summer of 1997, 103 people were killed. The average annual death toll on the Mont Blanc massif comes to almost three figures. Some winters more people perish in the mountains of Scotland than on the roads surrounding them. When Mallory climbed Everest, it was the last bastion of unconquerable earth, the 'Third Pole'. It is now a gargantuan, tawdry, frozen Taj Mahal, an elaborately frosted wedding-cake up and down which climbing companies annually yo-yo hundreds of under-experienced clients. Its slopes are studded with modern corpses: most lie within what has become popularly known as the Death Zone, the altitude bracket within which the human body enters a gradual but unstoppable process of degeneration.

Over the course of three centuries, therefore, a tremendous revolution of perception occurred in the West concerning mountains. The qualities for which mountains were once reviled – steepness, desolation, perilousness – came to be numbered among their most prized aspects.

So drastic was this revolution that to contemplate it now is to be reminded of a truth about landscapes: that our responses to them are for the most part culturally devised. That is to say, when we look at a landscape, we do not see what is there, but largely what we think is there. We attribute qualities to a landscape which it does not intrinsically possess – savageness, for example, or bleakness – and we value it accordingly. We *read* landscapes, in other words, we interpret their forms in the light of our own experience and memory, and that of our shared cultural memory. Although people have traditionally gone into wild places in some way to escape culture or convention, they have in fact perceived that wilderness, as just about everything is perceived, through a filter of associations. William Blake put his finger on this truth. 'The tree,' he wrote, 'which moves some to tears of joy is, in the eyes of others, only a green thing which stands in the way.' The same, historically, holds for mountains. For centuries they were regarded as useless obstructions – 'considerable protuberances', as Dr Johnson dismissively dubbed them. Now they are numbered among the natural world's most exquisite forms, and people are willing to die for love of them.

What we call a mountain is thus in fact a collaboration of the physical forms of the world with the imagination of humans – a mountain of the mind. And the way people behave towards mountain has little or nothing to do with the actual objects of rock and ice themselves. Mountains are only contingencies of geology. They do not kill deliberately, nor do they deliberately please: any emotional properties which they possess are vested in them by human imaginations. Mountains – like deserts, polar tundra, deep oceans, jungles and all the other wild landscapes that we have romanticized into being – are simply there, and there they remain, their physical structures rearranged gradually over time by the forces of geology and weather, but continuing to exist over and beyond human perceptions of them. But they are also the products of human perception; they have been *imagined* into existence down the centuries. This book tries to plot how those ways of imagining mountains have altered over time.

A disjunction between the imagined and the real is a characteristic of all human activities, but it finds one of its sharpest expressions in the mountains. Stone, rock and ice are significantly less amenable to the hand's touch than to the mind's eye, and the mountains of the earth have often turned out to be more resistant, more fatally real, than the mountains of the mind. As Herzog discovered on Annapurna, and I discovered on the Lagginhorn, the mountains one gazes at, reads about, dreams of and desires are not the mountains one climbs. These are matters of hard, steep, sharp rock and freezing snow; of extreme cold; of a vertigo so physical it can cramp your stomach and loosen your bowels; of hypertension, nausea and frostbite; and of unspeakable beauty.

❄

There is a letter which George Mallory wrote to his wife Ruth during the 1921 reconnaissance expedition to Everest. The advance guard of the expedition was camped fifteen miles from the mountain, between a Tibetan monastery and the tongue of the glacier which swept down from the base of Everest, where ice broke, as Mallory described it, 'like the huge waves of a brown angry sea'. It was an arduous place to be; cold, high and wind-blasted, the wind given body by particles of snow and dust so that it snaked between the rocks in grubby currents. Mallory had spent that day – 28 June – making the first approaches to the mountain on which he would die three years later. It had been an exhausting day: up at 3.15 a.m., and not back until after 8 p.m., covering many miles over glacial ice, moraine and rock. Twice he had fallen into pools of freezing water.

After the day's end Mallory lay, exhausted, in his cramped and sagging little tent, and wrote a letter home to Ruth by the granular light of a Tilley lamp. He knew that by the time his letter reached her in England a month later, his work on the mountain would probably have been completed for that year, one way or another. Much of the letter was taken up with an account of the day's efforts, but in his concluding paragraphs Mallory tried to describe to Ruth how he felt about being in such a place, attempting such a feat. 'Everest has the most steep ridges and appalling precipices that I have ever seen,' he wrote to her. 'My darling . . . I can't tell you how it possesses me.'

This book tries to explain how this is possible; how a mountain can come to 'possess' a human being so utterly; how such an extraordinary force of attachment to what is, after all, just a mass of rock and ice, can be generated. For this reason, it is a history which scrutinizes not the ways that people have gone into the mountains, but the ways that they have imagined they were going into them, how they have felt about them and how they have perceived them. For this reason it doesn't deal in names, dates, peaks and heights, like the standard histories of the mountains, but instead in sensations, emotions and ideas. It isn't really a history of mountaineering at all, in fact, but a history of the imagination.

'To me / High mountains are a feeling', declared Byron's Childe Harold, as he stared reflectively into the still waters of Lac Leman. Each of the following chapters tries to trace a genealogy for a different way of feeling about mountains, to show how that feeling was formed, inherited, reshaped and passed on until it became accepted by an individual or an age. The final chapter discusses how Mount Everest came to possess George Mallory, to cause him to leave his wife and family, and eventually to kill him. Mallory exemplifies the themes of the book, for in him all of these ways of feeling about mountains converged with unusual and lethal force. In this chapter, I have blended Mallory's letters and journals together with my own suppositions to write a speculative recreation of the three Everest expeditions of the 1920s in which Mallory took part.

To begin to trace these genealogies of feeling about mountains, we need to move backwards in time – back past me edging nervously along the sheet of snow in the Alps; back past Herzog standing on the top of Annapurna, the names of his illustrious predecessors chasing through his brain; back past Mallory at the base of Everest, scribbling his letter to Ruth on his camp-bed with the Tilley lamp roaring quietly away in the corner; back past four men falling down the cliffs of the Matterhorn in 1865; back towards the time when this modern repertoire of feelings about mountains was just beginning to form. Back, in fact, to the unseasonable cold of an Alpine pass in the summer of 1672, where the philosopher and churchman Thomas Burnet is guiding his young aristocratic charge, the Earl of Wiltshire, over the Alps and down to Lombardy. Because before mountains could become loved, a past had to be defined for them, and for that Burnet was to prove essential.

2

The Great Stone Book

Our imaginations may be awed when we look at the mountains
as monuments of the slow working of stupendous forces of
nature through countless millenniums.

LESLIE STEPHEN, 1871

August 1672 – the high noon of a continental summer. In Milan and
Geneva the citizens are sweltering beneath a strong European sun.
Many thousands of feet above them, among the snows of the
Simplon Pass – one of the major crossing points of the European
Alps – shivers Thomas Burnet. Shivering with him is the young Earl
of Wiltshire, great-great-grandson of Thomas Boleyn, the father of
the ill-starred Anne. The boy, his family have decided, needs educat-
ing and Burnet, an Anglican churchman possessed of a prodigious
and restive imagination, has taken what will be a decade-long sab-
batical from his fellowship at Christ's College, Cambridge, to act as
chaperone and cicerone to a succession of teenage aristocrats – of
whom the young earl is the first.

For Burnet it is an excuse to see the Catholic continent. They
will cross the Simplon Pass with their sullen guide and his train of

braying mules, and then travel southwards, past the long gleam of Lake Maggiore, through the orchards and villages of the foothills, across the green baize of the Lombardy Plains, and down finally to the pale and edifying cities of Northern Italy – Milan first among them – which the boy must see.

Before that, though, the crossing. There is little to recommend the Simplon Pass. A rudimentary hostelry exists at its highest point, but it isn't a pleasant place for a night's sleep. The cold is intrusive, and there are bears and wolves in the area. And the hostelry itself is really a shack, staffed by Savoyards who grudgingly double as shepherds and hoteliers.

Yet, despite these multiple discomforts, Burnet is happy. For here, among the mountains, he has discovered somewhere utterly unlike anywhere else: a place that has for the instant stalled his powers of comparison. This landscape is literally, to Burnet, like nothing else on earth. Despite the summer month, snow lies about in deep drifts, sculpted and frozen by the wind and apparently impervious to the sunshine. In the light it has a gold dazzle to it, while in the shadow it looks the creamy grey-white of cartilage. Rocks as big as buildings are scattered about, and throw complexities of blue shadow around themselves. The sound of distant thunder rolls in from the south, but the only thunderheads to be seen are thousands of feet beneath Burnet, massing over the Piedmont. He is, he realizes with delight, *above* the storm.

Down in Italy are the celebrated ruins of Rome, which Burnet knows the young earl must tour as part of his education in antiquity. Burnet himself is not immune to the magnificence of Rome's broken temples, and the gilded, weeping saints who fill the niches in the churches. But there is something up here, in what he will later describe as 'these sonic mountainous parts', amid the gargantuan rubble of the Alps, which to Burnet is infinitely more suggestive and overwhelming than Rome's ruins. Even though his age demands that he find them hostile and repulsive, Burnet is unaccountably affected by the mountains. 'There is something august and stately in the Air of these things,' he wrote after the Simplon crossing, 'that inspires the mind with great thoughts and passions . . . as all things have that are too big for our comprehension, they fill and overbear the mind with their Excess, and cast it into a pleasing kind of stupor and imagination.'

During his ten years on the continent Thomas Burnet and his various young wards would cross the Alps and the Apennines on several occasions. Gradually, the repeated sight of these 'wild, vast, and indigested heaps of Stones and Earth' fostered in Burnet a desire to understand the origin of this alien landscape. How had the rocks come to be so dispersed? And why did the mountains have such a powerful psychic effect on him? So deeply did the mountains strike Burnet's imagination and his investigative instincts that he decided he could not 'feel easie, till I could give my self some tolerable account how that confusion came in Nature'.

Thus it was that Burnet began work on his stylish, apocalyptic masterpiece, the first book to envisage a past for mountains, those most apparently timeless of objects. Burnet was writing at an ominous period in Europe. In 1680 and 1682 unusually lurid comets were seen in the skies. Edmond Halley, having taken celestial sightings from the top of a volcano, had tracked and named his own fiery messenger, and had (correctly) forecast its return in 1759. Thousands of pamphlets were printed across Europe predicting the catastrophes which would imminently blight the civilized lands – the deaths of monarchs, storm winds stripping the fields, drought, shipwrecks, pestilence and earthquakes.

It was into this saturated atmosphere of signs and portents that Thomas Burnet's *The Sacred Theory of the Earth* dropped in 1681, published at first in Latin in a discreet print-run of twenty-five copies, and carrying a pert little dedication to the King (which insinuated His Majesty's stupidity). Burnet's book looked not forward to possible future catastrophes, but backward to the biggest disaster of them all – the Flood. It was *The Sacred Theory* which began the erosion of the biblical orthodoxy that the earth had always looked the same, and it was *The Sacred Theory* which would crucially shape the ways in which mountains were perceived and imagined. That we are now able to imagine a past – a deep history – for landscapes is in part the result of Burnet's decade-long rumination on ruination.

Before Burnet, ideas about the earth lacked a fourth dimension – time. What, it was felt, could be more permanent, more incontestably *there* than mountains? They had been cast by God in their current poses, and would remain thus always and for ever. It was the biblical account of the Creation which, prior to the eighteenth century, determined how the earth's past was imagined, and according to the Bible the beginning of the world had been a relatively recent event. In the 1600s several ingenious attempts were made to compute a date of origin for the earth from the information given in the Bible. Of these the best known was by James Ussher, Archbishop of Armagh, whose dubiously scrupulous arithmetic resolved that the birth of the earth had begun at 9 a.m. on Monday 26 October 4004 BC. Calculated in 1650, Ussher's chronology for the creation of the earth was still being printed in the shoulder notes of English Bibles in the early 1800s.

The orthodox Christian imagination of Burnet's time had thus been inoculated against perceiving a history to the earth. It was widely believed that the earth was less than 6,000 years old, and that it had not aged visibly in that time. No landscape had a past worth contemplation, for the world's surface had always looked the same. Mountains, like everything else upon the earth, had been brought into being during that first frenzied week of creativity described in Genesis. They had been established on the third day, in fact, at the same time as the polar zones were frozen and the tropics were warmed, and their appearance had not altered much since, save for the cosmetic effects of lichen growth and a little light weathering. Even the Flood had left them untouched.

Thus ran the conventional view. It was Thomas Burnet's conviction, however, that the scriptural account of Creation as it was at that time understood could not explain the appearance of the world. In particular, Burnet puzzled over the hydraulics of the Flood. Where on earth, he wanted to know – where, literally, on earth – did the water come from for a Flood so profound that it could, as the Bible specified, 'cover the very highest mountain-tops'?

To achieve a global inundation of that depth, Burnet calculated, it would have taken 'eight oceans of water'. However, the forty days of rain described in Genesis would have provided at most only one ocean: not sufficient liquid even to lap at the feet of most mountains. 'Whither shall we go to find more than seven oceans of water that we still want?' asked Burnet. He reasoned that if there had not been enough water, then there must have been less earth.

And so he set forth his theory of the 'Mundane Egg'. Immediately after Creation, he proposed, the earth had been a smooth oviform spheroid: an egg. It had been flawless in appearance and uniform in texture, without hill or vale to disrupt its lovely contours. Its porcelain surface, however, belied a complicated inner architecture. The 'Yolk' of the earth – its very centre – was filled with fire, and in increasing circles about that yolk, like round Russian dolls, were arranged 'several Orbs, one including another'. And the 'White of the Egg' (Burnet was tenacious with his metaphors) was a water-filled abyss upon which the crust of the earth floated. Thus was the Burnetian earth composed.

At birth, asserted Burnet, this young globe was unblemished on its surface, but it was not inviolable. Over the years the action of the sun desiccated the crust, and it began to crack and fracture. From beneath, the waters in the abyss started to press more urgently upon the weakened crust until, at a summons from the Creator, came 'that great and fatal Inundation' – the Deluge. The inner oceans and furnaces finally ruptured the shell of the earth. Sections of the earth's crust plunged into the newly opened abyss, and the flood-waters roared up and over the remaining landmasses to create a 'great Ocean rowling in the Air without bounds or banks', as Burnet winningly described it. The physical matter of the crust was swirled about in a mêlée of rock and earth, and when the waters eventually receded they left chaos behind them. They left, in Burnet's phrase, 'a World lying in its Rubbish'.

What Burnet was suggesting was that the globe as the inhabitants of his age knew it was nothing but 'The Image or Picture of a great Ruin', and a very imperfect image at that. At a single stroke, in punishment for the impiety of the human race, God had 'dissolv'd the frame of the old World, and made us a new one out of its ruines, which we now inhabit'. And mountains, the most chaotic and charismatic of all landscape features, had not been created *ab origine* by God at all: no, they were in fact the residue left behind when the Deluge retreated, fragments of the earth's shell which had been swirled round and piled up by the colossal hydraulics of the Flood. Mountains were, in effect, gigantic souvenirs of humanity's sinfulness.

A rash of publications followed the English translation of Burnet's book in 1684. Irritated by his suggestion that the earth was defective in its present design, and by his challenge to conventional understanding

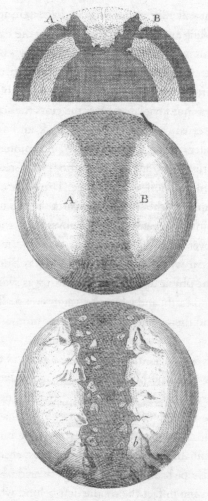

'The Deluge and Dissolution of the Earth',
in Thomas Burnet's *The Sacred Theory of
the Earth*, 2nd edn (1691). The illustration
shows three successive stages in the collapse
of the earth's crust into the watery abyss
(a). The lowest and last shows the creation
of the mountains (b) and the islands (c).

of the scriptures, many wrote to disprove his sacred theory. Quickly, the controversy made Burnet's ideas and the counter-arguments common intellectual currency – defenders and critics alike alluded to *The Sacred Theory of the Earth* simply as 'the Theory', and unspecified references to 'the Theorist' were understood to mean Burnet. Stephen Jay Gould estimates *The Sacred Theory* to have been the most widely read geologic work of the seventeenth century.

So it was that, for the first time, the intellectual imagination became involved in positing possible pasts for the wild landscapes of the earth. Attention was drawn by the Burnet controversy to the appearance of mountains. No longer could they just be wallpaper or backdrop – they had become objects worthy of contemplation in their own right. Importantly, it was also Burnet who fixed the perception of mountains as forms both awful and exciting in the minds of those who came after him: Samuel Taylor Coleridge, for example, was so stirred by Burnet's prose that he planned to render *The Sacred Theory* into a blank-verse epic, and the theories of the Sublime formulated by Joseph Addison and Edmund Burke were both shaped by Burnet's work. Burnet saw and communicated a majesty in mountainous scenery, and in doing so laid the groundwork for a wholly new way of feeling about mountains.

Burnet suffered for his brilliance. Cambridge had thrown a *cordon sanitaire* about itself to prevent the importation of harmful or counter-doctrinal ideas, and by questioning scripture Burnet had breached this line. After the Glorious Revolution he was forced to retire from court duties, and was then passed over for the Archbishopric of Canterbury. But his reputation as a writer would outlive his uneasy achievements as an Anglican divine. For in suggesting that the surface of the earth might not always have looked the same, Burnet started the ongoing inquisition into the history of the earth. 'I have,' he boasted in the preface to *The Sacred Theory*, 'retriev'd a World that had been lost, for some thousands of Years; out

Frontispiece to Thomas Burnet's *The Sacred Theory of the Earth*, 2nd edn
(1691). The seven globes represent, with a clockwise chronology, the
successive stages in the history of the earth as described in Burnet's book.

of the Memory of Man.' He was right to boast. Burnet was the first of the geological time-travellers, an explorer backwards in history – a conquistador of that most foreign of all countries, the remote past.

Although Burnet had challenged the belief that the visible world had always looked the same, he had not suggested that it was any older than the six millennia calculated by Ussher. It was not until the mid-eighteenth century that the first significant extensions of the earth's age took place. One of the chief dissenters from the so-called 'young earth' orthodoxy was the flamboyant French natural historian, Georges Buffon (1707–88). In his compendious *Natural History* (1749–88), Buffon sketched a panorama of the earth's history as divided into seven epochs, proposing that each of the days of Creation might in fact be a metaphor for a far longer period of time. Publicly, he estimated the earth to be 75,000 years old, although he sensed that this was too conservative a figure: in his notes was posthumously found a scribbled guess of several billion years.

Buffon's move was a canny one: by turning each biblical day into an epoch of indefinite length, he created the space and time necessary for geologists to begin their work of disinterring an authentic history for the earth, while at the same time staying within the bounds of respect for the scriptures. It was the work of Buffon and others like him which began the transformation of Ussher's implausibly precise dating of 4004 BC into a totem of idiotic biblical literalism.* For,

---

* Although, as Simon Winchester has recently pointed out, a 1991 poll returned that 100 million Americans believed God to have created man in his own image sometime in the last 10,000 years. The earth is thought by science to be around 5 billion years old; the first humans to have appeared *circa* 2 million years ago.

once the duration of the earth's past was no longer confined to 6,000 years, it was possible to speculate more systematically on what changes might have been wrought over wider spans of time. The science of geology could emerge and define itself in this newly old earth, proofed against accusations of blasphemy.

By the start of the 1800s, those thinkers interested in postulating a past for the earth had begun to separate into two loose schools of thought, conventionally called Catastrophism and Uniformitarianism. It should be said that geologists of the later nineteenth century – notably Charles Lyell (1797–1875) – tended to exaggerate the degree to which these two schools waged intellectual warfare on each other, and it is important to realize that, while opinions did differ, battle-lines were never clearly drawn between them.

Catastrophists believed that the history of the earth was dominated by major geophysical revolutions: one or many past *Götterdämmerung*s which had convulsed the earth with water, ice and fire, and all but extinguished life. The earth was a cemetery, a necropolis in which were interred countless now-extinct species. Drastic tidal actions, global tsunamis, severe earthquakes, volcanoes, the passing of comets: these were what had shaped and shaken up the earth's surface into its present disruption. One popular Catastrophic theory of mountain-formation suggested that, since the earth was cooling from a white-hot original state, its volume was slowly reducing and its surface was consequently prone to severe crumpling – just as the skin of an apple crinkles as it dries out. The world's mountain ranges were corrugations or crumples in the earth's skin.

The counter-theory to this violently paroxysmal vision of the earth's history was preached by the Uniformitarians. The earth had never been subject to a global catastrophe, they held. Earthquakes, yes; volcanoes, yes; tidal waves, yes – undoubtedly these phenomena had taken place throughout geological history. They were localized calamities, however: they had only racked and rearranged the landscape in their vicinity. Certainly, the earth's surface had been subject to drastic change – evidence for this was visible in any mountain range, or on any coastline. But this change had been achieved astonishingly slowly, by the forces of wear and tear which were presently at work on the surface of the earth.

Given sufficient time, argued the Uniformitarians, the conventional ordnance of nature – rain, snow, frost, river, sea, volcano, earthquake – could produce the largest effects. So what the Catastrophists took for evidence of disaster was in fact the result of a slow and enduring ground war. The cornerstone of Uniformitarian theory was that 'the present is the key to the past': in other words, the history of the earth could be inferred from the careful observation of present processes at work on its surface. It was a version of the water-dripping-on-stone idea: allow a river or a glacier enough time and it will slice a mountain in half. Time, great time – this was what the Uniformitarians needed for their theories to work, and so they ratcheted the beginning of the earth far further backwards than anyone had previously contemplated.

The most celebrated of the early Uniformitarians, usually credited with paternity of what is now called the Old Geology, was the Scotsman James Hutton (1726–97). Hutton possessed an instinctive ability to reverse physical processes, to read landscapes backwards, as it were. Like all of the founding geologists, Hutton was a prodigious walker, and for decades he strode back and forth across the Scottish landscape, attempting by a blend of induction and imagination to intuit the processes which had brought it to its present state. Fingering the white quartz which seamed the grey granite boulders in a Scottish glen, Hutton understood the confrontation that had once occurred between the two types of rock; saw how under fantastic pressure the molten quartz had forced its way into the weaknesses in the mother granite. To be with Hutton was to inhabit a world with a past so deep as to be terrifying. One of his colleagues and admirers,

John Playfair, famously described visiting a geological site on the Berwick coast with him. As Hutton explained the implications of the rock configuration, wrote Playfair, 'the mind seemed to grow giddy by looking so far into the abyss of time'.

Between 1785 and 1799 Hutton's three-volume magnum opus, *Theory of the Earth*, appeared: the distillation of decades of meditation on landscape formation. In it he proposed that the earth we presently inhabit is merely a snapshot in a series of an unknown number of cycles. The apparent permanence of mountains and coastlines is in fact an illusion born of our diminutive life-spans. Were we to live for aeons, we would witness not only the collapse of civilizations, but the utter rearrangement of the earth's surface. We would watch mountains being worn down by erosion to become plains, and we would see new landmasses being formed beneath the sea. Rubble eroded from the continents and laid down in sedimentary layers on the sea-floor would be lithified – turned to stone – by the exothermic core of the earth and then, over millions of years, would be lifted up to create new continents and new mountain ranges. Thus it was, said Hutton, that the shells which could be found embedded in the rocks of mountain-tops had not been washed there by the Deluge, but had been elevated from sea-floor to mountain-top by the patient, implacable processes of the earth.

Hutton put no parentheses around the age of the earth: according to his vision, the earth's history stretched backwards indefinitely into the past and unfurled indefinitely into the future. The final sentence of his book would toll through the centuries: 'The result therefore of our present enquiry is, that we find no vestige of a beginning, – no prospect of an end.' It was this inexpressible deepening of the earth's history that was geology's vital contribution to the common imagination.

❄

How did this geological revolution affect the way mountains were imagined? Once the geologists had shown the earth to be millions of years old and subject to immense and ongoing change, mountains could never be looked at in the same way again. Suddenly, these effigies of permanence had acquired an exciting, baffling mutability. Mountains, which seemed so durable, so eternal, had in actuality been formed, deformed and reformed over countless millennia: their current appearance was merely a phase in the perpetual cycles of erosion and uplift which determined the configuration of the earth.

A new generation of mountain-goers was drawn to the hills by the ghostly landscapes which had suddenly opened up under the scrutiny of geology. 'What I really saw as never before,' wrote Horace-Bénédict de Saussure in the 1780s, 'was the skeleton of all those great peaks whose connection and real structure I had so often wanted to comprehend.' Geology provided a reason and an excuse – scientific inquiry – for travelling to the mountains. 'A sentiment of curiosity, exceedingly natural, induces travellers from all parts of Europe to visit Mont Blanc, the highest point of the old world, and to examine the surrounding glaciers,' observed an English journalist in 1801. 'These places have recently acquired a new degree of interest – the geologue, the mineralogist, and mere amateur repair thither with avidity; and even women are amply indemnified for the fatigue of the journey by the pleasure arising from the view of objects entirely new to them.' To look at mountains was now also to look *into* them: to imagine their past. The English scientist Humphry Davy put it well in 1805:

To the geological enquirer, every mountain chain offers striking monuments of the great alterations that the globe has undergone. The most sublime speculations are awakened, the present is disregarded, past ages crowd upon the fancy, and the mind is lost in admiration of the designs of that great power who has established order which at first view appears as confusion.

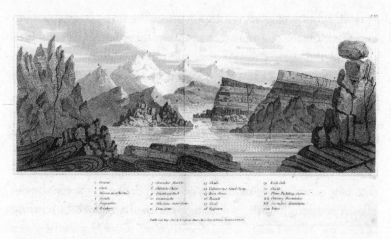

'Strata Types', frontispiece to Humphry Davy's *Elements of Agricultural Chemistry* (1813), showing the different rock layers which geology had made visible.

Here then was another vertigo – the giddiness inspired by deep time – to add to the more familiar and immediate kind one might feel on a steep mountainside. The experience of going to the mountains had become, as Burnet had suggested a century earlier, one not only of moving upwards in space, but also backwards through time.

James Hutton might have fathered geology, but he was by no means its most stylish exponent. Aside from its resonant final lines, Hutton's *Theory* was written in a prose as uniformly impenetrable as the Old Red Sandstone of which he was so fond. It would take thirty years and another legendary geologist to make truly popular geology's rapid advances and staggering exposés, and to entice even more people into the mountains. Far more than Burnet or even Hutton, it

was the Scottish geologist Charles Lyell who was responsible for edu-
cating the nineteenth century in the language and the imagination of
geology.

Charles Lyell was a lawyer before he was a geologist, and his foren-
sic training had equipped him with a writing style of extreme clarity
and elegance. Between 1830 and 1833 he published in three volumes
*The Principles of Geology: an Attempt to Explain the Former Changes of
the Earth's Surface by Reference to Causes Now in Operation,* a work
which carefully and beautifully laid out the arguments behind the
Uniformitarian view that the study of the present was the key to the
past. *Principles* quickly became required reading for the chattering
classes of its day and was widely translated: eleven revised editions
had been published by 1872.

Lyell's brilliance lay primarily in his marshalling of detail. As
Charles Darwin would do later in *The Origin of Species by Means of
Natural Selection* (1859), Lyell won over his audience with a combination of irresistibly accumulating facts – in this respect his writing
resembled the processes it was describing – and illuminating anec-
dotes. There was something appealing, too, in the democracy of the
knowledge Lyell was outlining. You did not need special equipment
or long training to decipher the earth's history: only an acute pair of
eyes, a basic knowledge of Uniformitarian principles, and curiosity
and courage enough to peer over the edge of the 'abyss of time'.
Given these minimal qualifications anyone could attend the most
exciting show on earth – its past.

To witness in action this new way of feeling about mountains, let
us turn to the year 1835, and to the town of Valparaíso, ledged precariously on the Pacific coastline of Chile. The town's name means
Paradise Valley, and a less fitting name could not have been found for
it. To begin with it does not occupy a valley, but rather the thin strip
of approximately horizontal ground that runs between the Pacific
combers and the range of red rock mountains which rise steeply up

behind the town. And it is positively not paradisal. The steady off-shore breeze which scours the surface earth, the steepness of the ground and the salty soil mean that there is no vegetation to speak of. There is little other life to be found here save for the human inhab-itants, who have made their homes in huddles of low white-washed houses with red-tiled roofs, which congregate in the stream-cuts and ravines. Near the shoreline, dories bob in rows, ready to service the big ships that come to anchor out in the deeper water – for Valparaíso, unlikely as it may seem, is Chile's principal sea-port. Over the whole scene hangs the clear, dry air of the coastal summer.

It is from Valparaíso on 14 August 1835 that Charles Darwin sets out on horseback for a long excursion into the Andean hinterland. Out in the bay is moored his ship, the ten-gun brig HMS *Beagle*, on which he is serving as scientific observer. While studying at Cambridge, Darwin had become interested in geology, and before he sailed south from Devonport on a ferociously stormy evening in December 1831, he packed the first volume of Lyell's *Principles* as reading for the long voyage out towards South America. He tested Lyell's theories in the field during a stop at the Cape Verde Islands, and by the time the *Beagle* first sighted the flatlands of Patagonia, Darwin's imagination was primed to interpret the landforms he encountered in Lyellian terms: to infer a deep past for their present appearance. 'I always feel as if my books came half out of Lyell's brains,' he would later write to a friend, Leonard Horner, 'for I have always thought that the great merit of the *Principles*, was that it altered the whole tone of one's mind & therefore that when seeing a thing never seen by Lyell, one yet saw it partially through his eyes.'

Leaving Valparaíso, Darwin first rides northwards along the coast for a day, in order to see the beds of fossilized shells which he has been told he must visit. They are astonishing – long banks of calci-fied molluscs which have been elevated, Darwin correctly deduces, by gradual crustal movement to their present resting-place several metres above the level of the sea. Having seen the shells – and having watched a gang of locals with pick and shovel plunder barrowloads of them for lime-burning – Darwin turns his horse inland, and canters up through the wide and fertile valley of Quillota ('whoever called Valparaíso Valley of Paradise must have been thinking of Quillota', he would observe later to his journal). The valley is densely packed with olive groves, and with stands of orange, peach and fig trees which have been manicured into tiny square orchards by the valley's inhabitants. On its higher slopes prolific fields of wheat flash in the sunlight, and above them rises the Bell of Quillota, a 1,900-metre peak from which there are reputed to be magnificent views. It is this mountain which Darwin has come to climb.

After spending a night in a hacienda at the foot of the mountain, Darwin procures a gaucho guide and fresh horses, and begins with difficulty to make his way up through the groves of thick-trunked palms and tall bamboo which flourish on the mountainside. The paths are not good, and by nightfall the two men are only three-quarters of the way to the summit. They pitch camp beside a spring, and beneath an arbour of bamboos the gaucho kindles a fire on which he fries beef strips, and boils water for *maté*. In the darkness the firelight dances off the walls of their arbour, and the bamboo seems briefly to Darwin like the architecture of some exotic cathedral, illuminated by flickering flames. The atmosphere is so clear and moonlit, the air so lucid, that Darwin can make out the individual masts of the ships anchored twenty-six miles away off Valparaíso, like little black streaks.

Early the following morning Darwin clambers up the greenstone blocks to the flat summit of the Bell. From there he looks across to the white towers and ramparts of the Andes, and down at the scars left on the flanks of the lower hills by the voracious Chilean gold-mining industry. The view astonishes him:

We spent the day on the summit, and I never enjoyed one more thoroughly. The pleasure of the scenery, in itself beautiful, was heightened by the many reflections which arose from the mere view of the grand range . . . Who can avoid admiring the wonderful force which has upheaved these mountains and even more so the countless ages which it must have required, to have broken through, removed, and levelled whole masses of them? It is well in this case to call to mind the vast shingle and sedimentary beds of Patagonia, which, if heaped on the Cordillera, would increase its height by so many thousand feet. When in that country, I wondered how any mountain-chains could have supplied such masses, and not have been utterly obliterated. We must not now reverse the wonder, and doubt whether all-powerful time can grind down mountains – even the gigantic Cordillera – into gravel and mud.

From his eagle's-nest perspective, Darwin's eye roves around not only in space but also within time. Indeed, the pleasure of viewing the *actual* scenery laid out before him is secondary compared with the visions he has of the *imagined* scenery – the masses of snow-capped peaks and ranges which must once have existed here but, thanks to the 'wonderful forces' of geology, no longer do. Darwin is, in effect, gazing at range on range of mountains of the mind, made newly and marvellously visible to him by Lyell's doctrines.

Moments like this litter Darwin's journals. One of the principal thrills for the many readers of his published account of the trip, *The Voyage of the Beagle* (a bestseller in its day), was to travel with Darwin not only to the storm-hammered tip of Tierra del Fuego and the silver deserts of Patagonia, but also back and forth within the recently discovered expanses of geological time. The HMS *Beagle* was one of the world's first time-travel ships – a prototype of the *Starship*

Enterprise, whose warp drive was fuelled by a mixture of Darwin's prodigious imagination and Lyell's insights.

Anyone who has spent time in wild landscapes will have experienced in some form this deepening of time which John Playfair sensed in Berwick and Darwin felt in Chile. Early one March I walked the length of Strath Nethy, a long Scottish valley which runs round the back of the Cairngorm mountains. In cross-section the glen, like all the glens in that part of the world, is shaped like a flattened U. It is shaped like this because until around 8,000 years ago the Scottish Highlands were overrun with glaciers, as were parts of Wales and Northern England, most of North America and significant sections of Europe. These glaciers moved gradually over the land: scooping it out, grinding it down, resculpting it.

Walking the glen that day, I could see, two-thirds of the way up either flank, the high-tide mark of the glacial ice, plotted by the boulders which had been cast up there in a ragged line like sea-shore flotsam. The flanks of the valley were also incised laterally with dozens of little stream-cuts. The stream-cuts had been harrowed into the bedrock granite during the millennia since the glaciers retreated from the valleys. They had been cut by the insistent fretwork of the rainwater which ran away down the sides of the ridges. Once it has found a channel, water works away at deepening it – carrying off particles of rock, using those particles to strike other particles free – until it settles into its groove, and its groove becomes its channel, and its channel its stream-cut.

Following the line of one of the stream-cuts, I scrambled up the eastern slope of the glen to the wrack-line. The heather was slippery with clumps of melting snow, and I often had to put a hand down

into it to steady myself. As I neared the boulders I startled a ptarmi-
gan, and it flew kekking up into the white sky, where it became a
silhouette.

By the time I reached the boulders my hands were cold. I rubbed
them noisily together, and then began to walk up the valley, from
boulder to boulder, imagining the ice filling up the glen like a bath.
Each rock was moated with dark earth, where the warmth it had
gathered during the day had leached out and melted the surrounding
snow. I kept walking along until the gradient steepened and I had to
drop off again into the valley floor. The path took me near a patch of
exposed rock perhaps ten square metres in area. I walked over, and
crouched down to examine it. The horizontal striations scored into it
showed that this rock had once been a scratching-post of the glacier
which had created the valley and was one of the places where it had
rubbed its tremendous underbelly along the ground.

I looked up from the rock. It had snowed recently, and the hills
visible beyond the confines of the glen were grey beneath a thin fall
of snow; their outlines softened. In the far distance their bulks could
hardly be seen against the white winter air; only a few dark strokes
defined them at all. They reminded me of charcoal sketch-work, or
the simple lines of a Chinese water-ink painting.

After two hours I reached the gateway to the valley, guarded to the
west by the cone of Stac-an-Iolaire, the Crag of the Eagle, and to the
east by Bynack More and Bynack Beg. Looking down towards the
forests of the north, I saw – russet against white – a herd of red deer,
perhaps half a mile away from me, jogging across the hillside, picking up their knees where the heather or the snow deepened. I stood
and watched for a few minutes the procession of the deer, the only
moving objects in the landscape, and was suddenly swallowed up by
time. Twenty thousand years ago, during the Upper Pleistocene era,
the heathered granite across which the deer were moving would have
been submerged beneath millions of cubic litres of ice. Sixty million

years ago floods of basalt lava would have been sluicing the land, as Scotland tore violently away from the landmasses of Greenland and North America. One hundred and seventy million years ago, Scotland would have been drifting through the northern tropics, and arid reddish deserts would have covered the area on which I was standing. About 400 million years ago, a Himalayan-scale range of mountains would have existed in Scotland, of which only the eroded stubs remain.

To understand even a little about geology gives you special spectacles through which to see a landscape. They allow you to see back in time to worlds where rocks liquefy and seas petrify, where granite slops about like porridge, basalt bubbles like stew, and layers of limestone are folded as easily as blankets. Through the spectacles of geology, *terra firma* becomes *terra mobilis*, and we are forced to reconsider our beliefs of what is solid and what is not. Although we attribute to stone a great power to hold time back, to refuse its claims (cairns, stone tablets, monuments, statuary), this is true only in relation to our own mutability. Looked at in the context of the bigger geological picture, rock is as vulnerable to change as any other substance.

Above all, geology makes explicit challenges to our understanding of time. It giddies the sense of here-and-now. The imaginative experience of what the writer John McPhee memorably called 'deep time' – the sense of time whose units are not days, hours, minutes or seconds but millions of years or tens of millions of years – crushes the human instant; flattens it to a wafer. Contemplating the immensities of deep time, you face, in a way that is both exquisite and horrifying, the total collapse of your present, compacted to nothingness by the pressures of pasts and futures too extensive to envisage. And it is a physical as well as a cerebral horror, for to acknowledge that the hard rock of a mountain is vulnerable to the attrition of time is of necessity to reflect on the appalling transience of the human body.

Yet there is also something curiously exhilarating about the contemplation of deep time. True, you learn yourself to be a blip in the
larger projects of the universe. But you are also rewarded with the
realization that you do exist – as unlikely as it may seem, you do
exist.

Charles Lyell's *Principles of Geology*, and the dozens of popular geological works which soon afterwards sought to emulate its success,
opened the eyes of the nineteenth century to the dramatic hidden
past of the earth. The common imagination began to respond to the
aesthetics of inordinate slowness; to gradual changes wrought over
epochs. And whatever one's position *vis-à-vis* the grand tectonics of
geological debate, or any of the many minor upsets and scuffles
which disturbed the science in the nineteenth century, what was
irrefutably wondrous – and terrifying – was the age of the earth: its
inexpressible antiquity. In little under half a century, geology had
unfolded the world backwards by billennia.

The seventeenth and eighteenth centuries had been the centuries
when space was extended, when the realm of the visible had suddenly
been increased by the invention of the microscope and the telescope.
We have images from that era which remind us of quite how astonishing that sudden stretching of space must have been. There is the
Dutch lens-grinder Antony van Leeuwenhoek, peering down his
rudimentary microscope in 1674 to see a host of micro-organisms
teeming in a drop of pond-water ('The motion of most of these ani-
malcules in the water was so swift, and so various upwards,
downwards, and round about, that 'twas wonderful to see . . .').
There is Galileo scrying upwards through his telescope in 1609, and
becoming the first human to realize that there are 'lofty mountains'

and 'deep valleys' on the moon. And there is Blaise Pascal's mingled wonder and horror at the realization that man is poised teeteringly between two abysses: between the invisible atomic world, with its 'infinity of universes, each with its firmament, its planets, and its earth', and the invisible cosmos, too big to see, also with its 'infinity of universes', stretching unstoppably away in the night sky.

The nineteenth century, though, was the century in which time was extended. The two previous centuries had revealed the so-called 'plurality of worlds' which existed in the tracts of space and the microcosms of atoms. What geology revealed in the 1800s was a multitude of 'former worlds' on earth, which had once existed but no longer did. Some inhabitants of these former worlds offered an excitement beyond the general thrill of antiquity. This was the range of monstrous creatures which had formerly lived on the earth: mammoths, mammals, 'sea-dragons' and dinosaurs (literally 'fearfully great lizards'), as they were christened in 1842 by the palaeo-anatomist Richard Owen. Fossilized bones and teeth had been plucked from the earth for centuries, but not until the early 1800s was it realized that some of these relics belonged to distinct, and extinct, species.

The French natural historian Georges Cuvier (1769–1832) did more than anyone to bring about this realization. For it was Cuvier who affirmed to the world the controversial fact of extinction, and in so doing created the conceptual framework needed to understand dinosaurs as fossil animals. Cuvier's test-case was the woolly mammoth: by comparing the structures of fossilized mammoth bones with those of contemporary African and Indian elephants, he proved that the fossil bones belonged to a different species. In 1804, to an astonished audience at the Institut National in Paris, Cuvier announced that huge and hirsute elephants – no longer alive upon the earth – had once inhabited France and had almost certainly stomped and herded through what were now the immaculate gardens

'The Rocks and Antediluvian Animals', frontispiece to Ebenezer Brewer's
Theology in Science (1860).

of Versailles. In terms of girth, Cuvier was a not inconsiderable man,
and inevitably he was soon nicknamed 'The Mammoth'.

Cuvier became a celebrity in his day, in part for his capacious
brain (he was reputed to have memorized the 19,000 books in his
library) but above all for his skill as an anatomist. Where James
Hutton had been possessed of a remarkable ability to deconstruct
rocks, Cuvier was able to reconstruct the megafauna of Europe
from their petrified bones: to reimagine what the beasts that once
roamed the earth might have looked like. He strung outsize skele-
tons together with wire, embedded archipelagos of bone in cement
frames, and with the help of illustrators developed the first draw-
ings of dinosaurs. To many, Cuvier's work appeared more like
thaumaturgy than taxidermy, for it conjured not only creatures
but whole ages to life. 'Is Cuvier not the greatest poet of our century?' Balzac would later write ecstatically of him. 'Our immortal
naturalist has reconstructed worlds from blanched bones. He picks

up a piece of gypsum and says to us "See!" Suddenly stone turns into animals, the dead come to life, and another world unrolls before our eyes.'

Stimulated by the new fervour for what had popularly become known as the Ancient Earth, fossil-hunting and palaeontology quickly became the European craze of the early nineteenth century. Every day, it seemed, a new dead species was discovered. An energetic sub-tribe of geologists, the fossil-hunters, sprang up. The fossil-hunters went with their knapsacks, hammers and soft brushes to where the rock was exposed: to the sea-side – like the rich Jurassic shale beds at Lyme Regis from which the renowned fossil-hunter Mary Anning prised ichthyosaurs and plesiosaurs – to creeks, quarries and river-cuts, and, of course, to the mountains. Athletically inclined fossil-hunters clambered up cliff-faces, past the different folds and pleats of rock, and wrote of how they felt themselves to be moving at speed through time, ascending an epoch with a single movement.

Many fossil-beds were pillaged by the collectors – the Victorian predilection for rendering species extinct extended even to already extinct species. Moneyed amateurs filled rooms with their finds, and for their smaller specimens invested in 'fossil chests': waist-height cabinets with rows of slide-out, glass-topped drawers, divided beneath the glass by matchwood partitions into dozens of little square holding-pens. In each pen, carefully labelled, was placed a fossil: a shark's tooth, say, or a fern impressed delicately on to a shard of shale. Fashionable little cemeteries of this sort stood in many affluent households, and people would come to gaze through the glass at these relics from former worlds, to ponder their own mortality and to contemplate the ineffable age of the earth.

The fossil craze is significant to our inquiry for two reasons. First, because it intensified the nineteenth-century fascination with the past ages of the earth. Fossils, Charles Lyell had adroitly observed in his *Principles*, are 'ancient memorials of nature . . . written in a living language', and palaeontology, like geology, taught people how to read a landscape as a history book: for what it told of the past. Indeed geology was *the* popular science of the first half of the 1800s. By 1861, even the Queen had a mineralogist by appointment. Geological tourism became a growth industry: those about to embark on a geological tour in the 1860s could pick from a range of lecture courses which would tutor them in the ways of rocks. For those who preferred the personal touch, Professor William Turl of Green Street in London offered (so his advert ran) 'individual instruction for tourists so that they can acquire sufficient knowledge to identify all the ordinary components of the crystalline and volcanic rocks to be encountered in the European mountains'.

The second and connected significance of the fossil craze was that it encouraged thousands of people outdoors, and fostered a more hands-on approach to rocks and cliffs. Indeed, the foundations of Western geology were laid down in the mountains, and mountaineering has always walked hand-in-glove with geology. Many of the pioneering early geologists – Horace-Bénédict de Saussure, and the Scotsman James David Forbes, for instance – were also pioneering mountaineers.* Saussure's four-volume *Voyages dans les Alpes* (1779–96) was both a founding work of geology and one of the first wilderness travel books. When the Geological Society of London formed in 1807, its members, aware that the implications of their science ran against the religious grain of the time, were keen to be perceived neither as fuddy-duddies nor as iconoclasts. They ended up styling themselves 'knights of the hammer': chivalric men of science

---

* Geology remained a driving force in mountaineering until well into the twentieth century – the first three Everest expeditions (1921, 1922 and 1924) were funded in part as scientific expeditions aimed at bringing back geological (and botanical) knowledge of the Everest region.

who sallied forth into the wilds in quest of knowledge. Robert Bakewell, in his *Introduction to Geology* (1813) observed that 'an additional recommendation to the study of geology, [is] that it leads its votaries to explore alpine districts . . .' As if to prove his point, the frontispiece to the first edition of his *Introduction* showed Bakewell sitting happily among the rock columns on the top of Cadair Idris.

Geology, therefore, for the early nineteenth-century public, came to suggest both a healthy outdoorsiness and a romantic sensibility: not just tinkering with old bones and stones. More than this, geology was perceived by many as a form of necromancy, which made possible a magical voyage into a past where one would encounter – as one knight of the hammer put it – 'prodigies more wonderful than fiction'. After the 1820s, when the rudiments of classical geology diffused in Europe and America, it was realized by increasing numbers of people that the mountains provided a venue where it was possible to browse the archives of the earth – the 'great stone book', as it became called.

I had two stone books as a boy. One was slim paperback called *A Guide to Rocks and Crystals*, and it provided descriptions and photographs of hundreds of different stones, whose resonant names I would roll round my mouth – *red and green serpentine, malachite, basalt, fluorspar, obsidian, smoky quartz, amethyst* – until I had learned them. I spent hours beachcombing on the Scottish coast, not for the serendipitous discoveries of the tide-line – the single flip-flop which had leapt off a passing liner, the neon globe of a fishing-float or the vulcanized corpse of a jellyfish – though these were certainly wonderful, but for the rocks which cobbled the beaches. Crunching across that geological pot-pourri with my guide in hand, I swooped upon stone after stone, gathering them up and stashing them in a canvas shoulder-bag I carried, where they clunked and squeaked against each other. It felt like being given free range in the world's finest sweet-shop: I could never quite believe I was allowed to take the stones away. I lugged them home, arranged them in troughs on the window-sill and kept them glossy and sleek with water.

I loved the colours of the stones, and their feel – the big flat ones which fitted warmly into the palm of the hand like a discus, and had rings of blue or red cutting through the background smoky grey; or the heavy granitic eggs, smoothed by epochs of oceanic massage; or flints, more jewel than stone, translucent as dark beeswax, and as deep to look into as a hologram. But what began truly to fascinate me, as I read more widely in geology, was the realization that each stone had a story attached to it: a biography which stretched backwards in time for epochs. I felt obscurely proud that my life had intersected with each of these inconceivably ancient objects; that because of me they were on a window-sill and no longer on a beach. Occasionally, I would take two stones and, cupping one in my hand, use it to shatter the other. There would be a crack, an orange sprig of fire and a smudge of rock-smoke. I would briefly be pleased that I had achieved what billennia of geophysical forces had not.

I paced over the Scottish hills and through the long glens of the Cairngorms looking for mineral treasures. My most sought-after specimens from the hillsides were lumps of rose quartz, tumbled into roundness by the rivers: beautiful with their chalky pink-and-white complexion, and their soft, pulsing luminosity. I also prized the Scottish granite, which with its fleshy pink feldspar and fatty flecks of quartz resembled a geological pâté. I read more widely about geology, and I began to understand the grammar of the Scottish landscape – how its constituent parts related to one another – and its etymology; how it had come to be. And I appreciated its calligraphy; the majuscule of the valleys and peaks, the intricate engravings of streams and rivulets, and the splendid serifs of ridge top and valley bottom.

From the summit or the slopes of every mountain I climbed with my family, my father would select a rock and carry it down in his orange canvas rucksack. He grouped them together, dozens of them, to make a rock garden. I remember a nubbed lump of gneiss, a black basalt pillow, a yard-long slab of silver mica as bright as salmon skin, and a hunk of dark igneous rock in which dozens of tiny quartz nodules were embedded. The finest of all, to my mind, was a rounded boulder of yellow-white quartz, as smooth and soft to touch as thick cream.

The other geological book I owned as a child was the chauvinistic *Boy's Guide to Fossils*. During one summer I spent in a cottage near the Scottish coast, it became my constant companion. Up among the cliff-top outcrops where the sediments lay with their rounded edges, my brother (seven) and I (nine) gathered belemnites. They were pointed and hard as bullet casings. We searched the seashore strata – hopelessly, I now realize – for trilobites. We levered rock nodes from the sea-cliffs with knives and smashed them open with hammers. We walked up to the hill lochs in the mountains above the sea, carrying little rods and minuscule black flies, and twitched trout from their water: dark little fish no more than a hand's-span in length which seemed, to my newly elongated imagination, at least a billion years old – more coelacanth than trout. But beyond the belemnites, there were no real fossil finds that year. No ammonites or ichthyosaurs. Certainly no archaeopteryx or giant prehistoric sharks. Our lack of success didn't stop me dreaming, of course: of pulling a plesiosaur skull from a soft chalk bank, or of striding over the Siberian perma-frost, stubbing my toe on the tip of a tusk, and looking down into the ice to see a mammoth staring tremulously back out at me.

Two summers after the Scottish holiday, our family set off to tour the National Parks of the American desert states. In Utah we saw the rock faces of Zion, the arches of Arches and the fretted pink obelisks of Bryce Canyon, which were arrayed up and down the valley like baroque missiles. I think it was near Zion that we pulled up at a road-side pump to feed our big American car with petrol. At one edge of the gravel forecourt was a man wearing a baseball cap. He was sitting on a dining-room chair, with an electric circular saw mounted on a frame in front of him, and a pyramid of rough rock spheres stacked like oranges to his left. We walked over to the man, and there was a conversation between him and my father. 'Pick a rock,' my father said, turning to me. The man stood up and watched me as I examined the rock pile. I wondered if they were dragon's eggs. I weighed one in my hand. It felt lighter than I expected. I whispered to my mother that it was light.

'That's a good sign,' said the man, taking the rock from me, sitting back down on the chair and placing his legs either side of the saw blade. 'Light means there's space inside. Have that one.'

He gunned the saw. Its silver-grey fangs seemed to spin first one way, then the other, and then blurred into a single immobile edge. The saw's engine began rhythmically to puff blue smoke into the air of the forecourt. 'Watch this,' my father mouthed to me over the noise of the saw. I wondered what would happen if the saw fell forwards into the man's lap. Using a handle, the man lowered the saw's edge slowly on to my rock egg, which he had vised into position. It took a minute or so for the saw to move, squealing, through the rock. When it was done the man cut the engine and raised the saw upwards, out of the rock. The rock dropped from the vise on to a blanket he had placed beneath it and fell apart like a halved apple. He dried off the halves with a yellow towel, and held them out to me. 'You've been lucky,' he said slowly. 'You chose well. You chose a geode. Most people aren't as lucky as you.' I held a half in each hand, and looked at them. Each half was hollow inside, like a cavern, and the walls of each cavern were lined with numberless tiny blue crystal teeth. As we drove out of the forecourt, gravel bits clattering up against the chassis of the car, I held the two halves together to remake the rough rock sphere, and then pulled them apart, astonished again and again by what I saw.

Between about 1810 and 1870, the scale of deep time was constructed and labelled. It will be familiar to anyone who has opened a geology textbook; as resonant a litany as the shipping forecast: Precambrian, Cambrian, Ordovician, Silurian, Devonian, Carboniferous, Permian, Triassic, Jurassic, Cretaceous, Tertiary, Quarternary . . . The compressive power of language – more powerful even than the geophysical forces it was describing – was set to work on the geological past, and hundreds of millions of years were effortlessly compacted into a few letters. A late developer among the sciences, during the nineteenth century geology rushed on precociously fast, naming and labelling as time unrolled further and further behind it. Popular geology handbooks proliferated, and the reading public was brought increasingly to understand what the more lyrically inclined geologists were starting to call the 'symphony of the earth' – the repeating pattern of uplift and erosion which produced mountains and seas, basins and ranges. Innumerable articles were published on geology and its revelations in periodicals across Europe and America. Everyone was made privy to the secrets of the earth's past. 'The wind and the rain have written illustrated books for this generation,' wrote Charles Dickens in a piece for his periodical *Household Words* in 1851, 'from which it may learn how showers fell, tides ebbed and flowed, and great animals, long extinct, walked up the craggy sides of cliffs, in remote ages. The more we know of Nature, in any of her aspects, the more profound is the interest she offers to us.'

As well as being excited by the spans of time uncovered by geology, the nineteenth-century imagination was aroused by the concept of geophysical force – the inconceivable power necessary to knead sandstone like pastry, to collapse trees into shiny seams of coal and to crush marine life into blocks of marble. Romanticism had left the collective nineteenth-century nervous system attuned to appreciate excess, and this inherited lust for the grandiose and the gigantic in part explains the enthusiasm with which geology was embraced.

In mid-century Britain, John Ruskin read widely in the writings of geology, and in turn began to write brilliantly himself about the slow-motion drama of mountain scenery. The 1856 publication of Ruskin's *Of Mountain Beauty* was, like the appearance in 1830 of Lyell's *Principles*, a seminal moment in European landscape history. 'Mountains are the beginning and end of all natural scenery', pronounced Ruskin at the outset, and he brooked no quarrel with that statement throughout the rest of the book. Where Lyell was a teacher, Ruskin was a dramaturge. Before his gaze, the landscape offered up the stories of its making. Meditating on the nature of granite, with its medley of minerals and colours, Ruskin dreamt of the violence inherent in its making: 'The several atoms have all different shapes, characters, and offices; but are inseparably united by some fiery, or baptismal process which has purified them all.' Basalt he perceived to have at one stage in its career possessed 'the liquefying power and expansive force of subterranean fire'. Seen through the optic of Ruskin's prose, geology became war or apocalypse; the view from the top of a mountain became a panorama over battlegrounds upon which competing armies of rock, stone and ice had warred for epochs, with incredible slowness and unimaginable force. To read Ruskin on rocks was – and still is – to be reminded of the agencies involved in their making.

In America, too, between 1820 and 1880 there emerged a dynasty of landscape artists – Frederick Edwin Church foremost among them – who drew their inspiration from the dramatic natural scenery of the States. While they were clearly influenced by the British triumvirate of Ruskin, Turner and John Martin, these painters were filled also with a distinctively American desire to express both awe at and pride in the landscape of their country: to celebrate God's chosen land. To this end, they produced immense and often lurid canvases of American wildernesses – the red rock citadels of the desert states, the mountainous throne-rooms of the Andes, the flaring skies and mirror lakes of the Rockies, or the vaporous magnificence of the Niagara Falls. Their giant pictures emphasized the puniness and transience of man: often one or two minuscule human figures can be seen in a corner of the canvas, dwarfed by the massive profiles of the landscape. These artists were also thoroughly versed in botany and geology: some of the pictures contained so much landscape detail that, when they were first exhibited, viewers were supplied with opera glasses so that they could see the extraordinary geological accuracy of the painting – a reminder of how intertwined were geology and representations of mountains.

Oil painting is an appropriate medium to represent the processes of geology, for oil paints have landscapes immanent within them: they are made of minerals. Oil paints were first devised in the fifteenth century, when Flemish painters – the van Eyck brothers foremost among them – tried mixing linseed oil with various natural pigments, and found they had created a substance which was not only more vibrant in colour, but also more malleable in terms of drying time than traditional egg tempera. Many of the pigments they blended with the oils were mineral in origin. Unburnt pit-coal was used to render the shadows of flesh, particularly by the Flemish and

Dutch painters of the seventeenth century. Black chalk and common coal were used to furnish a brown tint. The light blues employed to render mountains as films in the far background in the work of, say, Claude or Poussin would have come from copper carbonates or compounds of silver. The 'scumbling' effect of which the Dutch masters were so fond for their skyscapes (it gives a cloud-like texture to the skies which superbly imitates the consistency of cirrostratus) was achieved using ground glass as a pigment and ashes as a context. 'Sinopia', or red earth, was used to give rouging tints to faces or clothing, or to provide the first tracing of a fresco on to plaster. Geology, therefore, is intimate with the history of painting; in oil paintings of landscapes, the earth has been pressed into service to express itself.

An even closer coincidence between medium and message can be found in the 'scholar's rocks' which became popular in the T'ang and Sung dynasties of China. Seven centuries before Romanticism revolutionized Western perceptions of mountains and wilderness, Chinese and Japanese artists were celebrating the spiritual qualities of wild landscape. Kuo Hsi, a celebrated eleventh-century Chinese painter and essayist, proposed in his *Essay on Landscape Painting* that wild landscapes 'nourished a man's nature'. 'The din of the dusty world,' he wrote, 'and the locked-in-ness of human habitations are what human nature habitually abhors; while, on the contrary, haze, mist and the haunting spirits of the mountains are what human nature seeks.' This venerable Eastern esteem for wilderness explains the popularity of scholar's rocks, single stones which have been carved into intricate, dynamic shapes by the powers of water, wind and frost. They were harvested from caves, river-beds and mountainsides, and mounted on small wooden pedestals. The stones – which scholars kept on their desks or in their studies, much as we might now keep a paperweight – were valued for how they expressed the history and the forces of their making. Each detail on a rock's surface, each groove or notch or air-bubble or ridge or perforation, was eloquent of aeons. Each rock was a tiny, hand-held cosmos. Scholar's rocks were not metaphors for a landscape, they were landscapes.

Many of these rocks have survived and can be seen in museums. If you stare at one closely enough, and for long enough, you lose your sense of scale, and the whorls, the caverns, the hills and the valleys which nature has inscribed in them can seem big enough to walk through.

Not everybody, it should be said, was exhilarated by the advances of geology in the nineteenth century. There was a widespread feeling that geology, like the other sciences, had in some way displaced humanity. Scientific inquiry and methodology had been invited into the heart of the human project, and from there it had proved – in the most merciless and irrefutable way possible – that human beings were no more or less important than any other agglomeration of matter in the universe. It had eroded the Renaissance world-view of man as the measure of all things. The desolating expanses of time revealed by geology were more persuasive proof than any other of humankind's insignificance. To understand that mountains decayed and fell was inevitably to sense the precariousness and mortality of human endeavours. If a mountain could not withstand the ravages of time, what chance a city or a civilization? 'The hills are shadows,' wrote Tennyson in his elegy for stasis *In Memoriam*, 'and they flow / From form to form, and nothing stands; / They melt like mist, the solid lands, / Like clouds they shape themselves and go.' And 'From' flowed into 'form': philology was showing that language was subject to the same ceaseless shiftings as everything else. Not even words stood for what they once did. Nothing endured any longer except change.

By and large, however, the disclosures of geology were found inspiring rather than menacing. As well as explaining the forces of the earth, Ruskin urged his public to interpret landscapes for their absence as much as their presence: what had been subtracted from the hills by cataclysm or by the ceaseless work of erosion. In Ruskin's writing, hills on imaginary hills arose before one's eyes in a fantasia of contingency, might-have-been and once-was. Like a magnificent Prospero, Ruskin summoned up the ghosts of mountains past; had them arise in the space above the skylines and ridges of the present day. Wild nature, he taught, was a ruin of something once even more astonishing – a dilapidation of what he called 'the first splendid forms that were once created'. Even the Matterhorn, whose upwards flourish drew admirers in their thousands to the Zermatt valley, Ruskin pointed out to be a sculpture: gouged, chiselled and pared from a single block by the furious energies of the earth. As John Muir would do later in the United States, John Ruskin taught his many readers that the geological past was everywhere apparent – if only one knew *how* to look.

John Ruskin also believed that mountains moved. And this was perhaps his most important contribution to the formation of our mountains of the mind. Before publishing *Of Mountain Beauty*, Ruskin had spent years pacing the lower paths of the Alps; sketching, painting, observing, meditating. He had concluded that the apparently arbitrary jaggedness of mountain ridges was an illusion. In fact, examined with due diligence and patient eyes, mountains revealed their fundamental form of organization to be the curve, and not the angle as might be concluded by superficial observation. Mountains were inherently curved, and mountain ranges were shaped and arranged like waves. They were waves of rock – 'the silent wave of the blue mountain' – and not waves of water.

Moreover, said Ruskin, mountain ranges, like hydraulic waves, were prone to motion. They had been cast up by colossal forces, and were still being moved by them. That the movement of mountains could only be imagined and not witnessed was – as James Hutton had pointed out – a function of the minute life-span of a human being. They were not static, but fluid: rocks fell from their summits, and rainwater poured off their flanks. For Ruskin, this perpetual motion was what made mountains the beginning and end of all natural scenery. 'Those desolate and threatening ranges of dark mountain,' he wrote:

> which, in nearly all ages of the world, men have looked upon with aversion or terror and shrunk back from as if they were haunted by perpetual images of death are, in reality, sources of life and happiness far fuller and more beneficent than all the bright fruitfulness of the plain . . .

Ruskin's intuition that mountains moved was proved unexpectedly correct during the course of the twentieth century, in what is the final significant shift in Western imaginings of the past of mountains. In January 1912, in an incident now legendary among earth scientists, a German called Alfred Wegener (1880–1930) stood up before an audience of eminent geologists in Frankfurt, and told them that the continents moved. Specifically, he explained that the continents, which were composed primarily of granitic rock, 'drifted' on top of the denser basalt of the ocean floor, like patches of oil on water. Indeed, 300 million years ago, Wegener informed his increasingly incredulous audience, the landmasses of the world had been united into a single supercontinent, an ur-landmass, which he called Pangaea (meaning 'all-lands'). Under the divisive power of various geological forces, Pangaea had been riven into many pieces and these pieces had subsequently drifted apart, ploughing over the basalt to their present positions.

The mountain ranges of the world, Wegener argued, had been created not by the cooling and wrinkling of the earth's crust – a theory which had come back into vogue at the start of the twentieth century – but by the crash of one drifting continent into another, causing buckling around the impact zone. The low-lying Urals, for example, which nominally separated European Russia from Siberia, were, according to Wegener, the product of an ancient collision between two mobile continents which had occurred so long ago that the effects of mountain building in the impact zone had been largely flattened by erosion.

For proof, said Wegener, just look at the globe. Look at the dispersal of the continents. Move them around a bit and they fit together like a jigsaw puzzle. Slide South America towards Africa and its eastern coast locks into Africa's western perimeter. Wrap Central America around the Ivory Coast, and North America over the top of Africa and you have half a supercontinent already. The same trick, he pointed out, worked for India's angled western littoral, which fits snugly against the straight side of the Horn of Africa, just as Madagascar slots neatly back on to the divot on the south-eastern coast of Africa.

Wegener had harder evidence to support his claim. He had spent years working in the extensive fossil archives of the University of Marburg, and had deduced that identical fossil specimens had been found in the rock record at precisely the zones Wegener suggested had once been united: on the west coast of Africa, for example, and the east coast of Brazil the coal deposits and fossils matched. 'It is just as if we were to refit the torn pieces of a newspaper by matching their edges,' he wrote, 'and then check whether the lines of print ran smoothly across. If they do, there is nothing left but to conclude that the pieces were in fact joined in this way.'

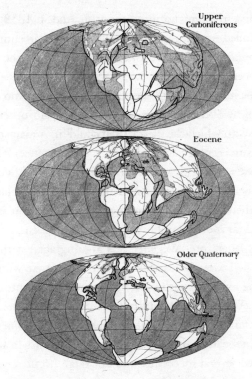

Reconstructions of the Map of the World for
three periods according to Wegener's
displacement theory. From Alfred Wegener's *The
Origins of Continents and Oceans*, trans. J. A.
Skerl, 3rd edn (London: Methuen & Co., 1924).

Wegener was not the first to suggest the interconnectedness of the
continents. The sixteenth-century cartographer Ortelius had noticed
the jigsaw-puzzle composition of the continents, and had suggested
that they were once attached, but had been sundered by drastic
floods and earthquakes. He was disbelieved. The endlessly perceptive
Francis Bacon mentioned in 1620 in his *Novum Organum* that the
continents could fit together 'as if cut from the same mould', but

seems to have thought no more about it. And in 1858, a French-American called Antonio Snider-Pelligrini devoted an entire treatise – *Creation and Its Mysteries Revealed* – to showing how the continents had once been united.

But in the mid-nineteenth century there was simply no context for such a radical overhaul of geological theory; no other pieces of knowledge with which the theory itself could fit. A mainstay of nineteenth-century geology was a belief in the existence of enormous land-bridges which had at one point joined the world's continents, but had since then crumbled into the oceans. These land-bridges explained the existence of the same species on different landmasses, and seemed far more plausible than mobile continents.

In 1912, therefore, Wegener was arguing against the grain of prevailing wisdom: if his theory were correct, it would nullify many of the founding assumptions of nineteenth-century geology. Worse still, Wegener was an intruder, a trespasser on the turf of the geologists. For his main field of research was meteorology – he was a pioneer in weather-balloon study and a specialist in Greenland, where he led several successful, and one fatal, Arctic research expeditions. How could a weatherman presume to dismantle at a single stroke the complex and magnificent edifice of nineteenth-century geology?

The opposition to Wegener's theory, as to that of Burnet so many years earlier, was immediate and voluble ('Utter, damned rot!', said the president of the American Philosophical Society, eloquently). But Wegener, a stoic visionary, remained phlegmatic in the face of early antagonism. In 1915 he published *The Origins of Continents and Oceans*, a careful explanation of his theory, and in its way as apocalyptic a reimagining of the earth's history as Burnet's *The Sacred Theory of the Earth* or Hutton's *The Theory of the Earth*. Between 1915 and 1929 Wegener revised his *Origin* three times to take into account advances in geology, but he was still ignored by the geological establishment. In 1930 he led another meteorological expedition to Greenland. Three days after his fiftieth birthday he and his team were caught in a severe Arctic blizzard, in which temperatures dropped to –60°F. Wegener became separated from his companions, and froze to death in the private wilderness of a white-out. His body was found by his colleagues when the storm receded. They entombed Wegener inside a mausoleum built of blocks of ice, topped with a twenty-foot iron cross. Within a year, the structure and its contents had disappeared into the interior of the glacier on which it was built – a means of burial that would no doubt have met with Wegener's approval.

It was not until the advent of the so-called New Geology during the 1960s that it was realized that Wegener had been at least half-right. As advances in bathysphere technology permitted the more systematized exploration of the ocean floor, it was discovered that the continents did indeed move and had indeed spun apart from a vast ur-continent. But the continents weren't – as Wegener had thought – independent entities drifting over a sea of basalt, like icebergs in water. In fact, the surface of the globe was discovered to be composed of some twenty crustal segments or plates. The continents were simply the portions of the plates which were sufficiently elevated to protrude from the sea.

These plates were named by the New Geologists. There was the African Plate, the Cocos Plate, the North American Plate, the Nazca Plate, the Iran Plate, the Antarctic Plate, the Juan de Fuca Plate, the Australian Plate, the Arabian Plate and the decidedly unfragile China Plates. Driven by convection currents or 'cells' within the semi-liquid mantle of the earth, and pulled by their own weight, these plates move around relative to each other. Where their edges meet beneath the ocean, either a mid-ocean ridge or a subduction zone is formed. At mid-ocean ridges the boundaries of two plates are continually being pushed apart by action in the mantle. Magma rises into the gap, and cools to form sea-floor basalt. Mid-ocean ridges are therefore raised above the surrounding ocean floor, like the seam on a cricket ball. A subduction zone, by contrast, is where the edges of two plates are forced together, and the less buoyant plate slides underneath the other. There, the rock of the subordinate plate is pushed down into the mantle, where it melts and comes bubbling back up in liquid form, causing super-heated wounds in the crust. These subduction zones form the oceanic trenches: the Aleutian Trench, the Java Trench, the Marianas Trench. At the bottom of these trenches – the Marianas Trench is deeper than Mount Everest is high – the atmospheric pressure is so enormous that, were you to materialize at that depth, your body would instantly be compacted to the size of a tin can.

Most of the world's mountain ranges have been thrown up by the jostling and collision of the continental plates. Thus, for example, the Alps were created when the Adriatic Plate (which carries Italy on its back) was driven into the Eurasian Plate. The oldest mountains are those which are now the lowest, for erosion has had time to reduce them. The blunted, rubbed-down spine of the Urals, for instance, speaks of great age. So too do the rounded forms of the Scottish Cairngorms. Perhaps surprisingly, among the youngest mountains on earth are the Himalaya, which began to form only 65 million years ago, when the Indian Plate motored northwards and smashed slowly into the Eurasian Plate – ducking underneath it and then butting it five-and-a-half miles upwards into the air. Compared to the earth's venerable ranges, the Himalaya are adolescents, with sharp, punkish ridges instead of the bald and worn-down pates of older ranges.

Like adolescents, too, they are still growing. Everest – which became the world's highest mountain less than 200,000 years ago – shoots up by a precocious five millimetres or so a year. Give it a million years – the blink of an eye in geological terms – and the mountain could have almost doubled its height. Except of course that won't happen, because gravity won't tolerate such a structure. Something will give: the mountain will collapse under its own weight, or be shaken apart by one of the huge earthquakes which rack the Himalaya every few centuries.

For years now I have gone to the mountains and been astonished by deep time. Once, halfway up the mica-rich peak of Ben Lawers in Scotland on a sunlit day, I found a square chest of sedimentary rock, hinged at its back with an overgrowth of moss and grass. Stepping back and looking at it from the side, I could see it was composed of hundreds of thin layers of grey rock, each one no thicker than a sheet. Each layer, I reckoned, was a paraphrase of 10,000 years – a hundred centuries abbreviated into three millimetres' depth of rock.

Between two of the grey layers I noticed a thin silvery stratum. I pushed the adze of my walking axe into the rock, and tried to lever the strata apart. The block cracked open, and I managed to get my fingers beneath the heavy top lid of rock. I lifted, and the rock opened. And there, between two layers of grey rock, was a square yard of silver mica, seething brightly in the sunlight – probably the first sunlight to strike it in millions of years. It was like opening up a chest filled to the brim with silver, like opening a book to find a mirror leafed inside it, or like opening a trapdoor to reveal a vault of time so dizzyingly deep that I might have fallen head-first into it.

3

The Pursuit of Fear

That Alpine witchery still onward lures,
Upwards, still upwards, till the fatal list
Grows longer of the early mourned and missed.

FRANCES RIDLEY HAVERGAL, 1884

I looked upwards. A tall, steep face of rock, striped vertically with snow gullies, angled up into the lightening sky. That was our route. My eye followed the face down. Without relenting in angle, it dropped some 600 feet to a small glacier which arced off the bottom of the face. The convex surface of the glacier looked hard, silvered and pitted like old metal, and it was pocked with stones which had fallen from the cliffs above. Further down, the glacier tumbled over a hundred-foot drop. There its surface turned a curdled grey, and the smoothness of the upper ice became ruptured into crevasses and blocks. I could see glimmers of blue ice far down inside the body of the glacier. That was where we would end up if we fell.

We had left the hut too late that morning. When we stepped outside, the sky beyond the mountains to our east was already livid with colour. It meant the day would be a hot one; another good reason to have avoided a late start, for the warmth would loosen rocks that were gripped by ice, and cause crevasses to yawn in the glaciers. Pushing for time and unroped, we half-jogged up over two steepening miles of glacier, trusting the lingering cold to keep the snow-bridges rigid. A final toil up a long snow ramp – tacking back and forth to make the slope less severe – brought us to the shoulder of our mountain, and the beginning of the route.

The main problem was scree, the debris of small stones and rock chips which collects on mountain sides. Scree is despised by mountaineers for two reasons. First, because it can easily be pushed off on to you by people climbing above. And second, because it makes every step you take insecure. Put a foot down on a shoal of scree, and it'll skid off as the scree scrapes over the rock beneath.

For about thirty minutes we moved steadily up the face. The rock was in poor condition, shattered horizontally and mazed with cracks. When I tried to haul myself up on a block of it, it would pull out towards me, like a drawer opening. Some of the rock ledges were covered with a moist sill of snow. My hands became progressively wetter and colder. The climbing hardware we had festooned about us clanked and tinkled on the rock. This, our breathing and the rasp of rock on rock were the only noises.

Then came a shout. '*Cailloux! Cailloux!*' I heard yelled from above, in a female voice. The words echoed down towards us. I looked up to see where they had come from.

Time doesn't stop or slow down when you are in danger. Everything happens as fast. It's just that – providing we survive them – we subject these periods of time to such intense retrospective scrutiny that we come to know them more fully, more exactly. We see them in freeze-frame. From this moment I remember a rivulet of water running darkly down the rock-rib in front of my eyes, the minute cross-hatchings on the fabric of my waterproof jacket and a little yellow Alpine flower tucked into a pocket of rock. And a sound – the crunching of the scree beneath my feet as I braced myself for impact.

There were just two rocks at first, leaping and bounding down the face towards us, once cannoning off each other in mid-air. And then the air above suddenly seemed alive with falling rocks, humming through the air and filling it with noise. *Crack*, went each one as it leapt off the rock face, then *hum-hum-hum* as it moved through the air, then *crack* again. The pause between the cracks lengthened each time, as the rocks gained momentum and jumped further and further.

Up above us, two French climbers glanced beneath their legs. They watched as the single rock which they had nudged off a ledge dislodged several other rocks, and those some others, and suddenly a gang of rocks of different sizes was leaping noisily off down the face. They couldn't see properly whether there was anyone below them: a protruding hood of rock prevented them getting a full view of the face. But it seemed unlikely that anyone would be coming up beneath them. They were the first down the mountain, having been turned back by a difficult pitch at the top. There had been no one coming across the glacier from where they had reached their high point. And no one would have been stupid enough to come any later than that. But they shouted anyway, out of decorum; like calling 'fore' on an empty golf course.

I continued to gaze up at the rocks as they fell and skipped towards me. A boy who had been a few years above me at school had taught me never to look up during a rockfall. 'Why? Because a rock in your face is far less pleasant than a rock on your helmet,' he told us. 'Face in, always face in.' He had led us all day on a horseshoe walk in Wales, and then when we returned, exhausted, to the car park and the minibus, he had marched back off into the hills in the sludgy dusk light with a rope over his shoulder, to climb until he could no longer see. A year later he and a friend were killed by rockfall in the Alps.

I heard Toby, my partner on the mountain that day, shouting at me. I looked across. He was safe beneath an overhanging canopy of rock. I couldn't understand what he was saying. Then I felt a thump, and was tugged backwards and round, as though somebody had clamped a heavy hand on my shoulder and turned me to face them. No pain, but the blow had almost jerked me off my stance. The rock, which had hit the lid of my rucksack, bounced off towards the blue crevasses far below.

Rocks were spinning past now, maybe a dozen of them. I looked up again. A rock was heading down straight towards me. Instinctively, I leant backwards and arched my back out from the rock to try to protect my chest. What about my fingers, though, I thought: they'll be crushed flat if it hits them, and I'll never get down. Then I heard a *crack* directly in front of me, and a tug at my trousers, and a yell from Toby.

'Are you all right? That went straight through you.'

The rock had pitched in front of me, and passed through the hoop of my body, between my legs, missing me but snatching at my clothing as it went.

I looked up again, and watched as the last, and biggest, of the boulders fell towards me. I was directly in its line again. About forty feet above me it took a big hop off a rock, and spun out into the air. As I watched it come it grew larger, and darker, until it was the size of my head. With a sharp report it struck the rock face once more, then took a lateral leap to my left, and whirred away past me.

I realized I was gripping the rock in front of me so hard that my fingers were white at their tips. My limbs were shivering and seemed barely able to support my weight. My heart pistoned. But it was over. I promised myself yet again that I would never come back to the high mountains. 'Let's get off this hill,' I shouted across to Toby.

Trekking cautiously back across the glacier, unnerved, my body still trembling from the adrenaline, testing the soft snow for crevasses, we heard the characteristic *whop-whop-whop* of a helicopter give the valley a rhythm. I began to sing aloud the chopper song from *Full Metal Jacket*: 'Surfin' Bird' – the Trashmen cover. Then I stopped. Get a grip, I told myself. You're not in Vietnam, you're in the Alps, just a guy who's gone up into the mountains to scare himself, and succeeded. The helicopter's not for you.

It wasn't, either. It beat a path of sound over the glacier and thumped its way off east, towards the pinnacle of the Zinalrothorn, where somebody else had died.

Late that night, back in the valley and unable to sleep, I got out of our tent and walked about the campsite, stepping carefully over the guy-ropes. Torches were on inside some of the other tents and they looked like little orange igloos against the blackness of the cold meadow. The sky was clear, and the tilted snowfields on the upper slopes of the mountains flashed the moonlight down into the valley like signalling mirrors.

As I walked, I thought back over the day. Toby and I had spent the evening in a bar, drinking pints of lager in celebration of our near-miss. The room was full of smoke and other climbers, clunking from table to bar and back again in heavy plastic boots, shouting out their tales over the music. We had sat and talked through the events of the morning: what if the big final stone hadn't leapt sideways, what if I'd been knocked off, would you have held me, would I have pulled you off? A more experienced mountaineer would probably have thought nothing of it, filed it away in the bulging folder of near-misses, and carried on regardless.

I knew I would not forget it. We had talked, too, about how much pleasure the fear had brought afterwards. And we had talked, as mountaineers always do, about how strange it is to risk yourself for a mountain, but how central to the experience is that risk and the fear it brings with it.

In his *Voyages dans les Alpes*, de Saussure wrote briefly about the chamois hunters of the Alps, men who pursued a notoriously perilous profession. The hunters were menaced by crevasses on the glaciers over which they chased their quarry, they faced death by falling from the steep slopes the chamois preferred, and death by exposure from the Alpine storms which could gather so quickly. And yet, de Saussure had written:

> it is these very dangers, this alternation of hope and fear, the continual agitation kept alive by these sensations in his heart, which excite the huntsman, just as they animate the gambler, the warrior, the sailor and, even to a certain point, the naturalist among the Alps whose life resembles closely, in some respects, that of the chamois hunter.

When I read this passage, it made absolute sense to me, despite the intervening centuries. As de Saussure said, risk-taking brings with it its own reward: it keeps a 'continual agitation alive' in the heart. Hope, fear. Hope, fear – this is the fundamental rhythm of mountaineering. Life, it frequently seems in the mountains, is more intensely lived the closer one gets to its extinction: we never feel so alive as when we have nearly died.

Of course the significant difference between de Saussure's chamois hunter and me was that for the hunter, risk wasn't optional – it came with the job. I sought risk out, however. I courted it. In fact, I paid for it. This is the great shift which has taken place in the history of risk. Risk has always been taken, but for a long time it was taken with some ulterior purpose in mind: scientific advancement, personal glory, financial gain. About two and a half centuries ago, however, fear started to become fashionable for its own sake. Risk, it was realized, brought its own reward: the sense of physical exhilaration and elation which we would now attribute to the effects of adrenaline. And so risk-taking – the deliberate inducement of fear – became desirable: became a commodity.

It is the summer of 1688, a momentous season in Europe. In Rotterdam, William of Orange is assembling a formidable invasion fleet to sail to England and prosecute what will become known as the Glorious Revolution. John Locke, too, is in Holland that summer, in exile, considering what to do with his anti-tyrannical tract, *Two Treatises of Government*. The Venetians are fighting the Ottomans up and down the Adriatic coast. And in North Italy, a young Englishman named John Dennis – who will find future fame as a playwright and aesthetician, and as the butt of Alexander Pope's jokes – is sitting before a snapping fire in a hostelry in Italy, having just crossed the Alps, and scribbling a letter to a friend in England who has never been near any mountains.

For a man who will make his living and his name from his pen, Dennis is finding it remarkably difficult to put words to what has happened to him. ''Tis an easy thing to describe Rome or Naples to you,' he writes, 'because you have seen something yourself that holds at least some resemblance with them; but impossible to set a Mountain before your Eyes, that is inaccessible almost to the sight, and wearies the very Eye to climb it.' Dennis faces the enduring problem of the travel-writer: how to say what something is like, when it is like nothing that your reader has ever seen? He concentrates at first on producing a physical description of the mountains, and runs through the conventional complaints of his age against their hostility, drawing his friend's attention to the 'impending Rocks', the 'dreadful Depth of the Precipices', and the 'roaring Torrents'.

But then, as Dennis tries to describe the exact feelings stirred in him as he reached a dangerously narrow part of the route, something unusual happens to his language:

> We walk'd upon the very brink, in a literal sense, of Destruction; one Stumble, and both Life and Carcass had been at once destroy'd. The sense of all this produc'd different motions in me, viz., a delightful Horrour, a terrible Joy, and at the same time, that I was infinitely pleas'd, I trembled.

Against all his expectations, Dennis discovered that walking 'upon the very brink' – just one stumble away from violent death – brought him an odd pleasure. No vocabulary exists to describe what he experienced, so Dennis has to invent one using the artificial logic of the oxymoron. He has to resort to paradox – to allow each 'motion' its equal and opposite emotion, and say that he felt 'a delightful Horrour' and 'a terrible Joy'.

We see here one of the earliest modern memoirs of pleasurable fear in the mountains. It is an account which, looking backwards from our age of adrenaline, appears quaint. John Dennis may not have been the first man to discover the congenial aspects to vertigo, but it was him and people like him, returning from the largely unknown world of high mountains with new experiences to tell of, who laid the foundations of future responses to mountains: to height and to fear. Dennis's glimpse that there was pleasure to be had from vertigo would, over the course of 300 years, blossom and amplify into our era's headlong pursuit of danger – people flinging themselves off

cranes attached to rubber-bands, off mountainsides attached to
ropes, and out of planes attached to nothing at all.

Around the middle of the eighteenth century something happened
which would both diffuse and formalize Dennis's understanding that
there was a pleasure to be found in fear. An intellectual doctrine was
proposed which revolutionized both the perception of wild landscapes and contemporary attitudes to fear. It is a doctrine which
continues silently to dominate both our imaginative relationship
with wilderness and our conceptions of bravery and fear. That influential doctrine was known as the Sublime (a word which means
'lofty' or 'elevated'), and it delighted in chaos, intensity, cataclysm,
great size, irregularity – the aesthetic antipodes, in other words, of the
preceding age's neo-classicism. Out of its tumult emerged a fierce,
and for a time peculiarly British, affection for wild landscape of all
types: oceans, ice-caps, forests, deserts and, above all, mountains.

In 1757 a young Irishman with a bright future published a short
work with a long title. *A Philosophical Enquiry into the Origin of Our
Ideas of the Sublime and Beautiful*, by Edmund Burke (1729–97),
tried to account for the passions evoked in the human mind by what
Burke called 'terrible objects'. Burke was interested in our psychic
response to things – a rushing cataract, say, a dark vault or a cliff-
face – that seized, terrified and yet also somehow pleased the mind by
dint of being too big, too high, too fast, too obscured, too powerful,
too *something*, to be properly comprehended. These were sublime
sights – hectic, intimidating, uncontrollable – and they inspired in
the observer, said Burke, a heady blend of pleasure and terror. Beauty,
by contrast, was inspired by the visually regular, the proportioned,
the predictable. So, for example, an Attic sculpture was beautiful, or

the balanced grace of the Parthenon, whereas an avalanche or a flooding river was sublime. In Burke's physiological terms, beauty had a relaxing effect on the 'fibres' of the body, whereas sublimity tightened these 'fibres'. 'Whatever is fitted in any sort to excite the ideas of pain, and danger,' he wrote:

> that is to say, whatever is in any sort terrible, or is conversant about terrible objects, or operates in a manner analogous to terror, is a source of the *sublime*; that is, it is productive of the strongest emotion which the mind is capable of feeling.

At the core of Burke's thesis was the proposal that these sublime sights caused terror, and terror was a passion which, he wrote, 'always produces delight when it does not press too close' (Burke was right in this; anyone who has experienced real fear for any length of time beyond the split-second will know how it commands your rapt and exclusive attention). So it would be impossible to appreciate the Sublime if one were, say, hanging by a handhold from a cliff-face. But if you came just near enough to a waterfall or a cliff-edge to suggest to your imagination the possibility of self-destruction, then you would feel a sublime rush. It was the suggestion of harm, melded with the knowledge that no harm was likely to come, which induced this delightful terror: the improbable parading as the possible. The English physician and philosopher David Hartley, writing in 1749, put it succinctly: 'If there be a precipice, a cataract, a mountain of snow etc. in one part of the scene, the nascent ideas of fear and horror magnify and enliven all the other ideas, and by degrees pass into pleasures, by suggesting the security from pain.'

Burke's smartly written treatise gave a verbal form and an intellectual respectability to the inchoate experiences which we saw John Dennis struggling to articulate seventy years earlier. Once Burke had coded the sublime – had provided a portfolio of words and ideas upon which the intellectual public at large could draw – it percolated quickly through the wider imagination. After *A Philosophical Enquiry*, no forest could be but dark and gloomy, no range of peaks but icy and majestic. Certain adjectives – sublime, awful, dreadful – became inseparably wedded to certain nouns – mountains, oceans, chasms. Philosophers and aestheticians across Europe turned their prodigious attentions to the question of the Sublime, and as a concept it began to sprawl in a suitably chaotic and ungovernable way across the neat partitions of classical aesthetics.

Burke didn't originate the concept of the Sublime; it had been around since the Greek rhetorician Longinus wrote his treatise *Peri Hupsous*, or *On the Sublime*, in the third century AD, and interest in the Sublime had subsequently been reinvigorated by Boileau's French translation of *Peri Hupsous* in 1674. But Longinus and his intellectual descendants had been concerned with the Sublime as a literary effect: how language, not landscape, could be lofty, grand or inspiring. What Burke did was to divert this pre-existent interest in grandness on to the experience of the eighteenth-century's newest of pleasures, the natural landscape. His famous little book provided a new lens through which wilderness could be viewed and appreciated. He gave previously vague and undistinguished forms of awe a local habitation (oceans, deserts, mountains, ice-caps) and a name (the Sublime).

The eighteenth-century rage for the Sublime not only transformed the way people perceived and wrote about landscapes, but also the way they behaved around them. When previously wildernesses had been shunned, now they were sought out as arenas of intense experience: places you could be temporarily disconcerted, or presented with the illusion of menace. 'I must have torrents, rocks, pines, dead forest, mountains, rugged paths to go up and down, precipices beside me to frighten me,' remarked Jean-Jacques Rousseau in 1785, 'for the odd thing about my liking for precipitous places is that they make me giddy, and I enjoy this giddiness greatly, provided that I am safely placed.' The French writer Jacques Cambry would wait for violent sea storms to blow in to the Breton coast, before going to stand on the brink of a sea-cliff. 'You think you can feel the earth quaking,' he wrote ecstatically, 'you flee instinctively; all your faculties are seized by a stunned feeling, fear, and inexplicable agitation.'

The Sublime provided a new impulse for eighteenth-century tourism. Instead of visiting the classical site, increasing numbers of tourists chose to spend their holidays tripping from cliff-top to glacier to volcano – from sublime sight to sublime sight. The ruins of mountains competed with the ruins of antiquity as places of interest. The number of visitors to Vesuvius, for example, increased dramatically in the 1760s and 1770s, there no longer to gaze dutifully downwards at the domestic details of antiquity – pondering the use of this spigot or that bowl in the daily round of a Roman housewife – but to rubberneck in helpless astonishment at the mountain itself. Some chose to get even closer to the peaks, and to climb them. In Chamonix, the town nestled beneath the needles and glaciers of Mont Blanc, guiding became a profitable business, as locals dragged foreigners keen for a sublime fix up to the viewing promontory on the Montanvert. And in Britain, seekers of the Sublime and of its slightly tamer cousin, the Picturesque, were responsible for opening up the mountainous areas of the Lake District, North Wales and Scotland. The Caledonian Tour, which took in the coastal beauty spots and inland wildernesses of Scotland, became particularly popular. Among the best-known of the first generation of Caledonian tourists was Dr Samuel Johnson, who undertook a journey to 'the Western Isles of Scotland' in 1773.

Six feet tall and some sixteen stone heavy, the formidable body of Dr Johnson was itself almost a sublime presence. When he arrived at Buchan, on the north-east coast of Scotland, Johnson had already visited Fingal's Cave on the Isle of Staffa and been rowed in calm seas through its famous Gothic archways. Now he and Boswell had come across country to see the Buller of Buchan, another renowned rock-formation. Johnson had wanted to go to China to see the Great Wall, so Scotland was always going to be a poor substitute. Nevertheless, he was impressed by the Buller. He described it thus:

> It is a rock perpendicularly tubulated, united on one side with a high shore, and the other rising steep to a great height, above the main sea. The top is open, from which may be seen a dark gulf of water which flows into the cavity, through a breach made in the lower part of the inclosing rock. It has the appearance of a vast well bordered with a wall.

Many of those who came to visit the Buller were content to view it from the security of the main cliff-edge. From there they could safely watch the sea boiling and sucking in the breach, and watch the fulmars which nested on the seawards cliff glide to and fro on their hunting forays.

Some among the bolder visitors, however, were tempted to walk out along the apex of the arch of rock. There was no real danger. True, in places the ridge narrowed to only two or three feet wide, and the ground underfoot was tussocky, uneven and crumbling near its edges. And when you looked down at your feet you could see the sea moving below the arch, so that it felt as though the arch itself was swaying liquidly back and forth, liable to pitch you to a watery death . . . But then that was the point of doing the walk in the first place; to deceive your mind into imagining its own annihilation. The ridge of the Buller, in other words, was the ideal place to experience the Sublime.

The Buller of Buchan.

To the dismay of Boswell, Johnson insisted that they make the crossing. Boswell shuffled slowly across, and declared it 'horrid to move along'. Dr Johnson, however, took it – like so many things in life – in his considerable stride, walking along without hesitation or stutter. For such a cumbrous man, he was remarkably agile: on the ground, as on the page, he was sure of his step. Afterwards, Johnson described the traverse in level-headed terms:

> The edge of the Buller is not wide and to those that walk round, appears very narrow. He that ventures to look downward sees, that if his foot should slip, he must fall from his dreadful elevation upon stones on one side, or into water on the other. But terrour without danger is only one of the sports of fancy, a voluntary agitation of the mind that is permitted no longer than it pleases.

The significant difference between Johnson and John Dennis was that Johnson briefly scared himself because he chose to do so. In the ninety years which intervened between Dennis and Johnson, under the influence of the Sublime, the pursuit of fear had begun.

Nevertheless, as far as mountains were concerned, the eighteenth century remained on the whole the century of appreciation from afar. For most people the principal attraction had not to do with setting foot upon the mountains, but with regarding them from a safe distance. The mountains were full of authentic and visible dangers – catastrophic shows of rockfall and avalanche, blizzards, precipices – and therefore they were reliable places to experience the Sublime. Down in the valleys you could stare up at the sky-scraping peaks, and from there you could hypothesize about what it would be like to fall from one of them or be caught up in an avalanche. 'What struck me most in Switzerland among the curiosities of nature were those horrid structures the Alps,' wrote a German traveller in 1785. 'One is awe-stricken at the view, and longs to impart this pleasant sense of horror to all one's friends.' Percy Shelley liked to show off about the Alpine dangers to which he had been exposed as a child. 'I have been familiar from boyhood with mountains and lakes,' he claimed boastfully. 'Dangers which sport upon the brink of precipices have been my playmate; I have trodden the glaciers of the Alps and lived under the eye of Mont Blanc.' This was all brag – in reality Shelley had always kept a prudent distance from edges – but his desire to style himself as a risk-taker was a sign of the growing enthusiasm for derring-do.

So energetically did the tourists of the eighteenth century take to the mountains, though, that within not too many years mountainous scenery became almost old hat. Summering in the French Alps in 1816, Byron was outraged at how blasé some of the visitors to the mountains could be. 'At Chaumoni –,' he dashed down in a righteously indignant letter to a friend:

in the very eyes of Mont Blanc – I heard another woman – English also – exclaim to her party – 'Did you ever see anything more *rural*' – as if it was Highgate or Hampstead – or Brompton – or Hayes. '*Rural*' quotha! – Rocks – pines – torrents – Glaciers – Clouds and Summits of eternal snow far above them – and 'Rural'!

In Byron's indignation, and in the Englishwoman's stylized enervation with the appearance of the landscape, can be seen the pith of what would become an ubiquitous impulse in nineteenth-century travel: the urge to leave the beaten track. Once looking at the mountains from the valleys had become just the same as looking at Highgate, or Hampstead Heath, or Brompton, or Hayes, once the superlatively jagged scenery of Chamonix left a spectator cold, new ways had to be found of experiencing the mountains: ways of refreshing those sublime sensations of 'delightful terror' which were no longer offered by spectacle alone.

The answer, of course, was to go into the mountains, and to put yourself at more risk. Once you were up among them, your touristic trip could turn into something much more serious: a stumble, perhaps, and then a fall.

During the first two years of the nineteenth century, Samuel Taylor Coleridge developed what he called 'a new sort of Gambling', to which he confessed he had become 'much addicted'. But then Coleridge had an addictive personality. He was addicted to conversation, addicted to thought and, devastatingly, addicted to laudanum. For a while, too, he was addicted to vertigo. Stimulation was the thing: the infinitely curious Coleridge was interested in experiences which stretched or heightened his perceiving mind, which somehow increased its acreage or sharpened its point – whether those experiences were induced by precipices or by pipes of opium.

Coleridge's gambling worked as follows. Pick a mountain, any mountain. Climb to the top of it and then, instead of 'winding about 'till you find a track or other symptom of safety' – instead of looking for the easy way down – wander on, and 'where it is first *possible* to descend', descend, and 'rely upon fortune for how far down this possibility will continue'. It was Russian Roulette, with the mountain-top the chamber of the gun and the ways off the mountain the bullets and the blanks.

On 2 August 1802 Coleridge's gambling got him into trouble. He had scrambled to the summit of Scafell in the Lake District – at 973 metres England's second highest mountain, and a threatening little rock peak when approached from the wrong angle. The weather was volatile that day: a lurid sky to the south suggested a storm was imminent. It was time to get down. By his own admission 'too confident, and too indolent to look around', Coleridge decided to gamble, and headed off to the north-east edge of the summit plateau. He couldn't have chosen a worse direction. For that line took him towards what is known now as Broad Stand, a steep giant's staircase of rock slabs and sloping ledges. Determined to keep to the rules of his own game ('rely upon fortune for how far down this possibility will continue'), however, Coleridge started to make his way down.

The descent began easily enough as he stepped from ledge to ledge, but soon the gaps between the ledges lengthened. Coleridge had to improvise. Faced with a sheer wall of seven feet, he let himself hang by his arms before dropping blindly to the next ledge. This shook him up physically: 'the stretching of the muscles of my hands and arms, and the jolt of the Fall on my Feet, put my whole Limbs in a *Tremble*'. It also committed him to finding a route down.

There was no way of reversing that move; a rubicon had been crossed. Coleridge kept moving down the cliff, but the situation was quickly becoming more grave – every drop 'increased the *Palsy* of my limbs'.

And then, suddenly, he found himself stuck. He was on a wide rock ledge with an unclimbable slab of rock above him. The wind was starting to whistle in his ears. Below him was a twelve-foot drop to a ledge so narrow 'that if I dropt down upon it I must of necessity have fallen backwards and of course killed myself'.

What to do? To be sure, nobody else would have done what Coleridge did:

> My Limbs were all in a tremble – I lay upon my Back to rest myself, and was beginning according to my Custom to laugh at myself for a Madman, when the sight of the Crags above me on each side, and the impetuous Clouds just over them, posting so luridly and so rapidly northward, overawed me. I lay in a state of almost prophetic Trance and Delight – and blessed God aloud, for the powers of Reason and the Will, which remaining no Danger can overpower us!
>
> O God, I exclaimed aloud – how calm, how blessed am I now – I know not how to proceed, how to return, but I am calm and fearless and confident – if this Reality were a dream, if I were asleep, what agonies had I suffered! What screams! When the Reason and the Will are away, what remain to us but Darkness and Dimness and a bewildering Shame and Pain that is utterly Lord over us, or fantastic Pleasure, that draws the soul along swimming through the air in many shapes, even as a Flight of Starlings in a Wind.

Stuck on the cliff-face, with a storm drawing nearer which would make the rocks slicker and even less safe, Coleridge didn't panic.

No, he lay on his back and reflected on the indestructibility of his faculty of Reason. Faced with extreme bodily danger, Coleridge retreated into the fastness of his intellect and looked out from there, from where the rocks and the storm and the drop all seemed like illusions. He *thought* himself out of a tight spot, in other words.

Indeed, when Coleridge emerged from his rational 'Trance', he noticed that several feet to his left along the ledge there was a slender gap in the rock, a chimney down which he could lower himself (it is now known as Fat Man's Peril). He took off his rucksack, 'slipped down as between two walls, without any danger or difficulty', and survived to tell the tale, though for the rest of the day he felt in a 'stretched and anxious state of mind'.

Coleridge's descent of Broad Stand is generally considered to be the first rock-climb. For Coleridge, his escape was proof of the majesty of reason over reality. He was wrong, of course. His escape had nothing to do with reason – he was just lucky enough to find a way out of his fix. You can't idealize cliffs and rocks out of existence, no matter how hard you try. Many people since Coleridge have discovered this. In a notorious incident in 1903, one hundred and one years after Coleridge's perilous descent, four climbers were killed while attempting to climb the steep slabs below Hopkinson's Cairn, also on Scafell. They were buried in the Wasdale Head churchyard, and onto each of their gravestones was chipped the same Miltonic epigraph: 'One moment stood they as the angels stand High in the stainless immanence of air; The next they were not, to their Fatherland Translated unaware.'

Coleridge's rock-climb began a century in which risk-taking in the mountains escalated. A hunger for willed and authentic fear came to usurp the more decorous pleasures of the Sublime. The proviso that one must, in Rousseau's words, be 'safely placed' in order to enjoy the frisson of risk became increasingly disregarded. Out to the mountains in growing numbers went the risk-takers. In his 1829 guide to Switzerland, the British publisher and travel-writer John Murray wrote with relish of how in the Alps 'the individual may be engulfed in some horrid chasm in the rending glacier, which instantly yawns to receive him, or the precipice may await him, should he escape the other perils so profusely scattered over the peaks of Switzerland'. Mariana Stark, the author of an 1836 guidebook to the Alps, advised lady mountain-goers 'to stare as much as possible over the edge of precipices'. In this way, Stark reasoned, your imagination would be so glutted with terror 'that you become capable of beholding height with sang-froid'. Intense beauty, altitude and solitude – certainly these were all important elements of the new glamour of mountains. But combined with them was the element of danger. The mountains provided an environment deliciously riven by risk, where you could test yourself against a profusion of hazards and difficulties.

It is above all this idea of risk-taking as a test which dominates nineteenth-century attitudes towards fear. The deeper one advances into the century, the more entangled become concepts of risk with concepts of selfhood and self-knowledge. In contemporary journals, biographies and expedition accounts, certain themes and attitudes towards wild landscape recur. Foremost among them is that of victory and defeat, of struggle and reward. In these books nature is figured usually as an enemy, or lover, to be vanquished or ravished according to how you saw it. While an alertness to the desolate beauties of wilderness remains in place, what moves decisively to the fore is a sense of a wild landscape, with all its hazards and asperities, as a testing-ground – a stage on which the self can be best illuminated. Crossing the snow-fields of the Alps or slogging over the polar tundra revealed what you were made of – and whether it was the right stuff.

An editorial in *Blackwood's Edinburgh Magazine* in November 1847, discussing the exploration of the Arctic, caught this mindset well: 'The evident design of Providence in placing difficulties before man is to sharpen his faculties for their mastery.'

Importantly, exposure to the risks and beauties of wilderness didn't only elucidate one's personal qualities; it could also actively improve them. Consider, for example, a letter which John Ruskin wrote to his father from Chamonix in 1863. 'That question of the moral effect of danger is a very curious one,' he began:

> but this I know and find, practically, that if you come to a dangerous place, and turn back from it, though it may have been perfectly right and wise to do so, still your *character* has suffered some slight deterioration; you are to that extent weaker, more lifeless, more effeminate, more liable to passion and error in future; whereas if you go through with the danger, though it may have been apparently rash and foolish to encounter it, you come out of the encounter a stronger and a better man, fitter for every sort of work and trial, and *nothing but danger* produces this effect.

Ruskin's equation of effeminacy with lifelessness, weakness and error is a sour reminder of how tightly braided ideas of bravery were with ideas of masculinity at that time. But his point is also distinctively Victorian in its belief that overcoming a danger made one 'a better' person. Nietzsche, a more famous metaphysician of fear than Ruskin, would later put it more punchily: what doesn't kill you makes you stronger. Risk-taking – scaring yourself – was, provided you survived, a potent means of self-improvement. And self-improvement was to the later Victorians, especially to the mountain-going middle classes, a powerfully attractive ideal. In 1859 Samuel Smiles published his instant classic, *Self-help*. Smiles's message was simple and, on the face of it, democratic. With ambition and with effort, anything could be achieved by anyone. 'Great men . . . have belonged to no exclusive class or rank in life,' he declared in his introduction. 'The poorest have sometimes taken the highest places, nor have difficulties apparently the most insuperable proved obstacles in their way.'

One of the fundamentals of Smiles's creed was that difficulty brought out the best in a person. 'It is not ease, but effort – not facility, but difficulty, that makes men,' he wrote. 'Sweet indeed are the uses of adversity . . . They reveal to us our powers, and call forth our energies . . . Without the necessity of encountering difficulty, life might be easier, but men would be worth less.' From here it was an easy step to the idea of deliberate self-testing: that one ought to seek out difficulty in order to maximize self-improvement. The line of least resistance always led downwards, according to Smiles. Those who took on and surmounted difficulties, by contrast, ended up bettering themselves.

Casting around for a metaphor with which to hammer home his idea, Smiles settled, tellingly, on mountain-climbing. 'Wherever there is difficulty, the individual man must come out for better for worse,' he wrote. 'Encounter with it will train his strength, and discipline his skill; heartening him for future effort . . . The road to success may be steep to climb, and it puts to the proof the energies of him who would reach the summit.' Smiles's doctrine of self-improvement through difficulty was admirably classless in its aims – anyone can be anyone – but it was assimilated most thoroughly by the Victorian bourgeoisie, many of whom put it to the test in the hazardous arena of the mountains.

As the thriving Empire brought with it greater domestic stability, prosperity and comfort, Victoria's burghers became increasingly fond of risk-taking. The middle classes needed a danger valve, as it were – somewhere they could let off the steam which built up through cosseted urban living – and the Alps were just the place, for there everyone could find their own levels of risk. 'The danger on the glaciers is more imaginary than real,' reassured the Baedeker guide to Switzerland in its 'Glaciers' section. Quite so: for most visitors that was just the point: one could imagine all manner of dreadful events taking place on the Alpine glaciers, and on the mountains through which they so gradually flowed – but it didn't happen often. The fact that people were killed now and again was inspiring for those who weren't, because it kept the possibility of death at least in sight, and that was essential to the mountain experience.

A measure of the mid-Victorian enthusiasm for vertigo can be taken from the success of Albert Smith, the rambunctious satirist and entrepreneur who from 1853 occupied the cavernous Egyptian Hall at Piccadilly with his show, 'The Ascent of Mont Blanc'. Smith, a sedentary man by inclination, had himself succeeded in climbing the mountain in August 1851, abetted by a battalion of guides and an intemperate amount of alcohol (Smith's liquid provisions for the expedition were: sixty bottles of *vin ordinaire*, six bottles of Bordeaux, ten bottles of St George, fifteen bottles of St Jean, three bottles of cognac, and two bottles of champagne). He broadcast his success across London on his return, and in March 1853 opened his show-hall account of the ascent to the public, replete with pretty female ushers in dirndls, a cut-out Swiss chalet (never mind that Mont Blanc was in France), dioramas of the mountain which were furled across the back of the stage, a shaggy St Bernard and – a final touch of Alpine verisimilitude – a brace of chamois that skittered about on the parquetry and shat at inconvenient times during the performance. A pit orchestra played the 'Chamonix Polka' and the 'Mont Blanc Quadrille', while Smith recited in his resonant voice the thrilling story of his climb.

The show was, in other words, an extravaganza of Alpine kitsch. But what it offered was a chance to experience risk vicariously. 'You

begin to ascend it obliquely,' Smith would boom to the rapt audi-
torium, describing his ascent of the Mur de la Côte. 'There is
nothing below but a chasm in the ice. Should the foot slip or the
baton give way, there is no chance for life. You would glide like
lightning from one frozen crag to another, and finally be dashed to
pieces hundreds of feet below in the horrible depths of the glacier.'
'*Oooh*,' shuddered the audience. In distinctly unprecipitous
Piccadilly, they could put themselves virtually in danger, could for
an hour or two be among the rocks and the steep ice of Mont Blanc
and then, when the lights came on, could stand up, shrug on their
coats, shiver metaphorically and leave. The thrill lay in being a spectator, not a partaker (and it is an enduring thrill: the same one
which still sells the tickets for every disaster movie, every account of
every catastrophe).

The public loved Smith's amalgam of the exotic and the awful.
The show had a six-year sell-out run, and took over £30,000. 'By his
own ability and good humour,' wrote Dickens approvingly, 'Smith is
able to thaw [Mont Blanc's] eternal ice and snow; so that the most
timid ladies may ascend it twice a day . . . without the smallest
danger of fatigue'. In the summer of 1855 Britain was, according to
The Times, gripped with 'Mont Blanc mania'. More and more
tourists were travelling to the Alps to see the superlative summit of
Mont Blanc; more and more, too, were trying to scale it.

While 1850 was the noon of the nineteenth century, 1859 was its
hinge. Smiles's influential book appeared, and so too did Charles
Darwin's *The Origin of Species by Means of Natural Selection*. One of
Darwin's most appealing and versatile ideas was the survival of the
fittest (a phrase which didn't in fact appear in *The Origin of Species*,

but was coined by Darwin's contemporary, the philosopher Herbert Spencer), and it was this premise which from the 1860s onwards put a new edge on the notion of risk-taking as test. For the mountains provided a laboratory in which an accelerated version of natural selection took place, and could be seen at work. What was simultaneously awful and enthralling about the mountains was how serious even the tiniest error of judgement could be. A slip that might turn an ankle in a city street could in the mountains plunge one fatally into a crevasse or over an edge. Not turning back at the right time didn't mean being late for dinner; it meant being benighted and freezing to death. On the loss of a glove, a day could pivot from beauty to catastrophe.

Everything was thrillingly amplified in the mountains: there the selective pressures were ubiquitous and much more immediate in their consequences. Being in the mountains was thus a powerful clarification of one's abilities and of one's fitness. And the weakest – well, the weakest went to the wall. 'The law of survival of the fittest,' growled Alfred Mummery approvingly of solo climbing in 1892, 'has full and ample chance of eliminating him should he be, in any way, a careless or incapable mountaineer.' The same survivalist values were being entrenched in America, especially in Alaska, where saloon-bars filled with gold-diggers and woodsmen provided fertile breeding grounds for a pungently masculine Darwinism. The bard of the Alaskan gold-rush, Robert Service, wrote an uncompromising little ditty on exactly this theme: 'This is the Law of the Yukon, that only the Strong shall thrive; / That surely the Weak shall perish, and only the Fit survive.' The American West and its attendant frontier myths have ever since been extremely masculine: knights doing battle on the freeway in their armoured trucks, classical body worship, and the howling wilderness.

What qualities was the successful mountaineer or explorer proven to possess? Manliness, one might answer straight away – that very

Victorian concept which would morph in the twentieth century into machismo. Climbing a mountain provided a confirmation of one's strength, an affidavit of pluck and potency, an assurance of resourcefulness, self-sustenance and manhood. When John Tyndall recollected his first ascent of the Weisshorn he did so in terms of a virginity being taken. 'I pressed the very highest snowflake of the mountain,' he wrote, 'and the prestige of the Weisshorn was forever gone.' H. B. George, discussing mountain travel at the turn of the nineteenth century, claimed it was the urge 'to explore the earth and to subdue it' which 'has made England the great colonizer of the world, and has led individual Englishmen to penetrate the wildest recesses of every continent'.

Patriotism, too, was involved. 'The authentic Englishman,' declared Leslie Stephen, 'is one whose delight is to wander all day amongst rocks and snow; and to come as near breaking his neck as his conscience will allow.'* Perhaps the most prized quality which was made visible by the landscape, however, was the combination of resilience and reticence which we now call grit. Grit was the ability to put one foot in front of the other for as long as necessary. To tread ceaselessly in the prints of the man in front. To know when to take the lead yourself and to be sufficient to that moment. And above all, not to complain. To play up, in other words, and to play the game. Tennyson, as so often, had a line for it in his poem

---

* Hitler believed strongly in the mystical power of mountains, and the image of the striving, suffering, physically remarkable mountain-climber lent itself well to fascism, with its twinned aesthetics of muscularity and maleness. During the 1930s the Reich sponsored teams of young German climbers – 'Nazi Tigers', as they became known – to attempt increasingly dangerous routes, the most notorious of which was the *Mordwand* (literally Death Wall) of the Eiger. They perished by the score. The mountaineer was also a favourite trope of Nietzsche's. 'The discipline of suffering – of great suffering,' he wrote, 'know ye not that it is only this discipline that has produced all the elevation of humanity hitherto . . . This hardness is requisite for every mountain-climber.'

'Ulysses': 'To strive, to seek, to find, and not to yield'. Grit was ingrained in the imperial generations of Britain from an early age – the boarding-school system churned out generation after generation of boys allegedly full of the stuff – and it was considered to be the moral substance which underpinned Britain's martial success, its zeal for exploration and its Empire-building: its prolific pinking of the map.

It was also grit which the mountains demanded of those who went among them. In 1843 James Forbes described an Alpine journey as 'perhaps the nearest approach to a military campaign with which the ordinary citizen has a chance of meeting'. Drained of energy as he climbed the final snow ramps of the Weisshorn, Tyndall kept himself going by remembering the traits which had made Englishmen famous in battle: 'It was mainly the quality of not knowing when to yield, of fighting for duty even after they had ceased to be animated by hope.' Leslie Stephen preferred to think of himself as a polar explorer. 'Struggling in the winter towards a hut,' he wrote, 'one is but playing at danger, but for the moment one can sympathize with the Arctic adventurer pushing towards the pole, and feeling that the ship which he has left behind is the sole basis of his operations.' The icescapes and rock faces of the mountains were in many ways so featureless, so entirely lacking in human specifics, that they were the perfect site for reimagining oneself at will, whether into a soldier battling on in the face of death, or an imperturbable and dauntless explorer.

For many nineteenth-century mountaineers, then, being among the mountains was little more than a role-playing game. The mountains provided a mythic kingdom, an alternative world in which you could reinvent yourself as whoever you wanted. They were a 'playground' – as Stephen christened the European Alps – in which grown men could play at danger: an arena of recreation, but also one of self re-creation. Nevertheless, it didn't matter how you imagined yourself or the mountains: the landscape could still kill you.

❄

I once went for almost a year without mountains. Stuck on the table-lands of Cambridgeshire, working without prospect of a break, I lusted after verticality. The only relief was the dark church towers which punctuated the horizon, and the white spires of the colleges, pirouetting away into thin air. One day in late January I cracked and caught a bus to Euston, where a friend and I boarded the sleeper to the Highlands.

We woke to find the train hustling and clanking its way through an icy glen. Snow rested in deep cross-sections to either side of the track; a white jacket unzipped by the snow-plough. The glen curved round ahead of the train, and when I leaned out of a corridor window, the wind cold on my face, I could see the rails carrying the sunlight off into the distance in two bright, converging tightropes.

From the train station we thumbed a lift up to the Cairngorm car park, and began the walk-in to the jagged black-and-white ramparts of the Northern Corries. It felt good to be out in the wind, which pushed at us in big soft buffets. High above the summits of the corries a crow surfed the turbulence, stiff-winged and silhouetted. When we reached the foot of the corries, we picked a narrow, near-vertical 300-foot gully which would take us up on to the plateau. From there we could, depending on the mood of the weather, head deeper into the hinterland or just turn back for home.

It was slow, hard going up the gully, even with axes and crampons to help us. The big southerly wind had scoured the plateau of snow and flung it all into the north-facing gullies, hundreds of tons of it, and it rushed incessantly down upon us like a thick white river, surging about our knees. It was, I reflected briefly as I stopped to gasp for breath, wonderful snow. Plumes of it whipped up and danced in mid-air, choreographed by the strange swirls and vortices of wind that filled the corries. The rock-ribs to the right and left of the gully were densely varnished with ice, and from every overhang was suspended a rigid chandelier of blue icicles.

By the time we reached the plateau, an hour later, the weather had severely deteriorated. It was snowing hard. Visibility had decreased to a hundred feet and the temperature had suddenly dropped. My eyebrows felt heavy, as though something were pulling them away from my forehead, and when I put a gloved hand up I found they were dense with ice. We knelt a few feet from the head of the gully, trying to coil the rope. In the cold it was as inflexible as a steel hawser. Its two ends lashed stiffly about in the wind which, having seemed so exhilaratingly playful a few hours before, had become a hurricane. I remembered the warning I had read in a guidebook to the area: *The highest recorded wind speed on the Cairngorm plateau is a gust of 176 mph: more than sufficient to flip over a car.*

There was no question of trying to make it back. It was impossible even to stand up – the wind would have bludgeoned us over the edge. And we couldn't go back down the gully. On hands and knees we crawled for a few hundred yards to where a bank of snow had drifted up and frozen, and spent an hour hacking out a rough snow-cave. For the next twelve hours we huddled together shivering in the cave, hands lodged in each other's armpits for warmth, waiting for the wind to drop. All that night I longed for the temperate and horizontal fens.

In Cambridge I had forgotten how hostile the Cairngorms could be. In my mind's eye I had seen them in their most benevolently beautiful state: graceful whale-backs of snow and ice, cast in a bronze winter sunlight. The actuality had been a very different matter. With mountains, the gap – the irony – that exists between the imagined and the actual can be wide enough to kill.

As the traffic in the Alps and other mountains became heavier over the course of the nineteenth century, so the mortality rate rose. From the start there had been dissenting voices: John Murray's *Handbook* to Switzerland, for example, pronounced those who went up Mont Blanc to be 'of unsound mind'. Such warnings went largely unheeded, though, and more and more people fell foul of what Edward Bulwer-Lytton called 'the sudden dangers none foreknow': the collapsing cornice, the unexpected rockfall, the avalanche.

The dangers of mountaineering were shockingly emphasized in 1865, two years after Ruskin wrote his letter to his father on the morally improving effect of danger, by the infamous Matterhorn disaster. While descending after the first ascent of the mountain, three Englishmen – a lord, a vicar and a young man from Cambridge – and a Swiss guide crashed 4,000 feet off a sheer face of the mountain to the glacier below. The three other climbers were saved only because the rope attaching them to the fallers snapped. When a rescue team reached the glacier, they found a trio of naked and mutilated corpses. The men's clothes had been ripped from them during the fall. Croz, the Swiss guide, had lost half his skull, and the rosary he wore was embedded so deeply into the flesh of his jaw that it had to be cut out using a penknife. Of Douglas, the lord, nothing was to be found except a boot, a belt, a pair of gloves and a coat sleeve.

The Matterhorn disaster, as it became known, took the shine off

the Golden Age of mountaineering. Britain in particular reacted
with a mixture of horror and fascination at this apparent waste of life.
Blue British blood had been spilt in the pursuit of altitude, and
many rightly sensed that there was considerably more spillage to
come. Charles Dickens, an armchair aficionado of that sanest of
endeavours, polar exploration, thought mountain-climbing ludicrous
and trumpeted his opinion about town. 'BRAG!' he bellowed
unsympathetically. 'The scaling of such heights . . . contributes as
much to the advancement of science as would a club of young gentlemen who should undertake to bestride all the weathercocks of all
the cathedral spires of the United Kingdom.' The weathercock news-
papers, which only a few months previously had been praising the
intrepidity of mountaineers, turned with the wind of the hour and
inquired dolefully why Britons were so bent on 'reaching the unfathomable abyss never to return', or denounced mountaineering as 'a
depraved taste'.

The public, however, was more fascinated than horrified by the
deaths, and displayed a predictable grim interest in the details of the
disaster. To many, moreover, the act of dying in the mountain had
conferred a majesty upon the men. A. G. Butler wrote an elegy for
the fallers which elevated them to the status of demi-gods and
likened mountaineering to a cosmic battle: 'They warred with
Nature, as of old with gods, / The Titans; like the Titans too they
fell, / Hurled from the summit of their hopes . . .' Never mind the
messy details of death – the horrifying seconds of frictionless plummet, the bones and organs turned into a mass of jelly by the impact –
in Butler's verses the fallers' fate was transformed into something
atavistic and magnificent. Mountain-climbing wasn't the sublimation
of student japery, as Dickens had denounced it, but an epic endeavour: an encounter with the utmost of all foes, Nature. For that, any
risk was worth it.

The Matterhorn disaster was a crucial moment in the history of risk-taking in the mountains. Had disapproval spread to become the orthodoxy, mountaineering might not have flourished as it subsequently did. In the end, though, it was Butler's hyperbolic adulation and not Dickens's contempt which carried the day. Mountain-climbing thrived, the fascination which mountains and risk-taking held for the non-mountaineering public was fortified, and the graveyards in the small Alpine villages filled up with a steady stream of climbing dead. Edward Whymper, one of the climbers who survived, later provided an epitaph for the Matterhorn disaster and for mountaineering itself. 'Climb if you will,' he wrote, 'but remember that courage and strength are naught without prudence, and that a momentary negligence may destroy the happiness of a lifetime. Do nothing in haste; look well to each step; and from the beginning think what may be the end.' Whymper followed his own prescription and lived a long and enthusiastically cantankerous life – many others have not been so prudent or so fortunate.

There are many ways to die in the mountains: there is death by freezing, death by falling, death by avalanche, death by starvation, death by exhaustion, death by rockfall, death by ice-fall and death by the invisible aggression of altitude sickness, which can cause cerebral or pulmonary oedema. Falling is, of course, the ever-present option. Gravity doesn't ever forget itself or go temporarily off duty. The French writer Paul Claudel put it nicely – we lack wings to fly, but we always have strength enough to fall.

Every year now, hundreds of people die in the world's mountains, and many more thousands are injured. Mont Blanc alone has killed over 1,000 people; the Matterhorn 500; Everest around 170; K2 a hundred; the North Face of the Eiger sixty. In 1985 nearly 200 people died in the Swiss Alps alone.

I have seen the climbing dead all over the world. They congregate in graveyards in mountain towns, or in ad hoc cemeteries in base camps. It's often impossible to retrieve or even find the bodies of those killed in the mountains, so many of the dead are present only as objects or tokens: rock faces with plaques neatly screwed on to them; names scratched into boulders; rude crosses made out of stone or wood; flowers huddled together under a poncho of cellophane. They are accompanied by the formulae of grief, which have done their duty so often, and which do it again without losing their power or their poignancy: *Here lies . . . Here fell . . . In memoriam . . .* All those uncompleted lives.

It's easy to sentimentalize or glorify the climbing dead. But what should be remembered – what's often forgotten – are the people left behind. All those parents, children, husbands, wives and partners who have lost their loved ones to the mountains. All those ruined lives which have to be completed. People who regularly take big risks in the mountains must be considered either profoundly selfish, or incapable of sympathy for those who love them. I recently met a woman at a party whose cousin had been killed in a fall the previous year. She was angry and baffled by what had happened. Why had he felt the need to mountaineer, she asked me, not wanting an answer. Why couldn't he have played tennis, or gone fishing? What made her even more angry was that his brother was still climbing. Her aunt and uncle were desolated by the loss of one son, she said, and the other one was still pursuing the pastime which had killed his brother. Or at least he had been until the week before, when he had broken both legs in a fall. She had been glad when she heard this news, she said, because she guessed it would stop him ever climbing again: it would save his life, would stop him – she hissed with quiet fury as she said this – being so selfish. Later, I heard that he had recovered the use of both legs, and was climbing again within a month of having had the plaster-casts removed.

In a situation like this there is an inescapable sense that some bad magic or mesmerism has been worked: that a love of the mountains has become something akin to brainwashing. It is an example of the dark side of mountaineering, a reminder of its potentially huge costs. There is no undeniable need to put one's life at risk on a mountain-side or a cliff-face. Mountaineering isn't destiny – it doesn't have to happen to a person.

I now almost fully acknowledge that there is nothing inherently noble about dying in the mountains: indeed that there is something atrociously wasteful about it. I have largely stopped taking risks. I rarely undertake climbs which require the security of ropes. I have discovered that it is eminently possible to spend time in the mountains and to be at far less risk than one would be, say, crossing city streets. I'm scared more easily, too: my fear threshold has been sharply lowered. That fizzing, nauseous, faintly erotic feeling of real terror grips me more quickly these days. Edges that five years ago I would happily have walked along, I now keep my distance from.* For me now, as for the vast majority of mountain-goers, the attraction of mountains is far more about beauty than about risk, far more about joy than fear, far more about wonder than pain, and far more about life than death.

The fact remains, though, that many people are still lured to take risks in the mountains, and do still die among them. Chamonix, in France, is probably the world's greatest mecca for mountain-lovers, and the only place I know where the flagpoles have ruffs of steel spikes on them to stop people climbing them. It is a dense small

---

* My new-found cowardice is not yet equal to that of Marcel Proust, who declared himself suffering a mixture of vertigo and altitude sickness after travelling from Versailles to Paris, the former being eighty-three metres higher than the latter.

town; a clot of apartment buildings, churches and bars stuck in a gap in the Alps. It always surprises me to see it there. You come across it unexpectedly, winding up the steep-sided road from Geneva, not thinking there's enough flat ground on which to build a house, let alone a town. And then suddenly there it is, lodged in the valley. Rising on every side of it are slopes of rock, smeared with glaciers, leading the eye upwards to the gleaming silver summit of Mont Blanc and to the ferrous-red pinnacles of rock which stand on every skyline.

On average, one person dies each day during each summer climbing season in Chamonix. You don't know they've gone, these people. There are no empty seats in the bars being protectively watched by red-eyed friends, no parents wandering stunned about the hot streets, wheezing with grief. The only clue is the *whop-whop* of rotor-blades as the rescue helicopters criss-cross the air above the town. Everyone in the bars looks up when a helicopter comes over; speculates briefly on where it's headed.

One spring I was trekking across the Glacier du Géant, the high-altitude glacial bowl which spreads between France and Italy in the mountains to the south-east of Chamonix. You can walk from one country to the other across this glacier bowl: it's about five miles wide. En route, you pass crevasses which are capacious enough to take a row of houses. Looking into them, you can see the cross-section of the glacier: the multi-coloured strata of ice – white near the surface, passing through shades of cobalt, ultramarine and sometimes sea-green. The ice layers at the bottom of these big crevasses consist of snow which fell several centuries ago.

All around you, out of the shining field of the glacier, jut the famous *aiguilles* of the Mont Blanc range – the needles and towers of russet rock which thrust thousands of feet into the air. On a clear day the colour scheme of the glacier bowl – red rock, blue sky, white ice – is as bright and defined as the *tricolore* itself. Most of the *aiguilles* have names. There is *Le Grand Capucin* – The Great Monk – who keeps a silent ministry beneath his habit of brown rock, and *La Dent du Géant* – The Giant's Tooth – which angles upwards like a caffeine-stained fang, or a 600-foot version of the accent that tops its name. People climb the *aiguilles*. Walking along the glacier, you can often see a tiny speck of red or white stuck into a seam on one of the rock faces, thousands of feet up.

That day we were traversing the glacier bowl from Italy to France. We had only just begun the crossing when I spotted, a hundred yards or so from the beaten track, what looked to be a clump of hardy flowers growing from the glacier. It seemed improbable; there was no earth for the flowers to grow in, only ice. I paced over to have a look.

It was a little green ball of clay, or plasticine, about the size of a fist, half-buried in the ice. Into it had been poked a dozen silk flowers, with short wire stalks. The silk of the petals must once have been colourful, but the weather had reduced all the flowers to a sepia brown. Slung round the stalk of one of them was a tiny card inside a plastic wallet: like one of the identity-tags that babies wear in maternity clinics. I nudged it over with the tip of my ice-axe. Moisture had got inside the wallet and made the ink run, but I could still make out a few blurred words: *Chérie . . . morte . . . montagnes . . . au revoir.*

I wondered what had happened to her. How she had died, and where. Who was grieving for her. Whether her whole family had come up here to plant this little garden for her. Then I walked back to the path and carried on towards France.

We crossed the glacier without incident. I returned home two days later. Waiting on my answer-phone was the news that somebody else I knew had died in the mountains. He had just completed a climb on Ben Nevis, and was unroping on the gentler ground at the top of the climb when a tiny, freakish avalanche pushed him back over the edge of the 1,000-foot gully he had just ascended. He was twenty-three. One of the burnt-yellow helicopters that the Scottish Mountain Rescue use had flown his body out from the Allt a' Mhuilinn, the glen that runs up into the granite horseshoe of Ben Nevis and Carn Mor Dearg.

I stood there with the phone in my hand after the message had ended, and pressed my forehead against the cool wall. I hadn't seen him since we had climbed together on the cliffs on Arthur's Seat in Edinburgh one New Year's Eve. Drunk and laughing, we had walked through the snowing streets of Edinburgh, seeing the flakes falling in each orange cone of street-light. We had marched up to the craggy side of Arthur's Seat, and there we had spent an hour or so climbing, clambering straight up the icy rock face or trying traverses. I remembered us both side by side, ten feet off the ground, leaning outwards from the cold rock to look for the next hold, hair combed straight back off our heads by gravity.

4

Glaciers and Ice:
the Streams of Time

In the hot summer of 1860 the glaciers of Chamonix were alive with
the rustle of crinoline. Up on the Mer de Glace, beneath an Alpine
sky undisturbed save by the elegant minarets of the nearby *aiguilles*,
little guilds of men and women clambered about on the acres of ice.
The men were dressed in dark tweed, the women in voluminous
black dresses, with thin gauzes of muslin dropping down from the
brims of their hats to protect their complexions from the Alpine
sun, which glanced up off the ice to scorch the insides of nostrils and
the undersides of eyelids. Both sexes wore cleated boots and everybody clutched a four- or five-foot alpenstock, fanged with metal at its
bottom end.

A guide – a Chamoniard – attended each group, pointing out the
sights of the glacier and ensuring that no one was lost to fatigue, or
to the yawning crevasses (though every so often someone was). At the
lower part of the Mer de Glace, where the ice was most violently ruptured, adventurous parties picked their way upward along precipitous
banks of ice, flanked on either side by blue abysses into which they
shouted and heard their voice returned from the depths in a *basso
profundo*. Further up the glacier, towards the Col du Géant, the sun
had sculpted the ice into a menagerie of legendary beasts and other
strange likenesses. 'Like the mutilated statuary of an ancient temple,'

wrote one visitor, 'like the crescent moon, like huge birds with outstretched wings, like the claws of lobsters and like antlered deer.'
Boulders, bigger than houses, which the locals claimed had been
struck off the surrounding mountains by the electric bolts of heaven,
lay about on the surface of the glacier, and it pleased those who
came back to Chamonix every summer to note how far downstream
their favourite rocks had perambulated in a year. When the good
weather held for days on end, the surface of the glacier would be
melted by the radiance of the sun, except for the ice beneath the
rocks, which would be left clasped aloft on thick gelid pedestals.
The daring ate their lunch in the shade of these rocks – glacier-
tables, as they were known – while the even more daring scrambled
up on to their flat tops to do the same.

The crevasses in the glacier were of considerable interest to the visitors. The braver of the women would edge towards their lips, held
either by a rope around the waist, or more usually by the strong arm
of their guide. Once on the brink they could peer into the crevasse,
could see how further down the dirty white snow changed its complexion and its colour to a translucent blue, or, if the light were
entering from a different angle, an intense green. The better
equipped among them pulled out a cyanometer to gauge the tint of
the icy walls, which they had already used to measure the remarkable
cerulean of the sky, or the pale blue light that leaked into the holes
their alpenstocks made in the snow.

Later that evening, sitting by the fire at the Hôtel d'Angleterre, the
visitors swapped stories of the people who had perished on the ice; of
how a French Protestant minister had slipped into a narrow crevasse on
the Grindelwald glacier, just wide enough to admit a man, and a guide
had descended after him on the end of a rope to find the minister's
body lying awkwardly in the far corner of 'a grand and spacious hall of
ice, of immense size, with a finely vaulted roof'; or of the young woman
who just the year before had been crushed to death by a block of ice

which had dropped from the arch of frozen water that marked the end of the Glacier du Bois, and which drew so many visitors.

For those who were disinclined to make the substantial climb up to the Mer de Glace, the Glacier des Bossons spilt itself over the brim of the valley and pushed down through the dark pines which forested its slopes and kept the avalanches pent up during winter, until it almost reached the Chamonix–Servoz road. From the base of the glacier, muscular rills of silty water escaped down the runnels they had carved on the northward side of the road: eventually they would mingle with the blue headwaters of the Rhône.

Here, right by the roadside, there were marvels aplenty: no need to exhaust oneself unnecessarily, agreed the parties that came to witness them. Chamoniards in breeches pointed them out – how the glacier toppled the ancient pine trees as though they were saplings and splintered them as though they were kindling; how, when the sun was high and hot, the ice could be heard creaking and groaning like ship's mahogany in a storm; how near its snout the glacier was disrupted into a thousand obelisks of ice.

There was, observed many of the visitors to the Glacier des Bossons, something frighteningly improper about its location, the way it made its slow and violent way down into the valley, leagues below its rightful altitude. Life had to go about its business in the shadow of this truculent, almost obscene, mass of ice; peasants had to gauge its likely career and build their huts and houses out of its way. The glacier got many of them anyway, for they drank its meltwater on a daily basis, thus silting up their kidneys and causing goitres to flourish beneath their chins.

None of this was a problem for the visitors, of course, who rather enjoyed fossicking through the Alpine *maquis* in search of the tiny, acidic strawberries that glowed like embers right in the shadow of the ice, or finding the troupes of deep blue gentians that grew only a few paces from the glacier side. And after all, these feelings of pleasurable horror at the spectacle of the moving ice – the deliberate inducement of which was a motive for visiting Chamonix in the first place – were soon forgotten when the coachman cracked his whip and the visitors' carriage rumbled off towards Geneva, the railway station and iceless England.

Not everyone was enchanted by the glaciers. Back in the 1830s, a disgruntled visitor had composed a quatrain for the album in the Hôtel Imperial: 'Give me the glace Tartoni makes, / And take your Mer de Glace for me, / I'd rather eat *his* ice and cakes / Than cross again that frozen sea.' That page of the album was now well thumbed, for the ditty had become something of a sight in itself – rumour had it that the man had been lost to an avalanche up near the Jardin the following day, and that this rhyme was his last word.

Were it not for the supposed death of the man, that page might have drawn attention to itself anyway, for it was an unusual senti-ment in an album filled to the margins with expressions of awe. The Imperial's guest-book, like that of every other hotel in Chamonix, was a *Festschrift* for the glaciers and the peaks, echoing with 'magnif-icents' and 'sublimes', just as the amphitheatres of the mountains echoed with them in the daytime. For the majority of visitors – whether climbers, strollers or just spectators – these mighty ice rivers left deep and abiding grooves of wonder in the mind. 'The *Glacier*,' wrote Karl Baedeker decisively in the preface to his *Handbook for Travellers to Switzerland*, the vade mecum of every tripper to Switzerland from 1863 onwards, 'is the most striking feature of the Alpine world, a stupendous mass of the purest azure ice. No aspect of Switzerland is so strikingly and at the same time so strangely beauti-ful.' What a peculiar obsession it was, though – how curious that people should feel the urge to admire and to disport themselves upon these masses of ice.

But then the glaciers were superb enigmas in an age which, beset by mechanization and materialism, was hungry for mysteries. Their history and their motion were imperfectly understood. No one really knew how they moved their bulks over the land, or even whether glacial ice was a liquid, a solid or some category-defying hybrid substance which both flowed (like a liquid) and fissured (like a solid). It had also since the 1840s become apparent that at some point in the spans of geological time glaciers had been far more extensive than they presently were. The existence all over Europe of polished and furrowed beds of rock, which looked as though they had been ploughed flat by an inconceivably powerful force, suggested this to be the case, as did the distribution of large angular blocks of rock upon the surface of the land, often dozens of miles from their nearest possible site of origin.

When I was twenty-two, I was part of a mountaineering expedition to the Tian Shan, the high and remote range which sweeps westwards out of China and into the Central Asian republics of Kyrgyzstan and Kazakhstan. We were flown into the mountains by helicopter, a rusting, clattery old bird that touched down briefly to drop us, before pulling up and away into the mist.

China lay to our east behind an elegant ridge of mountains, Kazakhstan to the north, hidden by a bulkier, more monstrous range. Slowly we made our way towards base camp – a herd of tents and lean-tos huddled on the black moraine of the Inylchek glacier.

The Inylchek is the world's third most voluminous glacier – a deep river of ice which pushes through the Tian Shan for some fifty miles. It is Y-shaped, and its two upper arms are fed by dozens of tributary glaciers that flow in slow-motion into it, and by minor ice-falls down which blocks of ice as big as cars descend at a stately rate. I lived on the Inylchek moraine for a few weeks, and at night, from inside the tent, I could hear the glacier running through its repertoire of sound effects: the slither as blades of slate slipped over one another, dislodged by an adjustment of the glacier's massive machinery; the groan, from deep inside the glacier, of ice separating from ice. It reminded me of James Forbes's lovely description of the Mont Blanc glacier in 1843: 'All is on the eve of motion.'

In comparison with the glacier's rhythms our movements around the camp – a pair of quick hands dealing out a pack of cards on an upturned rock, feet being stamped to keep them warm when the sun had dropped behind the mountains – seemed almost frivolously fast. Occasionally, though, would come a cataclysm, the mountains showing their own sleight of hand: the high scream of a block tearing away from an ice-fall, or the crack and rush of an avalanche.

Once, during the daytime, there was a soft crump and a big bass roar from far away to the east. We looked up. At that distance everything happened at a languorous, decelerated velocity. For what felt like minutes, the avalanche descended the face of Pik Pobeda. It was a big one, the biggest I had ever seen. Tens of thousands of tons of snow and rock falling in silence. It struck the glacier at the bottom of the face and, like a white carpet unrolling, the powder and debris from the avalanche billowed out horizontally for almost half a mile. Twenty minutes later the pall of white was still hanging in the air over the glacier. We muttered a few words of hope for the Spanish team that we knew were on the north face of Pobeda, and turned back to our game of cards.

At first glance glaciers appear destitute of life or interest; attractive only for their qualities of desolation and emptiness. They seem static, frozen like a photograph by the cold and the thin, transparent air. Eighteenth-century travellers regularly compared them to deserts. But like deserts, glaciers open themselves up to you when you look closely at them. You can never step into the same river twice, said

Heraclitus. Had he travelled a few latitudes further north, he would have said the same for glaciers. The ice is in that old paradox – a permanent state of flux.

On the Inylchek glacier, every time I stepped off the moraine and on to the ice, something would have changed. The glacier had a different character for each part of the day. In the cold mornings it was crisply white. At noon the sun carved the surface of the ice into groves of tiny, perishable ice trees, each one only a few inches high: a miniature silver and blue forest which stretched away for miles up and down the glacier. The late afternoon light – a rich, liquid light – turned the big dun rocks on the ice into tawny beasts, and made the pools of meltwater which gathered in the glacier's hollows glint like black lacquer. One night I was out on the glacier when it began to snow in big, heavy, wind-blown flakes. In the beam of my headtorch it looked as though I was moving at warp-speed through deep space.

Dusk was my favourite time on the glacier. The sun always fell fast, dropping suddenly behind a row of peaks, so it was a brief affair – forty minutes or so when shadows quickly densened beneath rocks, and the air temperature plunged. Down at the glacier's side, you could sense it battening down for the night. If you put a hand an inch or two above the ice, you could feel the cold pulsing off it, like marble. Out on the wide meltwater pools, the ice formed in zigzags just beneath the surface of the water, then thickened into heavy boiler-plates, locking in the deeper water. I once bent down to examine a shallow pool of water which had gathered in a dip, and watched for a few minutes as ice crept jaggedly inwards from its edges and knitted in the middle, like a fontanel closing, or a tiny ice age.

❋

Glacier-going was not just a nineteenth-century fad. It was back in the 1660s that reports first began to filter back to London of an outlandish phenomenon to be found in the very heart of Europe: the 'Icy and Chrystallin Mountains of *Helvetia*'. One of the first of these reports was a letter by a Mr Muraltus, published on 9 February 1673 in the *Philosophical Transactions* of the Royal Society, London's foremost intellectual institution. It was accompanied by a rough illustrative plate of the Lower Grindelwald glacier which showed an army of icy pinnacles marching down a steep-sided valley. 'The Icy Mountain,' began Muraltus confidently, 'deserves to be view'd.' He continued:

The Mountain it self . . . is very high, and extends it self every year more and more over the neighbouring meadows, by increments that make a great noise of cracking. There are great holes and caverns, which are made when the Ice bursts; which happens at all times, but especially in the Dog-days. Hunters do there hang up their game they take during the great heat, to make it keep sweet by that means . . . When the Sun shineth, there is seen such a variety of colors as in a Prism.

What must they have made of it in London, this moving mountain which by fits and starts overwhelmed the terrain about it and advertised its intent with 'great noise', which split the sunlight into its constituent colours and itself burst into shards without warning? The Londoners knew of ice, to be sure – the Thames froze most winters, often so thickly that carriages could be driven from Lambeth to Blackfriars. But that was manageable ice, convenient ice. Tents were pitched on its margins; out in the centre skaters could cut figures of eight on it, the ice crystals fizzing from their boots. London ice was a very different beast from this frozen, belligerent mountain that 'expands itself into . . . great Chinks, and that with a terrible Noise . . . frightens the whole Neighbourhood'.

By the start of the eighteenth century, glaciers had gained a reputation in Britain, and on 12 October 1708 William Burnet, son of the Bishop of Salisbury (and no relation to Thomas), took matters in hand. 'I resolved to go my self and see the Mountains of Ice in *Switzerland*,' he wrote to Dr Hans Sloane, eminent natural historian and then Secretary of the Royal Society, who published his letter in the Society's *Proceedings* that same year. 'Accordingly I went to the Grindelwald, a Mountain two Days Journey from Bern. There I saw, between two Mountains, like a River of Ice, which divides it self in two Branches, and in its way from the top of the Mountains to the bottom swells in vast Heaps, some bigger than *St Paul's* Church.'

Burnet, like John Dennis before him, was confronted with the difficulty of describing something that his readers – the scientific cognoscenti of London – had never seen. He picked his metaphors according to his audience, and could not have chosen a more suggestive, accessible image of size for the metropolitans of the Royal Society than '*St Paul's* Church'. Wren's cathedral was only two years away from completion in 1708, having already been thirty-three years in the building – every Londoner had seen its grey, graceful cupola lending curves and altitude to the city's low-slung skyline; every Londoner had marvelled at its proportions. Burnet's audience were thus furnished with a vivid vision of what the Grindelwald glacier resembled – 'a River of Ice' – and its size – bigger even than Wren's cathedral. This image of the glacier as frozen river would become for a few decades the staple simile for the ice mountains: apposite as it was, it passed straight into the common imagination.

For all his suggestiveness, however, Burnet had done nothing more than look. It did not occur to him to go near the ice, to touch it. It was not until thirty years later, in an act of swaggering braggadocio and self-promotion, that an Englishman would actually set foot upon the glacial ice, and write home about it.

One evening in the summer of 1741, out on the meadows of Sallanches – a small town between Geneva and Chamonix – a little laager of white tents was pitched near to the fields of wheat and rye which the June sun was just beginning to burnish. A pair of sumpter horses was tethered to a stake outside, their panniers bulbous with provisions, and three men with guns stood guard by them, peering into the accumulating gloom in an effort to keep sight of the locals, who were increasing in number with every half-hour. Occasionally, the young man whom the locals had come to see would push back the heavy canvas flap of one of the tents and take a turn about the campsite. He was swathed in the tight turban and voluminous robes of a Levantine potentate, and at his waist hung a dagger whose curve rhymed with that of his exorbitant slippers. His friend walked with him and they laughed together to see the astonished faces of their witnesses. The guards, who were already used to their employers' quirks, said nothing, and concentrated on making sure that no prying hands slipped inside the saddle-bags of the horses.

The pseudo-sultan was Richard Pococke, a compulsive traveller and an aspirant churchman. His companion was William Windham, the eldest and most fractious son of William Windham, the present paterfamilias of a Norfolk dynasty of William Windhams which stretched back to the fifteenth century. Windham the younger had been dispatched to Geneva by his exasperated father, where it was hoped he would pick up the manners and mores befitting a young gentleman from a politically inclined family, but where instead he did nothing but pick up whores, get into fights and keep an ear out for possible entertainments.

It had been Windham who had been keen to see the glaciers of Chamonix – according to the second-hand rumours in London they were simply astonishing. Despite their proximity, only a few Genevans had visited the glaciers; most of the staunch Calvinists of that city believed that God had seen fit to punish the rustically god-less inhabitants of Chamonix by visiting the ice-rivers upon them in a torpid and enduring plague. No one was prepared to accompany Windham to the glaciers, until he met Richard Pococke: a gentle-man, as Windham described him in his published account of their excursion, 'recently arrived at Geneva from his voyages into the Levant and Egypt, which countries he had visited with great Exactness'.

Well armed, well laden and backed up by a trio of Genevan hench-men, the two set off for Chamonix in a little cavalcade of horses on 7 June 1741. From Geneva they rode the four leagues to Bonneville, and thence proceeded along the River Arve, where they were 'entertained with an agreeable Variety of fine Landskips'. That first night, they camped on the fields at Sallanches, and it was there, to the wonder of the locals, that Pococke dressed himself up as a panjandrum (he had brought the clothes with him from Egypt, along with a wooden coffin containing a mummy from Saqqara and a stone statue of Isis).

Word had got about in the valley of their intentions to set foot upon the glaciers, and as they approached Chamonix, riding into the long afternoon shadow of Mont Blanc, a prior came to meet them and to convince them of their folly. But although their first sighting of the glaciers had hardly inspired them – the ends of them 'appear'd only like white Rocks', noted Windham disappointedly, 'or rather like Immense Icicles, made by Water running down the Mountain' – the two men were not to be deflected from their course. As Windham told it afterwards, 'relying on our Strength and Resolution, we determined to attempt the Mountain'.

Having bottled up a wine-and-water mix to fortify themselves at altitude, and leaving the Genevans to guard the camp, Windham and Pococke began to ascend the margin of the glacier, passing 'several Pieces of Ice, which we took at first for Rocks, being as big as a House', and hurrying in silence across the ravaged channels of avalanches, where boulders of ice and shattered tree trunks told of the violence which had passed through. It took them five hours of labo-rious and occasionally dangerous climbing to reach a high promontory. There they stood, pulled the cork from their bottle of watered-down wine, drank a toast and gazed over the cavorting ocean of ice before them.

Windham's account of his expedition was published in the *Proceedings* of the Royal Society, as well as in several other learned journals in Britain and the continent, and news of his venture spread through the country. Richard Pococke seemed less inclined to make much of his part in it all, not even mentioning the expedition in his second volume of travel reminiscences. He died of apoplexy in Ireland in 1765, but would be remembered for far longer than his life-span, both because of the slow-moving boulder on the Mer de Glace which bore his name (engraved there with hammer and chisel by the enchanted locals in memory of their favourite pasha), and because of the Lebanon cedars which he planted as seeds in Ardbraccan in Ireland, where their progeny still stand today – dark and unexpected verticals in a boggy and treeless territory.

'I am extremely at a loss how to give a right Idea of it,' wrote Windham of the glacier itself, 'as I know no one thing which I have ever seen that has the least Resemblance to it.' Like Burnet thirty years before him, Windham had to 'give an idea' of something which was like nothing else at all – a sight which all but confounded metaphor. He managed it by descriptive indirection, by going through another image: 'The Description which Travellers give of the Seas of *Greenland* seems to come the nearest to it,' he wrote. 'You must imagine your lake put in Agitation by a strong Wind, and frozen all at once.' It was a brilliant choice of comparison, for it drew upon the travelogues of those few travellers who had sailed west out of Plymouth and then north, towards the unknown upper reaches of the world, and had returned with stories of seas stiff with cold and air so frigid that one's breath froze and tinkled to the deck.

Windham's image of an agitated, frozen body of water would become the standard description for the Mer de Glace, and indeed for glaciers around the world. Windham was the first to contemplate the glacier as a suspended force, and his flamboyantly written account contributed to the growing sense in Europe of the high mountains as a world apart, an environment where the elements transmigrated one into the other: where water became ice and ice became water, and where the snows lay eternally in defiance of the Alpine sun. When Pierre Martel, a French engineer, made a similar trip to the glaciers three years after Windham, he tried to describe what he saw, but could 'think of nothing more proper' than Windham's image. Windham's metaphor, as metaphors will, controlled Martel's reading of the world.

In 1760 Horace-Bénédict de Saussure identified the Alps as a new world – a sort of 'earthly paradise' – and began his systematic exploration of them. De Saussure had certainly read Windham's letter, and had paid a visit to Pococke's rock on the Mer de Glace, and when he sought to characterize the appearance of the glacier he made use, in a finessed form, of Windham's image. The glacier looks, wrote de Saussure, like 'a sea which has become suddenly frozen, not in the moment of a tempest, but at the instant when the wind has subsided, and the waves, although very high, have become blunted and rounded.' It was this passage which Karl Baedeker quoted in every edition of his guidebook to Switzerland, and that therefore fixed and froze it in the minds of the thousands of Victorians who came to observe the wonders of the glacier: they could conceive of it in no other way. Windham had, from a distance of over a hundred years, whipped up the imaginations of the glacier-goers, and then frozen them with a single metaphor.

Although 'glacier' did not appear as a word in Dr Johnson's capacious *Dictionary* of 1755 – it had yet to push its way officially into the English language from the French – the idea of these fashionably disorderly seas of ice was by that year beginning to grip the imaginations of many Britons, for whom the appearance and the actions of glaciers seemed to answer some powerful cultural need. Once Windham and Pococke had blazed the trail, scores and scores of other tourists made their ecstatic pilgrimages to the glaciers and to Mont Blanc, the White Mountain: certainly the highest peak in the

Old World and thought to be lower only than the fabulous summits of the Andes.

In 1765 the *curé*'s house was the sole lodging for visitors in Chamonix: by 1785 there were three sizeable inns catering for the 1,500 tourists who came every summer to see the glaciers. Chamonix was a boom-town, and the locals cashed in. The honey they made, a golden, clarified liquid, was carried off by visitors and gained a reputation among gourmands as far away as Paris. The villagers would lay out the other natural wealth of the area on blankets in front of their houses: mostly fossils and crystals – pillars of smoky quartz and clear quartz, mocha stones, chunky onyx necklaces, geodes, tiny blocks of tourmaline – but also chamois horns, and the ribbed ram's horns of the mountain goat which spiralled up and out of its skull like ammonites.

Although visitors from across Europe came to behold the glaciers, it was undoubtedly the British who arrived in the largest numbers, and who were the most fervent in their adoration. Touring Switzerland in the winter of 1779, Goethe made his way to Chamonix with the intention of 'walking on the ice itself, and considering these immense masses close at hand'. He took 'nearly a hundred steps round about on the wave-like crystal cliffs' before retreating back to *terra firma* ('the more firmer, the less terror', one late-Victorian tourist would pun nervously in a hotel album a century later, clearly shaken by his trip on the ice) and clambering up to the Montanvert, the rocky outcrop which provided the best view of the Mer de Glace. There he met an Englishman who gave his name simply as Blaire, and who had 'erected a convenient hut upon the spot, from the window of which he and his guests could survey the sea of ice'. 'What a devotion to the spectacle of the ice!' noted Goethe in his journal.

❆

The Mer de Glace, engraving in G. S. Gruner's *Die Eisegebirge des Schweizerlandes* (1760). Note the sightseers in the bottom right-hand corner.

Perhaps a few hundred people have ever crossed the southern fork of the Inylchek glacier on foot. It is an awkward undertaking. There are no rocky hand-rails or balustrades on the ice-dunes which arise in their hundreds in the middle of the glacier – only smooth, convex surfaces of hard ice. Rivers of green meltwater roar and bluster around the base of the dunes, then disappear abruptly into the wide black sink-holes they have bored into the glacier. The individual dunes are joined by fine ridges of blue ice, rounded like the tiles on the apex of a roof. We crossed these ridges like tight-rope walkers, arms outstretched for balance and placing foot precisely in front of foot. When there was no other choice, we abseiled down into the gullies, leapt the rivers, and with axes and crampons climbed back up and out on to the summit of the next dune. The glacier was only two miles or so in width, but it took us seven hours to traverse it. We pitched a tent in the dark on sharp rocks at the foot of a mountain, beneath a moon as flat as a white plate. I slept fitfully, disturbed by the thin air and thoughts of falling, and woke to find that the frost had scribbled across the inside of our tent.

The following day the sky was blue, and the cold air was invisibly afire with sunlight. It was dangerous weather – after only half-an-hour exposed skin would redden, and then bubble overnight into blisters. We tugged our gloves on, swathed our heads in yards of fine white muslin gauze, strapped glacier-goggles over our eyes, and walked down the northern flank of the glacier for miles, in silence. In the mid-afternoon we reached a big glacial lake several acres in area, and we pitched camp on its shores, driving our tent pegs into the blue ice which surrounded it, and weighting down the flysheet with slabs of moraine rock. A fleet of jagged little icebergs navigated slowly about the surface of the lake, mimicking the peaks around them.

After we had pitched our tents, we lay about on the warm rocks by the brink of the lake, and built little towers out of shale. The others went to sleep. The air was still and hot at that time in the afternoon. I could see heat pulsing off the rocks in thick, gelatinous waves. The icebergs had stopped moving. The surface of the water was the colour of an anvil and as calm as steel. It seemed as though if I tried to dive into the lake, I would bounce and skitter across its surface, like a stone thrown on to ice. Only the ingots of sunlight lying on the clear floor of the lake expressed its depth; allowed the eye to get purchase on its dimensions. I sat up, hugged my knees to my chest, and stared into the water for what felt like hours. As I sat there, time seemed to pause. The sunlight seemed to petrify the landscape and the lake.

Only the clouds chimerically forming and reforming miles above me kept up any sort of movement or rhythm by which time could be calibrated. Otherwise, I might have belonged to any aeon. Nothing, it seemed to me then, could be more permanent, nothing more fixed than this tableau of dazzling ice and dark rock – a scene which had lasted for perpetuity and could only continue to do so. The landscape existed above and beyond me; I only happened to be there, a bystander genuinely of no consequence. Nothing more.

Then, unexpectedly, it began to rain: plump raindrops which splashed upon the pale grey of the rocks we were sitting on. The rain partitioned the air, bruised the stone, and plucked the lake up into a field of fleurs-de-lys.

There was a set of verses in the Apocrypha which sent a shiver down the spine of every God-fearing Briton who read it. It articulated a vision of divine punishment being visited upon a sinful earth in the form of icy death: a 'nitre of the north' which gripped the world and froze it. 'When the cold north wind bloweth,' the verses began, implacable and furious:

> and the water is congealed into ice, he poureth the hoar-frost
> upon the earth. It abideth upon every gathering together of
> water, and cloatheth the water with a breastplate. It devoureth
> the mountain, and burneth the wilderness, and consumeth the
> grass as fire.

Nothing was impervious to this apocalyptic ice, which obliterated with the same eager and remorseless energy as the unearthly fire of Revelations.

This Apocryphal vision of a global glacial catastrophe would, over the course of the nineteenth century, come to be realized as true. Geological science would reveal that an Ice Age was something which had happened at least once in the history of the earth, and physical science would suggest that it might happen again in the future. The later nineteenth century had to come to terms with the concept that humanity lived in an epoch bracketed by ages of ice. It was a concept so awful, and so total, that it took the common imagination – especially in green and clement Britain – decades to assimilate it. The horror was mitigated, for Christians at least, only by the knowledge that such an event would be a divine purgative – a purification by cold.

Visiting the Savoy glaciers in the blighted summer of 1816, Percy Shelley had no such religious insulation to keep himself cosy. 'Who *would* be, who *could* be an Atheist in this valley of wonders!' Coleridge had asked in the preface to his 'Hymn before Sunrise in the Vale of Chaumoni'. Reaching Chamonix in mid-July, Shelley had answered Coleridge's pompously modal question by signing himself into the hotel guest-book as '*Atheos*' – atheist.

The evening after his arrival Shelley paid a visit to the Glacier des Bossons. Of all the physical forms which he encountered in the Alps, the glaciers appear to have affected him the most profoundly. He brooded over his experiences among the mountains in two capacious, meditative letters, sent to his novelist friend Thomas Love Peacock, and his thoughts on the glaciers are worth quoting at length, because they were published, and read by many in Britain, and because they startlingly pre-figure the vision of a future ice age which was to haunt the later nineteenth-century imagination:

[The glaciers] flow perpetually into the valley, ravaging in their slow but irresistible progress the pastures and the forests which surround them, performing a work of desolation in ages, which

a river of lava might accomplish in an hour, but far more irre-
trievably; for where the ice has once descended, the hardiest
plant refuses to grow ... The glaciers perpetually move
onward ... they drag with them from the regions whence they
derive their origin, all the ruins of the mountain, enormous
rocks and immense accumulations of sand and stones ... The
pines of the forest, which bound it at one extremity, are over-
thrown and shattered to a wide extent at its base. There is
something inexpressibly dreadful in the aspect of the few
branchless trunks which, nearest to the ice rifts, still stand in the
up-rooted soil ...

If the snow which produces this glacier must augment, and
the heat of the valley is no obstacle to the perpetual existence of
such masses of ice as have already descended into it, the consequence is obvious; the glaciers must augment and will subsist,
at least until they have overflowed this vale.

I will not pursue Buffon's sublime but gloomy theory – that
this globe which we inhabit will at some future period be
changed into a mass of frost by the encroachments of the polar
ice, and of that produced on the most elevated parts of the
earth –

And so Shelley continued, spinning out his nightmare of an earth
turned into a necropolis of ice. He was writing with half a mind to
publication, and his language tends occasionally towards the melo-
dramatic, but there is no doubting the disturbance the glaciers caused
him. Given time enough, he thinks, there is nothing on earth to stop
these perpetually moving glaciers from pouring out of their rightful
environment, overflowing the vale, and melding with the ice-caps to
encase the world in ice. And time – as we have already seen – was
something that geological science had recently been discovering in
abundance.

The future freezing of the earth would have seemed more than usually plausible in that summer of 1816. The previous year Tambora, an Indonesian volcano, had erupted and its pall of dust and cinders had been carried across the world on the trade winds. The particles of debris coalesced into strange aerial shapes over Europe and America and sometimes performed dancing light shows, such as those regularly reported by explorers in the polar regions. Lurid, Turnerian sunsets burnt every evening, though the days were far colder than usual. The global temperature dropped by up to two degrees centigrade, harvests failed, and thousands died of famine or froze to death. There was no summer. Even the sun seemed disrupted – large sunspots were visible to the naked eye and in the streets of London people squinted up at them through shards of smoked glass.

Little wonder, then, that on that uncommonly cold July day Shelley's imagination saw in the glaciers the agents of the world's end. Byron, who was holidaying on the continent with Shelley that year, also sensed something terrifyingly inexorable in the way the 'glacier's cold and restless mass / Moves onward day by day', and the shroud of ash which had been pulled over the skies provoked in him a similar vision of death by freezing: the globe desolated by ice, and home to no man. 'I had a dream which was not all a dream', began his famous poem 'Darkness', which he wrote that same summer:

> The bright sun was extinguish'd, and the stars
> Did wander darkling in the eternal space,
> Rayless, and pathless, and the icy earth
> Swung blind and blackening in the moonless air;

Shelley and Byron's visions of a world plunged into deep-freeze were no doubt dismissed by some as the hypotheses of poets with too much time on their hands. Subsequent scientific discoveries, however, were to prove them not winsomely melancholic, but appallingly accurate.

The idea of the Ice Age did not diffuse into the cultural consciousness, but arrived with very little preparation, docking like an unexpected liner. The man widely held responsible for bringing the Ice Age to public knowledge was Louis Agassiz, a visionary and erratic Swiss scientist who had built a reputation as a palaeontologist before moving into the embryonic discipline of glaciology in the late 1830s. The better to pursue his research, he founded a rudimentary laboratory high in the Bernese Oberland: a wooden cabin perched on the shaley moraine of the Unteraar glacier. The cabin itself became part of his experiments on glacial motion, being conveyed downhill on its bed of rocks at – Agassiz calculated – a regal mean rate of 349 feet per annum until, during the spring of 1840, it collapsed in on its unoccupied self. (Agassiz arrived at his laboratory that summer to discover a heap of debris, the separate items of which were beginning to move in interestingly different directions. He was obliged to seek shelter elsewhere.)

It was high in the Oberland that Agassiz began to form his spectacular conclusions about the one-time extent of the glaciers. 'Since I saw the glaciers,' he wrote to an English geologist, 'I am quite of a snowy humor, and will have the whole surface of the earth quite covered with ice, and the whole prior creation dead by cold.' It was not an idle boast. In 1840 Agassiz published *Études sur les Glaciers* – or 'The Ice Book' as it was referred to by the British – a work which was rumoured to have been written in a single night of fervid creativity. That same year he toured Britain, lecturing on his radical new theory: that Europe, and quite probably much of the rest of the world, had as recently as 14,000 years ago been thickly sheathed in ice. The Alpine glaciers, in Agassiz's opinion, had been greatly extended, and the Arctic ice-cap had encroached south across the latitudes; relentlessly excavating, denuding and reorganizing, ironing out the plains of Eastern Europe, filling hills and dales alike with glaciers. Buffon's sublime but gloomy theory was being proved true, at least retroactively.

Agassiz's purpose was scientific, but his style, like his personality, was dramatic, as can be seen in an article he wrote for the *Edinburgh New Philological Journal* in 1841. The earth, he claimed, had been plunged into:

> a climate such as the poles of our earth can scarcely produce – a cold, in which everything that had life was benumbed, suddenly appeared. Nowhere did the earth offer creatures protection against the omnipotence of the cold. Whithersoever they fled, into the dens of the mountains, which formerly had served to many of them as a lurking-place, or into the thickets of the forest, everywhere, they succumbed to the might of the annihilating element ... A crust of ice soon covered the superficies of the earth, and enveloped in its rigid mantle the remains of organisms, which but a moment before had been enjoying existence upon its surface ... everything organic upon the earth was put an end to.

To the early Victorian mind, still very much in thrall to the Sublime, Agassiz's was a thrilling vision, excitingly awful in its totality. The ice had hunted life to its last lurking-place, had obliterated 'everything organic', and had rewritten the land. Agassiz's proposals were at first dismissed as ridiculous. But he possessed persuasive ocular proof – the striated rocks, the angular erratics, the inexplicable Till – and his campaign gradually began to gain support. 'You have made all the geologists glacier-mad here,' a Scottish scientist wrote to Agassiz after he delivered a lecture in Glasgow, 'and they are turning Great Britain into an ice-house.'

It is difficult for us to understand how drastically the idea of the Ice Age rewrote the nineteenth-century world-view. It affected almost

A three-layer panorama from 1860 showing the modern 'Adamitic' world (top layer) separated by the 'sharp sword' of the Ice Age (second layer) from the reptiles and mammals of the Tertiary and Secondary periods. Lithograph by W. R. Woods, from Isabella Duncan's *Pre-Adamite Man* (1860).

every scientific discipline – natural history, chemistry, physics – and obliged the rethinking of much of anthropology, natural history and theology. More immediately, familiar landscapes had suddenly to be looked at with very different eyes. In Llanberis in Wales, in Windermere in the Lake District, in the Cairngorms or in Switzerland, the evidence of the passage of the Ice Age could now be seen: scooped corries, U-shaped valleys, gigantic boulders, and the blade-like ridges which had been sharpened by glacial action. John Ruskin, in the fourth volume of *Modern Painters*, described how in the Alpine valleys 'there are yet visible the tracks of ancient glaciers . . . the footmark, so to speak, of a glacier is just as easily recognisable as the tracks of a horse that had passed along a soft road which yet retained the prints of its shoes'. Ruskin's image – the glacier as a horse, the hard mountain as a soft road – made the ancient superbly immediate; collapsed the deep past into the familiar present.

Glaciers became big news. Major cultural critics of the day – Ruskin, John Tyndall – discussed their import. Words were exchanged in the pages of the quarterlies over the cause of motion of glaciers and over the precise physical nature of glacial ice. Ruskin, with characteristic aplomb and perhaps with a desire to put an end to the pettifogging, declared them to be 'one great accumulation of ice-cream, poured upon the tops, and flowing to the bottoms, of the mountains.'

The considerable column inches devoted to glaciers between the 1840s and the 1870s, and the revelation of the Ice Age, increased the number of glacier-goers, who were eager to see at first-hand these masses of ice which had shaped the surface of the world. The 'little glaciers of the present day' were, as Tyndall put it, 'mere pigmies as compared to the giants of the glacial epoch', but that was just fine, for it pleased the imagination to attempt that enlargement of pigmy to giant. Visitors to the glens of Scotland imagined them being sculpted by glaciers that had long since deliquesced, and visitors to the extant Alpine glaciers imagined them for what they had once been: mighty rivers of ice encasing the earth.

What profoundly horrified the later Victorians – as it had horrified Shelley – was the possibility that the Ice Age might come again; this time as tragedy. In 1862 the physicist William Thomson, better known as Lord Kelvin, had made public his belief that the sun was cooling without renewal of its energy. Not only was there nothing new under the sun, but the sun itself was nothing new, and was ageing day by day. Owing to the slow and irreversible seep of entropy, the solar system was condemned to what had been christened 'Heat Death'. It was Buffon's nebular hypothesis all over again, except that this time it was not the globe which was cooling down, but its lantern and radiator, the sun. The universe was pulsing away on a limited wattage, science had proved, and the icy earth would at some point in the future swing blind and blackening through space.

Solar physics was a hot topic among articulate Victorians from the 1850s onwards. Kelvin's discovery (which would not be discredited until the discovery of radioactive salts by Rutherford in the early years of the twentieth century) made a universal winter – another Ice Age – historically foreseeable. The Poles themselves, 'the crystalline continents', were inaccessible, but out on the glaciers of the Alps, or the Caucasus, or the Karakorum, it was possible for the Victorians to confront their fears of obliteration; to acquaint themselves with the means of their future destruction. They felt the same horrified awe that we might feel in visiting the gleaming, ranked warheads of a nuclear arsenal. The return of the Ice Age, indeed, was their nuclear winter.

I first saw John Ruskin's drawing of the Glacier du Bois while leafing through the second volume of his thirty-nine-volume *Works*, appalled at the industry of the man. It is a startling sketch. Ruskin decided that it would be impossible to replicate the formal qualities of the ice itself: conventional realism would be thwarted by its appearance. So he sought instead to depict the relationship between the observer and the observed; to present not the ice as it was, but the ice as he saw it – to paint the act of perception.

In 1842, J. M. W. Turner, whom Ruskin venerated, had completed one of his finest canvases, *Snow Storm: Steamboat off a Harbour's Mouth Making Signals in Shallow Water, and Going by the Lead.* There is, at first glance, no steamboat in this picture, only snow storm. The canvas is aswirl with dark colours, a viscous whirlpool of cloud canted up to the vertical. Only after a few seconds, and with the help of the title, does the ship become visible, its round dark mill-wheel barely discernible through the spume, the fire from its furnaces gilding only a tiny area of heaving sea. Once the ship has been seen, then the long black-brown limb of storm reaching down from the thunderheads is understood to be nothing of the sort, but the billowing smoke-stack reaching upwards. Finally, at the very centre of the whirlpool, one spots deliverance – a hint of blue, the tinted iris of the storm, an eye-shaped glimpse of good weather. Not enough to make a Dutchman a pair of trousers, but blue sky nevertheless.

Ruskin's drawing of the glacier is clearly modelled on Turner's painting of the snowstorm. There is the same forceful sense of vortex, of centripetal energy. Spindrift – the loose particles of snow and ice blown by wind – lisps over every surface. A chough or raven flies just on the event horizon of the picture, as does a bristly old tree bole – both apparently about to be swirled inescapably down into the pale plug-hole of the sun. Even Ruskin's signature, in the bottom left-hand corner, is bending under the strain, its ends being tugged inwards by the pull of the drawing. In the background the mountains stand in profile, like white knives, echoed by the pinnacled surface of the glacier. Ruskin comes nearer in this drawing than any other artist I have ever seen to catching the experience of being on a glacier. He brilliantly compounds its paradox of stasis and dramatic force. On a glacier, one is always aware of motion in the midst of stillness: there is, as Gerard Manley Hopkins observed of an Alpine ice-river, 'an air of interrupted activity'.

I fell into a crevasse once, walking over the snowed-up surface of a Swiss glacier and whistling, as I tend to do on glaciers, the Doors' song 'Break on through to the Other Side'. I did. There was a creak, and then an awareness of collapse beneath my feet, like a trap-door opening.

The Glacier du Bois, etching from a drawing by John Ruskin (1843).

I dropped vertically, and jammed at belly-level in the ice, the air punched from my lungs by the fall. My lower half had entered another element. It felt colder, much colder down there. My feet, heavy with boots and crampons, kicked in emptiness, until I realized this might dislodge me and I let them hang, toe-downwards, and spread my arms out across the snow, in the upper world. There was a sensation of unknowable depth beneath me and I was gripped by a terrible vertigo. It was the same feeling as when, aged thirteen, I stepped from the brink of a yacht into sea several miles off the coast of Corsica, where the charts showed a submarine trench of 4,000 feet. The water was clear, tinged with blue. My brother and I dropped two silver centimes and with scuba masks watched their slow bright tumble, head over tail, for what seemed like hours through the water. Suddenly I was seized with panic, with the fear of losing my buoyancy and tumbling helplessly downwards after the coins. I had to be pulled from the water by my father, who cupped me under my armpits and lifted me out in one fluid movement, trailing a tail of sea water.

My climbing partner hauled me gracelessly from the glacier, like a body from a swimming-pool, and I lay on the snow gasping, almost asthmatic with fear. That night, safe in an Alpine hut but sleepless on a thin mattress with other climbers turning all about me, my mind got to work on what had happened, luxuriating in the conditional tense. Had I dropped into the crevasse, the glacier would have gone about its business as surely as if I had not been there. Its internal machinery would have annihilated my body. Had I fallen, like the French Protestant minister, into a crevasse the size of a 'grand and spacious hall', the sides would have closed in over the months, and the space would have diminished from ballroom, to bedroom, to broom cupboard, to coffin.

❄

Glaciers compounded two concepts that were especially exciting to the nineteenth-century imagination: great force and great time. In *Travels through the Alps of Savoy*, the Scottish glaciologist James Forbes drew attention to this last aspect of them. 'A glacier is an endless scroll,' he wrote, 'a stream of time upon whose stainless ground is engraven the succession of events, whose dates far transcend the memory of living man. Assuming the length of a glacier to be roughly twenty miles, and its annual progression 500 feet, the block which is now discharged from its surface on the terminal moraine may have started from its rocky origin in the reign of Charles I!' To walk down the 'wide gleaming causeway' of a glacier, therefore, was to walk backwards in time. To descend into a crevasse was to encounter ice that had been compacted when the Civil War was in progress. To behold a gargantuan avalanche or an ice-fall, as did Robert Ker Porter, an English aristocrat and soldier travelling in the Caucasus in the late 1810s, was to witness the collapse of ages – 'the snows and ice of centuries, pouring down in immense shattered forms and rending heaps!' Glaciers and the mountains around them forced the human mind to think in different ways, and at different speeds.

There is a lovely anecdote about Mark Twain, who visited Switzerland with his family in 1878. Having climbed high up the eastern side of Zermatt valley, they pondered the easiest way back down. 'I resolved,' Twain remembered in *A Tramp Abroad*, 'to take passage for Zermatt on the great Gorner glacier.'

> I marched the Expedition down the steep and tedious mule-path and took up as good a position as I could upon the middle of the glacier – because Baedeker said the middle part travels the fastest. As a measure of economy, however, I put some of the heavier baggage on the shoreward parts, to go as slow freight. I waited and waited, but the glacier did not move. Night was coming on, the darkness began to gather – still we did not budge. It occurred

to me then, that there might be a time-table in Baedeker; it would be well to find out the hours of starting. I soon found a sentence which threw a dazzling light upon the matter. It said, 'The Gorner Glacier travels at an average rate of a little less than an inch a day.' I have seldom felt so outraged. I have seldom had my confidence so wantonly betrayed. I made a small calculation: One inch a day, say thirty feet a year; estimated distance to Zermatt, three and one-eighteenth miles. Time required to go by glacier, a little over five hundred years! The passenger part of this glacier – the central part – the lightning-express part, so to speak – was not due in Zermatt till the summer of 2378, and that the baggage, coming along the slow edge, would not arrive until some generations later . . . As a means of passenger transportation, I consider the glacier a failure . . .

Twain, with a characteristically charming lack of gravity, was satirizing an attitude towards nature which has since come to predominate: we expect nature to do our bidding, to fall into step with us. Or we override it with technology, and render its rhythms superfluous. Our need for speed has led us to esteem the streamlined, the dynamic in all things, and that estimation has accelerated us out of sync with the natural world.

But slowness and stasis have their own virtues too, their own aesthetic, and it is well to be reminded of that from time to time. Early one spring I caught a minibus out of Beijing. It drove north past the frozen Mi yun reservoir – acre after acre of silver ice – which provides Beijing with much of its water, and up into the pleated landscape along whose narrow ridges the Great Wall marches. After three hours the bus turned off the main asphalt road and hairpinned laboriously up a rubbled track.

We stopped, finally, in the shadowed floor of a gorge. High above us on its north wall was a squat watchtower, supervising the land around as it had done for 800 years. Spilling off the rim of the gorge was a frozen waterfall: thick pipes of dirty yellow ice three or four hundred feet in length, and between them vertical stripes of clean blue ice. The whole frozen fall looked like a Gothic pipe-organ, with its tubes and wind-tunnels radiating extravagantly up and out. The air was warm, and from the tips of the lowest icicles meltwater ran in continuous streams.

We strapped on crampons, picked up a pair of axes each, and spent the day climbing the fall. During a break I took off my climbing gear, and scrambled down to explore the frozen river into which the waterfall plunged. Seen from an oblique angle, the ice appeared blue ridged with silver. I dropped down on to it.

Where the ice filled the gaps between the shoreline stones it was the milky white colour of cataracts. The big resident boulders out in the middle of the river, which would in summer have generated whirlpools and rapids, were surrounded by smooth planes of transparent ice. Looking down into the ice I could see its deepness, marked by the birch leaves suspended in it and by plump white air bubbles which ascended like strings of pearls. There was a clatter, and I glanced up. A mink poured itself out of the shadows on one side of the river, skittered across the damp ice and galloped off over the flat stones on the other side. It printed them with wet pawmarks, black decals which in the dry air faded quickly back into the colour of stone.

My sense of wonder at the frozen waterfall and the halted river derived from the absolute stasis of something that would normally be absolutely turbulent. Perhaps our quickening obsession with speed has to do with our end-of-the-worldliness: the latent sense, unique to our modern age, that apocalypse might come either by ice (the death of the sun) or by fire (nuclear holocaust). I had wondered about this, though I had not found anyone else who did until, reading through Théophile Gautier's journalism, I came across a passage from 1884:

How strange is this wild urge for rapid locomotion seizing people of all nations at the same instant. 'The dead go swiftly', says the ballad. Are we dead then? Or could this be some presentiment of the approaching doom of our planet, possessing us to multiply the means of communication so we may travel over its entire surface in the little time left to us?

Terrifying in their slow implacability, ripe with history and, at least to the properly primed imagination, thrillingly beset with hazards – it was unsurprising that glaciers attracted such a quantity of avid guests to them in the nineteenth century. Above all, glaciers offered somewhere that was utterly different. As Ruskin wrote admiringly of the Zmutt glacier, 'the whole scene [is] so changeless and soundless; so removed, not merely from the presence of men, but even of their thoughts'. When in 1828 John Murray and his wife trekked into the middle of the glacier of Talèfre, they sat down among the seventy-foot ice pyramids to slug from a flask of brandy, and reflected on the splendour of their situation:

> Amid these awful and icy solitudes, no voice was heard but our own. The stillness of death reigned around, save only that it was, at distant intervals, broken by the thundering crash, announcing the fall of a distant avalanche, or the rending of the mighty glacier. In this vast amphitheatre, walled in by mountains of snow, here and there penetrated by the peaked summits of their aiguilles, reigns an eternal winter, the accumulated snows of many ages, the wreck and run of rocks, and all the magnificent personification of dread desolation . . .

Solitude, deathliness, sterility, barrenness, inhumanity – these were the qualities of a landscape which Romanticism had made so appealing. The polar wastes exemplified this landscape ideal, but in the nineteenth century, as now, the poles were unapproachable to all save the most determined and well-financed explorers. It was the glaciers of Europe, South America and Asia which provided the nearest and finest approximation to the poles. People came – as they still come, as I have come – to enjoy them in their tens of thousands, and to die by the dozen: drawn to the ice by feelings that had, like the glaciers themselves, accumulated over the centuries.

5

Altitude:
the Summit and the View

Now away we go towards the top. Many still, small voices are
calling 'Come Higher'.

JOHN MUIR, 1911

'They sit there like Buddhas in the snow,' Sasha told us. 'I have
myself seen more than a dozen of them.' He meant bodies, the bodies
of climbers, most of them Russian, who have died on the summit
ridge of Pik Pobeda: Victory Peak, the highest point in the Tian
Shan mountains. Sasha wasn't trying to impress us. He knew he had
no need of that. For three-quarters of the year he was a lecturer in
mathematics at a Moscow institute, and every summer for three
months – the weather window – he came to the Tian Shan to climb
harder and harder routes. He spoke almost irreproachable English,
had outsize, bottle-thick glasses, and always wore a scrawny down
jacket and a pair of patched *salopettes*.

We looked up at the ridge, some five miles away. At high altitude
the depressurized air acts as a lens, bringing distant objects closer.
From where we were on the glacier we could see the hunched, bulky
outline of Pobeda immaculately, each serac and snow-field on its

seven-mile-long summit ridge picked out. The evening light had sluiced the snow pink, so that it looked curiously benign, like strawberry ice-cream. We stood there, five of us, our breath pluming in the cold air, thinking about the bodies. I imagined them leaning casually against snow-banks, as though they were just sleeping, as though you might shake them awake. I imagined them sitting there along the summit ridge like cairns, marking the way to the top.

It was more likely, though, that their bodies had been contorted by the cold, their clothes had been pulverized by storms and sunlight and lay in tatters around them, and their skin had been bleached and beaten off their bones.

'I remember hearing of one man,' Sasha said, gesturing up at the ridge. 'He reached the summit in bad conditions, thick snow, with two others. They could see another big storm coming from the east, so they turned round straight away and followed their own tracks back along the ridge. After five minutes' walking, he went blind in one eye. Click! Just like that – blackness. Like turning off a light. His retina had gone. A couple more paces and click! – the other one went too. Both retinas ripped off by the pressure. They led him for a while, but he would never get down with no eyes. Finally he just sat down in the snow to die.'

Sasha shrugged his shoulders. 'He's still up there. That is how it is at height.'

Sight is often all you have at high altitudes. The other senses are abolished. It is too cold to feel anything, too high to smell anything, your taste-buds are dulled, and there is no sound except for your own breathing. Sight is essential: you need your eyes to spot the few scarves of cirrus which might be the outriders of a storm, or to place your feet methodically one in front of the other during a blizzard, or to look at the view – which is likely to be one of the reasons why you are up in such a dangerous, aerial world in the first place.

Like altitude, memory can lend a peculiar sharpness to certain images. When I was seven I clearly remember my grandfather showing me a black-and-white photograph, perhaps ten inches by five, of a snow ridge in the Alps which he had climbed – the Biancograt of the Piz Bernina. The ridge was so sharp that it appeared to cut the sunlight in two: one side of the ridge blazed whitely, the other was cast in shadow. In the background was only the sky, and at its summit the ridge tapered to a snow cone. From the tip of this cone unfurled a white flag of cloud. With his little finger, my grandfather pointed out the flag. He told me it was a stream of ice crystals being blown off the mountain by the wind. To me this peak, dipping its point up into the empty air and flying its flag of ice, seemed extra-terrestrial. I could not believe my grandfather had climbed it.

Most summers when I was young we would drive up to visit my grandparents in the Scottish Highlands, and use their house as a base for days in the hills. My grandfather kept his climbing equipment in a garage that was always cold and smelt of engine oil. There were his skis, for a long time taller than me, and the seal-skins which he slipped over their bases. He explained to me how the nap of the skin meant the skins would slide over the snow only in one direction: when he wanted to ascend, they stopped him slipping backwards. His ski-poles were straight and wooden, with metal tips and wide, circular buckets of rattan. Two crampons always sat together near the skis, the grey metal oiled, articulated and fanged. They were like two little monsters. And there was his ice-axe, three feet long and heavy as an oar, its wooden shaft coated in varnish and the steel adze scarred with use.

My grandfather grew up in Montreux on the eastern shore of Lake Geneva, and on his way to and from school he passed a monument to an Englishman and his son who had fallen to their deaths while descending the grassy lower slopes of a peak near Arolla. Each summer he would go up into the mountains in the company of Big Labby, a Dutch friend of the family whose nickname did little justice to his size. At the age of nine my grandfather climbed his first 3,000-metre peak in the Alps, the Haute Cime of the Dents du Midi. On its summit he met General Charles Bruce, the man who led the Everest expeditions in 1922 and 1924. The grand old general, shot about and scarred after sustained active service in the British army, had a few quiet words with Labby and my grandfather, and then romped off down the steep side of the mountain. My grandfather descended tentatively by the easy way, nursing the encounter to himself. He has always held that unexpected meeting to mark the start of his climbing life.

Over the years I discovered more about the scars in that ice-axe. My grandfather had climbed in the Himalaya, North America and all over Europe. There was a gully route named after him in the Ala Dag range in Turkey, which he explored during his wartime leave. Shortly after marrying my grandmother, who had herself climbed extensively in the British Isles, the Venezuelan Andes and the volcanoes of the West Indies, he took her on a climbing holiday to the Valais region of Switzerland. Early in the week a storm hustled in and kept them confined to the remote Turtmanntal hut for three days, with only a single large onion to eat between them. He advised me against planning 'this sort of jaunt' for my own honeymoon. For his seventieth birthday, he and my grandmother joined an expedition to the mountains of Bhutan. Unseasonally heavy snowfall blocked them into a valley at over 4,000 metres; finally the Indian army had to be persuaded to airlift them out using helicopters. I recall anxious afternoons back in England – us sipping tea aimlessly, not really speaking, waiting for the phone to ring.

My grandfather's veneration of high places has never wavered. It is not something he has seen fit to question, although friends of his have died and been appallingly injured in the mountains. One friend, forced to spend a night in an ice-cave high on a Himalayan peak, lost sixteen fingers and toes to frostbite. He was twenty-two at the time. I met him once, fifty years after the event. Instinctively I put out my hand to shake his, and was shocked to feel the bulbous palm, the shiny nubs where the fingers had been.

I tried to talk to my grandfather about it once: about why he loved being at height, about why he had spent – and risked – his life struggling to reach so many summits. He didn't really understand the question, or even that it was a question. To my grandfather the attraction of altitude was beyond explanation, or had none. How is it, though, that summits and views have gained such an attractive force over the imagination of so many? Or as Tennyson put it in a tone of mild incomprehension – for although mountains obtrude now and again into his poetry, he was not constitutionally a man for the heights, preferring to pass his holidays on the Isle of Wight – 'What pleasure lies in height . . . in height and cold?'

We might answer Tennyson's question simply by saying that the urge to explore space – to go higher – is innate to the human mind. The French philosopher of space and matter, Gaston Bachelard, considers the desire for altitude to be a universal instinct. 'A human being,' he writes, 'in his youth, in his taking off, in his fecundity, wants to rise up from the earth. The leap is a basic form of joy.' Certainly, the equation of height with goodness is embedded in our language and consequently in the way we think. Our verb 'to excel' comes from the Latin *excelsus,* meaning elevated or high. Our noun 'superiority' is from the Latin comparative *superior,* meaning higher in situation, place or station. 'Sublime' originally meant lofty, distinguished or raised above. And so on. Conversely, a clutch of pejorative words are associated with depth: 'lowliness', 'inferiority', 'base', dozens more. We construct our models of progress on a gradient. We move on up, or we sink back down. It is harder to do the former than the latter, but that makes it only more admirable. One does not, under any linguistic circumstances, progress down. Most religions operate on a vertical axis in which heaven or their analogue of that state is up, and its opposite is down. To ascend, therefore, is in some fundamental way to approach divinity.

More recently, the mountain summit has become a secular symbol of effort and reward. 'To peak' is to reach the high point of an endeavour. To be 'on top of the world' is to feel incomparably well. Undoubtedly, the sense of accomplishment which comes from reaching a mountain-top has historically been a key element of the desire for height. This is unsurprising – what simpler allegory of success could there be than the ascent of a mountain? The summit provides the visible goal, the slopes leading up to it the challenge. When we walk or climb up a mountain we traverse not only the actual terrain of the hillside but also the metaphysical territories of struggle and achievement. To reach a summit is very palpably to have triumphed over adversity: to have conquered something, albeit something utterly useless. It is the imagined significance of the summit – which is, after all, nothing but a patch of rock or snow raised higher than any other by the contingencies of geology; a set of co-ordinates in space; a figment of geometry; a point without a point – which has largely given rise to the industry of ascent.*

A sense of success is not the only pleasure which lies in height, however. There is also a joy to be found in the sensory experience of

---

* Not everybody likes climbing mountains, of course. Somebody funny, I can't remember who, remarked sagely that 'When a man's circumference bears more than a certain ratio to his altitude, he prefers the plains in the bottom of his soul.' This said, the invention of funiculars, cable-cars, chair-lifts and all the other heavy machinery of ascent is testimony to the urge felt to get high even by those not naturally predisposed to walking up mountains.

altitude: a bliss which isn't competitive, but contemplative. Height makes strange even the most familiar of scenes. To look over a city you have lived in all your life from the top of a tower is to see it afresh. The poet George Keates, a friend of Voltaire, put it well when he wrote that at height 'a new Creation bursts upon our Sight'. View the features of a landscape from the top of a mountain, and they look very different – rivers resemble ribbons, lakes silver blades and boulders flecks of dust. The land resolves itself into abstract patterns or unexpected images.

One October I reached the summit of Bla Bheinn, a mountain on the Isle of Skye. It was a bright day, but the top 300 feet of the mountain were swaddled in cloud, and I didn't realize until I entered the cloud that the summit was also blanketed with snow. When I reached the top I stopped and stood for a while, wrapped in white snow and white cloud. I could not see more than twenty feet in any direction. It was hard to make out where the land ended and the sky began, except where black rocks jagged through the whiteness. As I stood there, a blizzard of snow-buntings whirled unexpectedly across in front of me, their black under-wings startling against the snow's whiteness, the little flock turning as one bird. Black and white, the chessboard colour scheme of high mountains.

And then suddenly, briefly, the clouds cleared from around me. The coastline was laid out like a map to north and south, the dark fingers of the land clasping the silver fingers of the Atlantic. A window opened in the cloud cover far out at sea, and the sun projected a golden island of light down on to the water. Then it closed again, and the cloud closed round me, and I turned away to begin the descent.

We are now less amazed by the perspective from above, bombarded as we are with images taken from aeroplanes or satellites. But imagine how startling it must have been to the early summiteers, who had never seen anything like this aerial view, suddenly to find themselves looking down on the world. To these travellers the visionary amplitudes of altitude felt like approximations of divine sight. Reading through early accounts of ascent, time and again one encounters the successful mountain-climber comparing himself to what the Greeks called the *kataskapos* – the looker-down, the heavenly observer, suddenly and marvellously blessed with a cartographer's perspective on the world.

For a long time, Noah held the altitude record. Opinion differs sharply as to the location and height of the biblical Mount Ararat, upon the slopes of which the Ark was deposited by the subsiding flood-waters. And according to the expedition log (the Book of Genesis) Noah never actually made it to the summit. Nevertheless, it was indisputable that he had been to a considerable altitude. William Whiston, an eighteenth-century Cambridge cosmogonist, calculated that the mountain upon which the Ark came to rest was six miles high – that is, nearly 32,000 feet: 3,000 feet or so higher than Mount Everest. Had Whiston's arithmetic been correct, and had the Ark been laden as described in Genesis, its humans and other animals would have died swiftly of hypothermia, hypoxia and the other fatal effects of extreme altitude. Shem, Ham, Japheth and Noah's other implausibly fertile sons and daughters would not have gone forth and multiplied. The world would not have been restocked with flora, fauna or humanity.

So perhaps Whiston erred on the high side. But then early estimates of altitude, like early estimates of geological time, were deeply muddled. This is unsurprising. There was no need for accurate calculations of height. Almost no one climbed mountains, and for those few who did it was not a comparative undertaking. Measuring the depths of seas, or the extent of coastlines, was far more necessary than measuring height. Pliny the Elder claimed the highest mountain in the world reached 300,000 feet above sea-level: out by over 270,000 feet. Until the eighteenth century the volcanic Peak of Tenerife was thought by many to be the highest mountain in the world because it rose straight from the sea so prominently on one of the major maritime trade routes. It is in fact well under half the height of Everest.

To those early travellers who were obliged to go to altitude – the merchants and pilgrims who crossed the Alpine passes on their way to and from Rome, for example – it was obvious from the nausea, dizziness and headaches they experienced that there was a bad fit between height and the human body. Of the many early accounts of what is now referred to as AMS – Acute Mountain Sickness – perhaps the most vivid is to be found in the diary of Jose de Acosta, who in 1580 found himself unable to complete a journey in the Andes due to an attack of what the Andeans called *puna*. 'I was surprised with such pangs of straining and casting', wrote de Acosta, 'as I thought to cast up my heart too, having cast up meate fleugme and choller, both yellow & greene.' Travellers sought to combat the effects of altitude by clasping vinegar-soaked sponges to their mouths and noses; this seems to have done little to mitigate the symptoms of altitude, or to increase the pleasures of the journey.

There is scant evidence that any widespread aesthetic appreciation of views was in operation in Europe before the eighteenth century. Those who did find themselves at height among the mountains were often more concerned with the prospect of survival than with the prospect. The idea of the beautiful view, which now seems to us as instinctive a reaction to a landscape as is possible, does not seem to have had currency in the common consciousness, or at least not to have been triggered by mountains. Quite the opposite, in fact: until well into the 1700s, travellers who had to cross the Alpine passes often chose to be blindfolded in order to prevent them being terrified

by the appearance of the peaks. When the philosopher Bishop
Berkeley traversed Mont Cenis on horseback in 1714, he recorded
being very much 'put out of humour by the most horrible precipices'.
Even the anonymous author of *Les Délices de la Suisse* (1730), probably the earliest tourist brochure for Switzerland, was appalled by the
'prodigious height' of the Alps, and their 'eternal snows'. 'These great
excrescences of the earth,' he wrote, 'to outward appearance have neither use nor comeliness.' He chose to advertise instead the neatness
of the towns, and the happiness and health of Swiss cattle.

The usual starting-point for histories of altitude is the Italian poet
Petrarch's description of his ascent, with his energetic brother
Gherardo, of Mont Ventoux – a benign 1,910-metre lump in the
Vaucluse – in April of 1336. Upon reaching the summit of the
mountain, Petrarch was amazed by the vista:

> As if suddenly wakened from sleep, I turned about and gazed
> toward the west. I was unable to discern the summits of the
> Pyrenees, which form the barrier between France and Spain; not
> because of any intervening obstacle that I know of but owing
> simply to the insufficiency of our mortal vision. But I could see
> with the utmost clearness, off to the right, the mountains of the
> region about Lyons, and to the left the bay of Marseilles and the
> waters that lash the shores of Aigues Mortes, altho' all these
> places were so distant that it would require a journey of several
> days to reach them.

Petrarch and Gherardo descended in the gathering darkness to an inn
at the foot of the mountain, and by the light of a candle the poet

jotted down his account of the day. Petrarch's ascent is undoubtedly momentous for the history of height. Its importance is tempered, however, because of the insistence with which Petrarch turns his experience into a religious allegory. Nothing in his description – the path he takes up the mountain, the view from the summit, the clothes he wears – can be only itself: rather, all are significant details in an account bristling with symbolism. Some scholars suggest that the ascent did not take place at all, but was simply a convenient fictional framework over which to drape Petrarch's metaphysical musings, and an opportunity to draw a pious moral. 'How earnestly should we strive, not to stand on mountain-tops,' Petrarch concluded, 'but to trample beneath us those appetites which spring from earthly impulses.'

To witness the first flashes of interest in mountain-tops not just as spiritual emblems but as actual physical forms which are affecting to behold, we must look to the 1600s, when the template for the famous Grand Tour – the edifying trip around the cities and landscapes of continental Europe which, in the late seventeenth and the eighteenth centuries, it became usual for moneyed (or disgraced) young men to take – was just being forged. These Grand Tourists would return as the bearers and disseminators of new cultural attitudes towards landscape in general and mountains in particular. Among the first generation of young Britons who chose to sample the Tour was the diarist John Evelyn, whose journal would bring him such posthumous fame (it was written between 1641 and 1706, discovered in a laundry-basket in 1817 and published for the first time the following year).

One November evening in 1644 Evelyn and two companions were trotting past the outer walls of the Rocca castle in the mountains of northern Italy. Through the evening air came the sound of a big church bell, rung by one of the Capucin monks who lived on an island in the nearby lake of Bolsena. Only a few weeks earlier, while crossing the Alps into Italy, Evelyn had been repelled by the 'strange, horrid and fearful' appearance of the mountains. In his diary entries for those days he had railed against the Alpine peaks, rehearsing the conventional seventeenth-century objections to mountains: that their steepness prevents the free range of the eye; that they are 'desarts' – barren of life and of no use to anyone.

What a surprise it was to Evelyn that so soon after that unpleasant experience he should find himself thrilled by height. For, as he rode further up the mountain, he was rewarded with one of the most exciting and beautiful effects of altitude – the cloud inversion, when the mountain-goer discovers him or herself suddenly to be above the clouds.

> We pass'd into very thick, soled [solid] and darke body of Clowds, which look'd like rocks at a little distance, which dured [stayed with] us for neere a mile going up; they were dry misty Vapours hanging undissolved for a vast thickness, and altogether both obscuring the Sunn and Earth, so as we seemed to be rather in the Sea than the Clowdes, till we having pierc'd quite through came into a most serene heaven, as if we had been above all human Conversation, the Mountaine appearing more like a greate Iland, than joynd to any other hills; for we could perceive nothing but a Sea of thick Clowds rowling under our fete like huge Waves, ever now and then suffering the top of some other mountaine to peepe through, which we could discover many miles off, and betweene some breaches of the Clowds, Landskips and Villages of the subjacent Country: This was I must acknowledge one of the most pleasant, new and altogether surprizing objects that in my life I had ever beheld.

Reading the travelogues of the seventeenth and early eighteenth centuries, one stumbles occasionally across moments like this, when a mind discloses its instinctive relationship to a form of landscape; slips briefly out of the straitjacket of received opinion and creates new ways of feeling. The excitement about height which Evelyn experienced would remain unusual, however, until in the mid-eighteenth century it moved swiftly to the foreground and became an orthodoxy which continues to hold sway today: the adoration of height for height's sake. When this shift of perception came, it would require as much originality *not* to be delighted by height as it had previously required to find it delightful.

During the eighteenth century altitude became increasingly venerated. Of course, the Church had always made sure it took the high ground, physically and morally. On the hot hills of Italy and in the steep-sided valleys of Switzerland stood churches, chapels and crosses, surveying the land beneath them. And in cities across Europe the spires of cathedrals stretched longingly – aspired – towards the heights of the Christian empyrean. But a newly secularized feeling towards height was emerging, according to which the individual discovered pleasure and excitement in height for its own sake, and not as a paraphrase of heaven.

This fresh attitude to altitude was a radical change of heart, and one which made itself felt in almost every cultural sphere, from literature to architecture to horticulture. In the early part of the century the so-called 'hill poem' established itself as a popular minor genre, in which the poet – much as Petrarch had done four centuries earlier – would describe first the physical act of walking up a hill, and then the cogitations that the view from the summit evoked in him. The hilltop, with the broadening of vision that it offered, also became attractive for leisure-seekers. Viewpoints and viewing stations were formalized and institutionalized across Europe, including ones at Etna, Vesuvius and Naples. Here were places where your eye could traverse pleasingly between different orders of life: where events, objects and existences which were usually dispersed in space and time could be experienced simultaneously and at a single glance. Altitude made possible the *panorama*: the Greek word for 'all-sight' or 'all-embracing view'. From an Alpine mountain-top, wrote the Swiss naturalist Conrad Gesner, one might observe on a single day the four seasons of the year. The great seventeenth-century French traveller Maximilien Misson noted that from the rough stone balconies of the Chartreuse St Martin, perched high above Naples, a spectator could survey the outline of the city itself – its harbour, breakwater, lighthouse and castles – then move southwards down the coast, over the scalloped coastline with its white rocks, and then northwards, to the black bulk of Vesuvius, with thick lines of smoke coiling upwards out of its crater like fakirs' ropes.

In Britain during the second half of the century, under the influence of the picturesque movement, a chic raggedness of design came to supplant the carefully proportioned ground-plan of the Enlightenment garden. The Enlightenment had bequeathed to the Big Houses of Britain a neat horticultural geometry – patterned rose gardens, spokes of gravel pathways radiating out from fountains that leapt agilely and repetitively from font to pond, clean vistas of card-table lawn scrolling away to invisible ha-has – but in the light of the later eighteenth century all this manicuring came to be deplored as too ordered, too regular. Many of the more modish landowners chose to turn their manicured estate lands into symbolic wildernesses. Grottoes, waterfalls, hermits and shattered obelisks, gloomy copses and rocky knolls: suddenly all this wildness was far preferable to neatly trimmed and aligned box-hedges or grandiosely uniform lawns. And when these landowners commissioned the conversion,

'Sightseers on the Upper Crater of Mount Etna', in J. Houel's *Voyage pittoresque des isles de Sicile, de Malte et de Lipari* (1787).

they usually asked for a miniature crag or some similar vantage point from the top of which the extent of their gorgeously unkempt demesne could be viewed.

One such landowner was Richard Hill – the 'Great Hill', as he inevitably became called – who succeeded to the Hawkstone Estate in Shropshire in 1783 and swiftly embarked on a fifteen-year re-development programme. While Richard orchestrated the digging of a two-mile-long lake and continued to make money through what one contemporary mysteriously called his 'lucrative arith-metick', his enthusiastic sisters – the two Miss Hills, as they were known – collected fossils, shells and other geological curios, which they then embedded in the soft interior walls of a cave complex that existed on the estate. It took them three years to complete their redecoration; when it was done Richard hired a hermit to live in the caves and (as the contract had it) 'to behave like Giordano Bruno'.

The sublimest jewel in Hawkstone's crown was its 300-foot-high white sandstone outcrop – Grotto Hill. From the top of Grotto Hill, on a clear day, a panorama of thirteen of England's shires was visible. Visitors flocked to the estate (as they still do) to marvel at the vista, and to induce in themselves a pleasurable little frisson of vertigo. Among the earliest of Grotto Hill's summiteers was Dr Johnson, who for once provided a stock response to an experience. 'He that mounts the precipices at Hawkestone,' intoned the good doctor:

> wonders how he came hither, and doubts how he shall return . . . He has not the tranquillity, but the horror of solitude, a kind of turbulent pleasure between fright and admiration. The Ideas which it forces upon the mind, are the sublime, the dreadful, and the vast.

Remember that this was a 300-foot cliff in rolling, sheep-dotted Shropshire, not an Alpine peak with no hope of rescue or retreat. But then Johnson's hyperbole was cast in the language of his time. Here in provincial England was to be found at least an approximation of the enjoyment which some were already seeking out on grander mountainsides.

A new style of feeling about altitude was taking hold, and the popularity of Hill's hill was one of its many expressions. 'What are the scenes of nature that elevate the mind in the highest degree, and produce the sublime sensation?' asked Hugh Blair, lecturing in Edinburgh in the 1760s. 'Not the gay landscape, the flowery field, or the flourishing city, but the hoary mountain . . . and the torrent falling over the rock.' What really elevated the cultivated mind in the second half of the century was elevation. More and more people began to expose themselves to the pleasures – and the dangers – of height, and the notion of a summit as a goal in itself began to emerge. One sweltering summer afternoon in Cumbria, late in the century, Samuel Taylor Coleridge climbed to the top of a peak, and was rewarded as dusk fell with the view of an electric storm moving across the Lake District: jagged blue filaments of lightning flicking on and off, and the thunder like distant timpani. It was, he wrote exultantly when he got back down, 'the most heart exciting of all earthly things I have beheld'. In the Alps, Mont Blanc was ascended by the Frenchmen Michel-Gabriel Paccard and Jacques Balmat on a cold day in 1786: Balmat waving his hat from the summit to the villagers of Chamonix so many miles below, and Paccard unable to write down the temperature on the summit because his ink froze before it reached the paper. The very next year an efficient young English officer called Mark Beaufoy scaled Mont Blanc with a minimum of fuss. Asked why he had done so, he replied, as though it were a truth universally acknowledged, that he 'was moved by the desire everyone has to reach the highest places on earth'. Summit fever was catching.

Switzerland – 4 a.m. The sky was clear and already there was the promise of great heat in the day to come. We emerged into the cold black air from our tent, which was pitched on a flat area of the glacier. We had our head-torches on, which gave each of us a little cone of light by which to see. Specks of ice drifted in and out of the beams like phytoplankton. Although the moon was powerful, we still needed these torches, and their brightness ruined our night-vision. When I turned my light off and looked around, there was total darkness and then, like a developing photograph – the image swimming into sharpness in the chemical bath – the forms of the peaks around us came into focus.

Chief among these, to our south-west, was the Nadelhorn and its slightly smaller neighbour, the Lenspitze. These two 4,000-metre peaks are joined by a long, crenellated rock ridge, so that the massif resembles a frozen tidal wave of ice and stone many thousands of feet high: a tsunami which geology has halted.

In the dark, in the glare of our head-torches, we prepared ourselves: slipping on harnesses, looping and tying rope, leashing axes to our arms. Not for the first time I was reminded of medieval knights preparing for combat. There was a ritual to be observed, and each of us attended to the other like a squire to his master: checking and double-checking buckles and knots, tugging on straps, muttering quiet, urgent questions. It felt, excitingly, as though we were going into battle up there on the summit of the Nadelhorn.

We began moving slowly in the semi-darkness across the glacial bowl which spreads out from the base of the wave. The frozen snow creaked beneath our feet. The rope trailed between us, catching occasionally on lumps of ice. Far away to the south I could see two glow-worms: the head-torches of a more serious party who were climbing straight up the curved inside face of the tidal wave, using axes and crampons to bite their way up 3,000 feet of near sheer ice. They would be hoping to move quickly and to reach the summit ridge before the hot morning sun played on the ice like a blowtorch, and turned it to butter beneath their feet.

It was very cold; perhaps ten degrees below. I sensed sweat pricking on my forehead from the exertion and freezing instantly – when I raised my hand I could feel my skin was crisp with a thin varnish of ice. Other parts of me had frozen as well: my balaclava had become a steel helmet, and my gloves gauntlets.

Our first task was to make steady time over the glacial bowl, and then to climb a steepening snow slope at its far side which led to a high pass called the Windjoch, famous for the north-westerlies which scour it. After a couple of hours' work we reached the pass and, duly,

The Nadelhorn (4,327 metres/14,196 feet) at the right-hand end of the ridge; the Lenspitze (4,294 metres/14,087 feet) at the left-hand end.

out of the depleting darkness roared a powerful wind. We climbed steadily on up the north-east ridge as the day formed about us. The rocks looked slippery in the early morning light, which gleamed off the film of ice clinging to each of them. By the time we reached the summit, an airy little cone of rock and ice, the air had become hot around us.

We lay there for half an hour or so in the warmth, hands clasped behind our heads. I rubbed crystals of salt from my face and looked around. To our south was the face of another big mountain which bulged with domes of snow. Behind them was the sky, now a pure blue except for one large and evolving cumulus cloud. I looked across and watched as it seemed to explode slowly out of itself, polished bosses emerging from somewhere inside it to complicate further its already complicated surface. I felt sure that if I unclasped a hand and reached out, I could run my hand over that surface and sense each whorl, ridge and valley on it. Then I looked down back into the glacial bowl which we had traversed in the dark that morning. There was no movement. It seemed an enormous basin of space and stillness into which, briefly, I wanted to dive.

Altitude has one effect which even the most fervent fan of the horizontal can't deny: you can see further. From the tops of mountains on the Scottish west coast you can look out towards the Atlantic and see the curvature of the earth, can watch the dark rim of the sea's horizon bending at either end. From the summit of Mount Elbrus in the Caucasus you can look into the Black Sea to your west and to your east into the Caspian Sea. From the top of a Swiss Alp you begin to discuss the world with an uncommon largesse – Italy is to my left, Switzerland to my right, France straight ahead. Your topographic units are suddenly countries instead of counties. Indeed, on a clear day, the only limits to how far you can see are the mechanical limits of your vision. Otherwise you are panoptic, satellitic, an all-seeing I: simultaneously thrilled and terrified by what Marshall McLuhan called the 'vast, swallowing distances of visual space'. And that is an unforgettable sensation.

Great height gives you greater vision: the view from the summit empowers you. But in a way, too, it obliterates you. Your sense of self is enhanced because of its extended capacity for sight, but it also comes under attack – is threatened with insignificance by the grand vistas of time and space which become apparent from a mountaintop. The traveller-explorer Andrew Wilson felt this keenly in the Himalaya in 1875:

At night, amid these vast mountains, surrounded by icy peaks, shining starlike and innumerable as the hosts of heaven, and looking up to the great orbs flaming in the unfathomable abysses of space, one realises the immensity of physical existence in an overpowering and almost painful manner. What am I? What are all these Tibetans compared with the long line of gigantic mountains? And what the mountains and the whole solar system as compared with any group of great fixed stars?

This is the human paradox of altitude: that it both exalts the individual mind and erases it. Those who travel to mountain tops are half in love with themselves, and half in love with oblivion.

❄

The adoration of the summit, which intensified over the eighteenth century, reached its peak in Europe in the early decades of the nineteenth. There is a painting from 1818 by the German Romantic artist Caspar David Friedrich, usually called *The Traveller above a Sea of Clouds*, which is now, thanks chiefly to the greetings-card industry, familiar to almost everyone. Friedrich's *Traveller* became, and has remained, the archetypical image of the mountain-climbing visionary, a figure ubiquitous in Romantic art. He now looks implausible to us, ridiculous even: the little rock hummocks protruding from the nimbus at his feet, his absurdly clichéd stature – one foot raised; a big-game hunter with his foot upon the cavernous ribcage of his dead beast. But as a crystallization of a concept – that standing atop a summit is to be admired, that it confers nobility on a person – Friedrich's painting has carried enormous symbolic power down the years in terms of Western self-perception.

Two years before Friedrich painted his archetype, John Keats started worrying that he was suffering from writer's block. He decided that altitude might relax his mind, and took to imagining himself at height when he wanted to write: a Romantic version of counting sheep to get to sleep. It worked – or at least it gave him a subject to write about:

> I stood tiptoe upon a little hill,
> ... I gazed a while, and felt as light and free
> As though the fanning wings of Mercury
> Had played upon my heels: I was lighthearted
> And many pleasures to my vision started ...

Height, at least in its imaginary form, was the laxative which Keats's blocked mind thought it needed: the 'mountain-top' again proved to be a spiritual vantage-point as well as a physical one.* Shelley, too, was profoundly affected by the qualities of altitude. 'Wind, light, air,' he declared, 'stir violent emotions in me.' Air is the distinctive element of his poetry (as water is of Byron's). Vaporous and ethereal, his writing returns again and again to the 'upper air', to the 'keen sky-cleaving mountains', the 'ermine snow' and the 'cold sky' – his poetry sublimates itself into gaseousness, spirals exultantly up into nothing. On first looking up at the Alps in 1816, as he rode in along the Chamonix–Servoz road, Shelley was overwhelmed. His hands were fortunately not in charge of the reins, and he was free to goggle at the mountains. He described his reaction in a famous letter. 'I never knew – I never imagined what mountains were before,' he wrote. 'The immensity of these aerial summits excited, when they suddenly burst upon the sight, *a sentiment of extatic wonder, not unallied to madness.*'

It isn't hard, with the benefit of hindsight, to see why altitude was so attractive to Romantic artists such as Friedrich, Keats and Shelley. As a concept it coincided perfectly with the Romantic glorification of the individual. A summit was somewhere one could stand out –

---

* When Keats came to climb actual mountains, he found them not as amenable to inspiration. Of an attempted ascent of a Lake District peak in 1818, we have this account: 'I should, I think, [have got] to the summit, but unfortunately I was damped by slipping one leg into a squashy hole.' This is one of the more harmless disjunctions between mountains of the mind and real mountains.

could be outstanding. The mountain-top also provided an icon for the Romantic ideal of liberty: what could more obviously embody freedom and openness? 'Men are not made to be crowded together in ant-hills . . . the more they congregate the more they corrupt each other,' Rousseau had noted, an observation which would gain in potency and relevance as urbanization increased over the course of the nineteenth century. Cities teemed with merchants and thieves, but the mountains! – the mountains were devoid of sin. The mountain-top became a ubiquitous symbol of emancipation for the city-bound spirit, a crystallization of the Romantic-pastoral desire to escape the atomized, socially dissolute city. You could be lonely in a city crowd, but you could find solitude on a mountain-top.

And of course it was upon a summit, in solitude, that the Romantic fondness for meditation could be both indulged and encouraged. Time and again in Romantic documents we find the traveller exclaiming at the inrush of lofty thoughts induced by height. 'What great spectacles fill the soul of the philosopher who is on top of a peak!' declared Pivery de Senancour in 1800. Horace-Bénédict de Saussure had been even more ecstatic two decades earlier: 'What language can reproduce the sensations and paint the ideas with which these great spectacles [mountains] fill the soul of the philosopher who is on top of a peak? He seems to dominate our globe, to discover the sources of its motion, and to recognise at least the principal agents that effect its revolutions.' Romanticism fused into the imagination of altitude a new element of attractiveness: that one was almost guaranteed enlightenment – spiritual or artistic epiphany – by getting high.* The mountain-top and the viewpoint became accepted sites of

* The last word on the creative power of the Alps should probably go to Wagner, who included alpenhorns in the score for *Tristan und Isolde*. '[The works] I conceived in that serene and glorious Switzerland, with my eyes on the beautiful gold-crowned mountains,' he bashfully declared after the first performance, 'are masterpieces, and nowhere else could I have conceived them.'

contemplation and creativity: places where you were brought to see further both physically and metaphysically. From the Victorian family eating their picnic on the North Downs and casting their eyes over London to the pioneering alpinist toiling upwards towards a virgin summit, all visitors to altitude were drawn in part by the conviction that they would be rewarded both with far sight and with insight: that mindscapes as well as landscapes would be revealed to them.

In 1836 Charles Darwin could claim with some confidence that 'Everyone must know the feeling of triumph and pride which a grand view from a height communicates to the mind.' What a change that was from Bishop Berkeley's displeasure at the 'horrible precipices' over which he passed in 1714. In little more than a century, height had come to connote a host of attractive characteristics. It equalled escape, it equalled solitude, it equalled spiritual and artistic epiphany. Height was also held to have physically hygienic properties: at altitude, the air was thought to be cleaner – and to be a cleanser. 'There is assuredly morality in the oxygen of the mountains,' announced John Tyndall in 1871. From the 1850s onwards, numerous high-altitude sanatoria were established in the European Alps, at which tubercular or asthmatic patients – among them Katherine Mansfield and Robert Louis Stevenson – resided, absorbing the mountain sunlight, breathing the mountain air and thrashing out big ideas over dinner. When my great-grandfather was diagnosed with chronic bronchitis, he was advised by his doctors to move to Switzerland. The air was no help; he died in 1934, and was buried in a mountain cemetery with a view of the peaks. But it was because of this that my grandfather was brought up in Switzerland, and it was there that he contracted his love of the mountains, which I in turn would catch from him.

By the closing decades of the nineteenth century, the veneration of height was almost automatic. For those inhabitants of Europe who didn't care to run the risks of stepping on to a hillside, or couldn't afford to, the experience of being at height was available in a multitude of forms. Books of landscape photographs and engravings, expedition journals and knockdown editions of Romantic poetry all provided stay-at-homes with at least second-hand versions of the facts and the feelings about altitude. Following the lead of earlier continental mountain painters such as Salvator Rosa and Josse de Momper, nineteenth-century artists including Philippe de Loutherbourg, J. M. W. Turner, Alexander Cozens and John Martin filled their canvases with precipitous scenery, using distorted scales, unconventional viewpoints and disrupted horizons to unbalance their viewers and pull them into the vertiginous worlds of their images. At the Leicester Square Rotunda or the Panorama Strand in the 1820s and 1830s, spectators could wander in the darkened central circular platform, while around them for 360° stretched a multiple vanishing-point painting of the Mont Blanc massif – an 'alporama'. There for an hour or two they could fill their heads with the startling geometries of the mountainscape: the glint of snow and ice, and the black ribs of rock. The ambition of the alporama was hyperrealism, and it was successful – visitors had been known to experience acute disorientation, and even vertigo. And after the 1850s, what one passenger called the 'delightful velocity' of the railways hastened the return journey to Zermatt from sixty-six days to fourteen, and the entrepreneurship of one Thomas Cook – dubbed 'The Napoleon of Excursions' – brought the masses to see the Matterhorn: such a bracing shock after the low-altitude skylines of Britain's cities.

A common heritage of feeling was passed down through the generations and spread across a swathe of people. The difference between those who died on the mountains, those who took a Thomas Cook tour to the Alps and those who merely read about mountains or gazed at their representations was one of degree and not one of kind. All were susceptible to the spell of altitude, and all were part of its casting. There was a near-perfect marriage between the attention-seeking mountaineers and the ascension-seeking public. A new kind of altitude sickness had come to grip the common imagination, for so long antagonistic to the mountains: one in which the nausea came from *not* being at height. John Ruskin alluded to it when he confessed that in a totally flat landscape, he felt 'a kind of sickness and pain'.

In 1827 a young man named John Auldjo, fresh out of his degree at Cambridge and enthused by the descriptions he had heard about the Alps, arrived in Chamonix with the intention of becoming the seventh Briton to summit Mont Blanc. Soon after reaching the town, he was sought out by a local who had survived a badly fractured skull from rockfall on Mont Blanc in 1791. The old man pushed his dented head close to Auldjo's face, and warned him not to attempt the ascent. Auldjo scoffed – though he did take the precaution of hiring six guides to ensure his safe passage up the mountain.

A battalion of guides could not have saved Auldjo from the afflictions he suffered on the mountain, however. Altitude sickness, hypothermia, snow-blindness and narcolepsy were visited upon him on the way up; heat-stroke, dyspepsia, loss of motor control and eventually total collapse were added to those ailments on the way back down. He made the summit, but it was due only to the concerted efforts of his six guides that Auldjo survived. When Auldjo was at his hypothermic worst, and utterly incapable of movement, his guides huddled round him and heated him up using their own body warmth. Thus thawed, he was able to descend the final few hours of the mountain. He staggered back to a hero's welcome in Chamonix, spent two days recuperating, then bid a tearful farewell to his guides and set off for London.

On his return to England, Auldjo wrote up an account of his ascent which divided its time between describing his extreme suffering and describing the extreme beauty of the mountain. On the debit side, Auldjo noted manfully, the climb had been exceptionally arduous, and 'the cold excessive'. However, he declared, all in all his suffering had been worth it for the view from the summit of Mont Blanc had revealed to him scenes 'of dazzling brilliancy, too much almost for the eye to encounter and such as no powers of language could adequately portray'.

Concluding his story, Auldjo observed that 'perhaps will it not be decreed presumptuous in me to say that this brief narrative may be consulted with advantage by all those, who influenced by a congenial spirit of adventure, may be disposed to engage in a similar undertaking.' Presumptuous it certainly was not: Auldjo's mixture of derring-do and sublime sensibility proved popular, and his book sold very well. Not only did his account help to enhance the fascination of Mont Blanc in the public imagination, it also familiarized the idea that a view – that 'dazzling brilliancy' he had seen from the summit – might be worth risking one's life for. The number of summit attempts from Englishmen described a steep upwards curve in the years following 1828 – Auldjo's book had caught the imagination of the country.

Among those who read it was a young Londoner called Albert Smith, whose imagination was so inflamed by Auldjo's description that he was moved to travel to Chamonix himself and attempt the mountain. In 1851 he climbed it successfully, and with considerably less discomfort than his hero, Auldjo. Smith's ascent, as we know, became the subject of his best-selling show, which opened in London in March 1853. News of the mountain also spread to America, and among those who read the account of Smith's ascent, and his theatrical descriptions of the incomparable view from the summit, was Henry Bean, who, on 5 September 1870, accompanied by his American friend Mr Randall, a Scots Reverend named George MacCorkendale, three porters and five guides, started his ascent of Mont Blanc.

It all began so well. After an easy climb in pristine weather, the group overnighted at the Cabin des Grands Mulets. Having set off again in warm sunlight the following morning, the group were observed from the telescopes of Chamonix to have reached the summit of the mountain at 2.30 p.m. and they turned immediately to begin their descent. Then, with a terrible swiftness, a thundercloud closed around them and they were lost from view.

Were we able, twenty-four hours later, to start off up the mountain and follow the path taken by Mr Bean and Mr Randall, we would leave the town of Chamonix and ascend steeply through the dense pine forests that texture the piedmont, over the ruptured ice of the Glacier des Pèlerins. Here we would enter the lower cloud of the storm which still wrapped the mountain, pass quickly and nervously beneath the echoey couloir of the Aiguille du Midi, which is sending down irregular fusillades of rockfall, and finally we would enter the blizzard which has enfolded the top of Mont Blanc, and which is so severe that once within it there is only whiteness in every direction.

And here, somewhere on the expressionless snowscapes of the Col du Dôme, we would find Mr Bean. He is hunched in a snow-hole that he and one of the porters have dug using their alpenstocks and their stiffened hands as shovels. Mr Bean is on the outside facing inwards, barely grasping the stub of a pencil. His fingers are white and violet with frostbite, and rigid. His clothing is frozen into a herringbone-tweed carapace, which makes movement of any sort difficult. Leaning on the back of the porter, who is hunkered in the snow-hole with him, Mr Bean is writing a few words to his wife in a notebook that he has carried up the mountain. His pencil moves slowly and stiffly across the page. The *scratch scratch* of coarse lead on coarse paper is inaudible against the raving of the wind. He adds to the words he has already written:

TUESDAY, SEPT. 6. I have made the ascent of Mont Blanc, with ten persons – eight guides, and Mr. MacCorkendale and Mr. Randall. We reached the summit at half past 2. Immediately after quitting it, we were enveloped in clouds of snow. We passed the night in a grotto hollowed in the snow, which afforded us but poor shelter, and I was ill all night.

SEPT. 7 – MORNING. The cold is excessive. The snow falls heavily and without interruption. The guides take no rest.

EVENING. My Dear Hessie, we have been two days on Mont Blanc, in the midst of a terrible hurricane of snow, we have lost our way, and are in a hole scooped in the snow, at an altitude of 15,000 feet. I have no longer any hope of descending.

At this point Mr Bean's handwriting becomes larger, loopier, less steady:

Perhaps this note-book will be found and sent to you. We have nothing to eat, my feet are already frozen, and I am exhausted; I have strength to write only a few words more. I have left means for C's education; I know you will employ them wisely.

I die with faith in God, and with loving thoughts of you.
Farewell to all. We shall meet again, in Heaven . . . I think of
you always.

What is both fascinating and macabre about this sequence of events
is how clearly it allows us to see certain seductive, dangerous ideas
about altitude being passed on from person to person – like the
Black Spot in Robert Louis Stevenson's *Treasure Island* – until at last
they result in tragedy. It illustrates how emotional attitudes about
concepts as indeterminate as height, views and summits are trans-
mitted. John Auldjo is stirred by the accounts he has read by others
who have seen or scaled the Alps, and decides to climb Mont Blanc.
His own narrative inspires Albert Smith to emulate the feat, and
Smith by means of his celebrated Piccadilly Show inspires tens of
thousands of people to see Mont Blanc first-hand. Among those
influenced by Smith is Henry Bean, who is moved to leave his wife
and embark on his awfully big adventure. Auldjo and Smith survive;
Bean, MacCorkendale, Randall and their eight nameless helpers die.
All of these men were attracted to the mountains by two intertwined
ideas: first, the abstract notion that reaching the summit of a mountain was a worthwhile end in itself; and second, the belief that the
view from a great height – the 'scenes of dazzling brilliancy' which
Auldjo described – could be sufficiently beautiful to merit risking
one's life to see it.

Like everybody else who has perished in the mountains – the
Russian Buddhas frozen on the top of Pik Pobeda; the father and son
whose memorial my grandfather walked past on his way to school –
Bean was sent to his death by ways of feeling set in motion many
years before his birth. Because in the ways we perceive and react to

forms of landscape we are prompted, primed and reminded by those
who have gone before, no death in the mountains is isolated from
historical circumstance. Although we might like to believe that our
experience of altitude is utterly individual, each of us is in fact heir to
a complex and largely invisible dynasty of feelings: we see through
the eyes of innumerable and anonymous predecessors. The unexpected pleasures which Evelyn discovered at height; Friedrich's iconic
image of the traveller on his rocky promontory; Shelley's aerial
poetry; Auldjo's ecstatic vision from the top of Mont Blanc – all of
these played a part in transforming the way altitude has been imagined. Now, at the start of the twenty-first century, the imagination of
millions is susceptible to what the mountaineer and writer Joe
Simpson calls the 'beckoning silence of great height': the inverted
gravity of mountain-going – the attractive force that pulls you ever
upwards.

6

Walking off the Map

All the most exciting charts and maps have places on them that
are marked 'Unexplored'.

ARTHUR RANSOME, *SWALLOWS AND AMAZONS*, 1930

The most exciting map I have ever held was a photocopied sheet
which supposedly represented the far east of the Tian Shan mountains, near where Kyrgyzstan borders China and Kazakhstan. It was
exciting because it was so rudimentary – there was a cross to signify
a peak, a circle for a lake and a line for a ridge. No contour lines curl-
ing around the mountains. No shading to represent dangerous cliffs.
And definitely none of those reassuring Ordnance Survey acronyms:
FB for footbridge, PO for post office and PH for pub.

In the centre of the map was outlined the Y-shaped valley carved
out of the mountains by the Inylchek glacier. This central highway
of the Tian Shan was well enough known. It had first been penetrated by the Russian explorer P. P. Semenov in 1856 and 1857 (he
became known afterwards, in the literal way of nineteenth-century
Russian nomenclature, as Semenov-Tian-Shanskii). Undeterred by
the bands of Kyrgyz brigands which roved the territories around

Lake Issyk-Kul, Semenov had pushed as far east as the Santash pass. This area had long been a contested march between China and the different potentates of the Central Asian plains; it was allegedly on the Santash pass that Tamburlaine had instructed each man of his army to add a stone to a pile on their way to war with China. When his depleted army crossed back over the pass after the campaign, each man picked up a stone. Tamburlaine counted the stones which were left, and thereby knew exactly how many soldiers he had lost in China.

It was Semenov's reports which enticed subsequent Russian explorers and cartographers to the region, including the malevolent but brilliant Nikolai Przhevalsky. A proudly European Polish-Russian of Cossack descent, Przhevalsky detested the Asian peoples among whom he spent so much of his life. In his last book he suggested exterminating all Mongolians and replacing them with Cossacks, a policy which Stalin – rumoured to be Przhevalsky's son – would go some distance towards enforcing. Przhevalsky overcame his abhorrence of non-Europeans sufficiently to lead four expeditions across Central Asia, including one to the far east of Kyrgyzstan. He died among Asians too, in 1888, in Karakol, the town at the eastern tip of Lake Issyk-Kul which in Russian is now named after him. His shining black statue surveys one of that town's dusty squares, and there is a little-visited museum devoted to his memory, filled with the bric-à-brac of his trade: saddle-bags, maps, weapons and – oddly – troupes of stuffed animals.

After Przhevalsky came the Munich-born explorer Gottfried Merzbacher. The impulse which drove Merzbacher into these mountains was not a political one – Przhevalsky had been a key player in the Great Game – but rather a desire to know. Merzbacher had read Semenov's accounts of the region, and had been fascinated by his description of the 'gigantic nodal point' of the Tian Shan range, a spotless and colossal pyramidal mountain of pink marble which he had named Khan Tengri – the Lord of Heaven. The Russian geologists who later visited the area confirmed Semenov's speculations but, like Semenov, lacked the mountaineering skills to penetrate far enough into the hostile range to reach the peak.

From 1902 to 1903, with the help of two Tyrolean guides and an escort of Cossacks, Merzbacher attempted to pick a way through the maze of ridges and glaciers to Khan Tengri. The mountains did not give up their secret easily: Merzbacher was avalanched, attacked by hornets, hounded by abysmal weather, mutinied on by his staff and nearly crushed by a rock earthquake which also triggered an ice-fall. Most seriously of all, as far as Merzbacher was concerned, his toothbrush was lost in a river crossing. But he survived all of these adversities, and in August 1903 he discovered the Inylchek glacier and, at the end of it, nearly on the border with China, he found the Lord of Heaven.

The Inylchek glacier provided Merzbacher with a road into the mountains. Over many millennia it had bulldozed and levelled all the terrain it had encountered, grinding down with infinite patience mountains more than 20,000 feet high. Without it, Merzbacher would not have been able to get near Khan Tengri. Even with its aid, it took him many days of hard walking to ascend the glacier.

When we came to the Tian Shan we were whisked up the Inylchek glacier by helicopter: a fast forty-minute flight which first followed the grey melt-river that came bellowing out of the glacier's snout, and then the grubby blue ice of the glacier itself. For all its convenience, it was not a happy journey.

The helicopters flew out of a remote Russian military base located in a valley deep in the Tian Shan. The base had been established during the Sino–Soviet tensions of the 1960s as a listening-post for eavesdropping on Chinese communications. I was in Kyrgyzstan as part of a small and – in retrospect – dangerously under-experienced team. We had come with the intention of bagging unclimbed peaks. After flying in to Almaty, the capital of Kazakhstan, we had travelled for several days by train, bus, taxi and foot, to Karakol. From there, it had taken a seven-hour journey in an eight-wheeled lorry, over the rubbly mining roads which led through the western reaches of the mountains, to get to the military base. The night we arrived, we talked to a pair of tall, stern Americans who had flown back down to the base from the glacier. They told us the flight was far more dangerous than the mountains, and that among the rocks on the south bank of the glacier they had seen the corpses of three helicopters.

At 6 a.m. on the morning of our flight, I pushed aside the tent-flap to see our pilot, Sergei, apparently Sellotaping the tail-rotor back on to the helicopter. He gave a cheery smile and a thumbs-up. Half an hour later, when the ground crew seemed satisfied that the helicopter was in no way airworthy, fifteen of us were weighed – ominously – on an ancient set of abattoir-scales, and then ushered aboard. Also travelling with us, it appeared, were fifty watermelons, dozens of pallets of food and a dead goat. Finally, the ground crew heaved a 100lb red gas canister into the cabin. It was placed between my legs as the rotor-blades began their slow build-up of noise. 'In the case of a crash, hug it like your mother,' yelled the head mechanic through the helicopter door before he slammed it shut. It was clearly an exit line he'd used before.

During the flight, I clasped the canister between my thighs with the tenacity of a wrestler. I felt lucky – at least I'd die first and fastest. As we reached the nose of the glacier, a cold updraft caught the helicopter and the whole vehicle shuddered; for a second I thought we were going to plummet from the sky. But it stabilized, and flew on to touch down on the turbulent ice. We opened the doorway to the roar and thump of the rotors, and leapt down heavily one by one on to the glacier, where the downdraft was sending ice crystals scurrying away in ever increasing circles.

This glacier was the Y-shaped area marked in the centre of my rudimentary map. I–N–Y–L–C–H–E–K: the letters were strung out along its length. The peaks which bordered the glacier were named and spot-heighted. Beyond them, however, the details faded out. No

names. No heights. Just crosses, lines and circles. And beyond that –
blankness. The unknown.

Later that day, once we had set up our tents, I followed a faint track
which led up the moraine towards China. After half a mile or so it
turned behind a rocky spur and into a glacial cirque. I stood and
watched the business of the cirque for a while – chunks of serac calving
from a small hanging glacier, leaving patches of fresh blue ice behind
them; a chough with its bright orange beak mewing to an invisible
mate; a rough pyramid of shale shivering and reassembling itself as the
main glacier shifted beneath it. As I walked on, the flimsy sunlight
flashed off something close to me. There was a small metal plaque
fastened to an outcrop of mud-brown rock. And another, and another.
I walked over to the rock. It was a cemetery for those who had died on
the mountains. There were fifteen plaques bolted to the rock: thirty-
one names. Most of the dead were Russian; there was also a German,
two Americans and an Englishman. Niches had been chipped into the
rock beneath all but one of the Russian plaques, and objects had been
placed in them as offerings or elegies: the grim haberdashery of death.
There was a cheap plastic doll, its peroxide-blond hair and scarlet dress
startling against the quiet tones of the rock. Two blackened candlewicks
in a fat puddle of red wax. A brittle head of edelweiss. A ceramic
Madonna, permanently weeping tiny lapis tears.

The Englishman had no niche, just a plaque on which rust was
dully blooming. 'Paul David Fletcher, Tian Shan, 16 August 1989,' it
read. And below that, in bolder letters, 'Англичанин' – 'Englishman'.
Why had he come here, I wondered briefly? What had he expected to
find in this place? Not death, certainly. My mind kept returning to the
plaques I had seen, particularly to Fletcher's, I suppose because of the
automatic selfishness of the memory: because he of all the dead resembled me the most closely. I wondered again what, ten years ago, had
drawn him to the Tian Shan, thousands of miles from England. What
had he imagined that inaccessible landscape held for him?

I wandered back to camp, and was introduced to our guide, Dmitri. Dmitri was built like a polar bear and bearded like Santa Claus. He claimed to be the ice-climbing champion of the Arctic Circle, and I was inclined not to doubt him, at least not aloud.

❄

A few nights after arriving on the glacier, we were sitting around a table with Dmitri in his hut, a ramshackle structure of tarpaulin and planking. It was blizzarding outside. Even with the screech of the storm-wind, we could still hear the sounds of the mountains – the musketry of rockfall and, less frequently, the bomb-rumble of an avalanche. In the middle of the table, illuminating the proceedings, was a halogen lamp; a wasp's nest in a glass jar, glowing yellow-white. When I stared at the lamp and then glanced away at the darkness of the hut, the impression of the gauze haunted my sight, so bright it was branded temporarily on to my retina. I looked around the table; the intense light lit the front of our faces, and the backs of our skulls faded away into darkness.

On the table Dmitri had placed two tin bowls. In one were triangles of orange melon, and in the other a dozen creamy garlic cloves. Dmitri husked an onion. Its flesh was very white. Holding the bulb of the onion together with the finger and thumb of one hand, he cut it across four times with a knife. Then he let his hand go, and tapped the onion with the knife, like a magician touching a top hat with his wand. Eight white wedges of onion rocked backwards on to the table, like the petals of a flower opening. Finally he lined up five little thick-glass tumblers, and filled them with a vodka so strong it was viscous, like petrol.

We drank and ate. Afterwards, my eyes watering from the onion and the vodka, I asked Dmitri about what lay beyond the ink lines of my map, on the blank page.

'There is nothing there. Only unclimbed peaks.'

'Can we get there?'

'Of course. We can walk in,' he looked round at us, with gentle contempt in his eyes, 'or better, but for dollars, we can fly in, by helicopter. Last year we dropped a group there' – he waved his hand vaguely towards the south – 'and they climbed four new peaks in a week. If you like we can go to the next valley along, beyond the ridge. It is not explored.'

The following morning, I stood with Dmitri on the moraine of the glacier, my hungover head ringing in the sunshine, and asked him where the unexplored valley was. He pointed south-east to where a high bowed ridge of snow cupped the blue sky. No one had ever been into the territory beyond that ridge.

Suddenly I felt almost sick with the desire to go there. I sat down on a glacial boulder, which was already warm from the sun. I unfolded my map, and looked from the ridge to the map, and to the ridge again.

The whiteness of the sheet said it perfectly. We would be the first people to set foot on that snow, to lay eyes on those mountains. We would climb invincibly and brilliantly; we would summit four difficult peaks and christen one each. Afterwards our names would always be associated with those mountains, that valley. Our memory would be indivisible from the landscape we had travelled so far to see.

We didn't go, of course. It would have been too expensive and it would also, given our inexperience, have been almost suicidal. Instead we climbed a peak across the glacier which had been climbed only once before, seven years previously, by a Czech team. With each step I tried to forget the memory of their going, and pretend to myself that we were the trailblazers, the pioneers, the path-breakers: that we were the first to have stood on that summit and been stunned into silence by that view. But we weren't, and at the time that disappointed me more than I could say.

The view up the Inylchek glacier towards the unexplored valley. The valley begins behind the first unclouded peak on the skyline.

The unknown is so inflammatory to the imagination because it is an imaginatively malleable space: a projection-screen on to which a culture or an individual can throw their fears and their aspirations. Like Echo's cave, the unknown will answer back with whatever you shout at it. The blank spaces on a map – 'blank spaces for a boy to dream gloriously over', as Joseph Conrad once called them – can be filled with whatever promise or dread one wishes to ascribe to them. They are places of infinite possibility. The pungent longing I felt for that immaculate valley beyond the ridge was a longing for my own disguised dreams. And my dreams, of course, were driven by the desire to go somewhere no one had gone before, to do something no one had done before: the desires for priority and originality which are so deeply entrenched in the Western imagination.

The concept of the unknown has not always possessed an allure in and of itself. For centuries the chief incentives for exploration were economic, political or egotistical ones: the desire for money, or territory, or glory. The unknown *per se* held no allure; wise explorers plotted out their journeys on the maps of the familiar. Once again, it was the later eighteenth century which incubated the longing for the unknown in the Western imagination. During the second half of the 1700s in Europe there emerged a new and distinctive appetite for remote countries, for different territories, tastes and sensations – for orders of experience we might now call exotic; meaning literally *on the outside*. In short, for discovery. This sharpening desire for discovery reflected various frustrations. Chief among these was a spreading fatigue at the pieties and stagnancy of urban bourgeois existence. The known and the predictable became qualities to be kicked against, and a hunger grew for regions where one could expect the unexpected. The unknown came to be seen as a gateway to these alternative orders of experience. Charles Baudelaire put it well several decades later: '*Au fond de l'Inconnu pour trouver du nouveau.*' Through the unknown, we'll find the new.

From the 1770s onwards, this potent intellectual lust for the unknown was translated dramatically into action. The sixty years straddling the turn of the eighteenth century were the golden age of exploration. Through the ice-thickened water of the Arctic north, among the Pacific islands and across the deserts of Africa, adventurers and explorers travelled in search of wealth and beauty. Above all, these people were driven by a desire for novelty. Their paramount goal was to penetrate the unknown, and to see the unseen. Discovery became an end in itself, an ethos which accorded with the intellectual fascination of those decades for originality in all its forms. The ideal Enlightenment being, observed the essayist William Duff in 1767, should occupy himself in 'exploring unbeaten tracks and making new discoveries'. In 1764, shortly after he had ascended to the throne, George III initiated a campaign of sea-bound exploration. The mandate he gave his explorers was a simple one: 'to make new discoveries in the southern hemisphere'. So electrified was a young Scotsman named James Bruce at the prospect of being the first man to 'yield a discovery' in George III's reign that he took himself off to explore the mountains and rivers of Abyssinia.

The explorers who visited these wild regions were the film-stars of their age; at once glamorous and notorious. When they returned – if they returned – they wrote up their exploits, and illustrated them with fold-out maps on which were marked, in lines of dots and dashes, their sallies into the unknown. In 1822 the British Arctic explorer John Franklin got back to London after three years on the Arctic tundra. It was rumoured that he and his starving crew had survived on a diet of boot-leather, lichen and, eventually, each other. Franklin's account of the expedition was a bestseller, and second-hand copies changed hands for far more than the original asking price. Lieutenant William Edward Parry, a doggedly passionate Arctic explorer, became so famous from his repeated trips north that he was mobbed by fans in the street.*

---

* On his first expedition to Greenland, Parry brought with him a flag on which was painted an olive branch. With this he hoped to convince the 'Esquimaux' of his peaceful intentions. It appears not to have occurred to Parry that the symbolic associations of an olive branch might fail to be recognized by people who lived in an ice world almost entirely devoid of vegetation, let alone of trees. It is an earlier version of the mixture of idiocy and cultural arrogance which leads some turn-of-the-millennium Englishmen abroad to believe that, if spoken very slowly, English functions as a form of intuitive Esperanto – miraculously comprehensible to all from Novosibirsk to Timbuktu.

Even after the supposedly golden age of exploration had drawn to a close in the 1830s, the idea of the geographical unknown remained an energizing force in nineteenth-century foreign policy. Britain, France, Russia, Spain, Belgium: all the great expansionist powers of that century dedicated themselves to tingeing the blanks on the map with their chosen colour – green for France, orange for Russia and pink for Britain. (In America, of course, a different struggle was taking place: the struggle to push the frontier of so-called civilization towards the Pacific – to squeeze the unknown out of existence against the western seaboard in the name of Manifest Destiny.) Volley after volley of expeditions was fired off by the imperial nations in a bid to stake, claim and supposedly civilize the unknown regions of the world.

As each blank was filled in, so a new one was nominated to take its place. The source of the Nile, the North-West Passage, the North and South Poles, Tibet, Everest: each generation of the nineteenth century found a new geographical mystery to puzzle over and obsess about. The German explorer Julius von Payer spoke for much of the reading public, as well as for his fellow explorers, when he remarked that 'No more exciting situation can be imagined, than that of an explorer in unknown lands especially when nature seems to have surrounded him with an impenetrable wall, and the earth is as yet untrodden by man.'

The British, seemingly more than any other imperial power, were fuelled by the desire to make the whole globe known; to grid it and to girdle it with maps. In 1830 the Royal Geographical Society was founded 'for the advancement of geographical science', and before Victoria's reign was long under way the aim of filling in the remaining white spaces on the world map had been raised to the status of both cultural orthodoxy and policy issue. 'If there is talk of an unknown land into which no Englishman has penetrated,' declared a *Times* editorial from 1854, 'he must be the first to visit the place.' In 1846 John Barrow, at the time the Second Secretary to the Admiralty, proclaimed that 'The North Pole is the only thing in the world about which we know nothing; and that want of all knowledge ought to operate as a spur to adopt the means of wiping away that stain of ignorance from this enlightened age.' Barrow wasn't telling the truth – Antarctica and the Himalaya were far less known about than the North Pole – but his impassioned rhetoric nicely catches the fervour with which the mid-century British wanted to solve the globe's mysteries.

Undoubtedly, the widespread fetishization of exploration and discovery during the nineteenth century affected contemporary perceptions of mountains. For those who could not be fully fledged explorers, but who felt the pull of the unknown, going to the mountains offered an attractive paraphrase of the experience of exploration. And what made mountains especially appealing for European explorers *manqués* was their proximity to home. You didn't need to travel impossibly far to get to the mountains, or convince an Admiralty funding board of the worth of your trip. What was needed to experience the mountainous unknown was not a prolonged horizontal journey – the year it might take to sail south to the Antarctic, for example, or the many weeks battling north through ship-high waves and ship-wide icebergs to the Arctic – but a briskly vertical one. In just a day, and equipped only with determination, a pair of sturdy shoes and a knapsack of victuals, you could ascend from the benevolence of a Swiss meadow to the Arctic asperities of a high Alpine peak.

In many ways, too, the mountains offered a more authentic experience of the unknown than other more apparently daring exploits. 'Gentlemen now walk across Siberia with as little discomposure as ladies ride on horseback to Florence,' wrote James Forbes in 1843:

Even the Atlantic is but a highway for loungers on the American continent, and the overland route to India is chronicled like that from London to Bath. The Desert has its post-houses, and Athens has its omnibuses. But in the very heart of Europe is an unknown region . . . Whilst Parry, and Franklin, and Foster, and Sabine, and Ross, and Darwin brave the severities of arctic and antarctic climates, to reap the knowledge of the various phenomena of earth and atmosphere, climate and animals . . . are we perfectly informed of all these particulars even in our own quarter of the globe? Undoubtedly not.

In Forbes's words can be heard an *ennui* at the civilization of the wider world (the Atlantic has become a highway, Siberia a pavement, Italy a manège, Athens a traffic-jam), a sentiment which would gain in power as the century wore on. But there is also an audible excitement at the discovery of the *terra incognita* of the Alps which was buried in the heart of civilized Europe, previously hidden from view by the camouflage of altitude.

In the Alps were innumerable virgin peaks, and beyond the Alps lay the unmapped, unexplored, unclimbed expanses of the Greater Ranges – the Andes, the Caucasus, the Himalaya . . . An editorial in the first edition of *Peaks, Passes and Glaciers* (1859), a popular anthology of writing by members of the Alpine Club, drew attention to the 'unlimited field for adventure' offered by mountaineering in the Alps, 'not to mention the numerous ranges which the Englishman's foot is someday destined to scale'. Plus, presumably, the rest of the Englishman's body.

Drawn by this abundance of *terra incognita*, from the 1850s until the 1890s Italian, French, German, Swiss, American and British mountaineers swarmed over the Alps; bagging, climbing, naming and, most significantly of all, mapping.

On early European maps, mountains were represented figuratively as molehills, or little brown blossoms of rock. The Cottonian World Map (*circa* 1025–50), for example, depicts several crude caramel-coloured hummocks, about which strolls a winged and humpbacked monster loosely resembling a lion. Where knowledge faded out, legend began: the fantastical creatures which populated these early maps were embodiments of the unknown: little cartoons of ignorance. By the fifteenth century, however, these magical portmanteau beasts – body of a lion, head of a snake – would be more or less extinct from maps, chased off their edges by the spread of knowledge, though they would survive for far longer in the imaginations of mariners, explorers and travellers.

Even after the beasts had disappeared, mountains continued to be represented figuratively, as were forests (as miniature groves of stylized fir trees) and seas (as rows of blue wavelets frozen in mid-lap). The mountains of these early maps were drawn as they might appear if one were looking at them from the level of a valley: the 'plan view' – the view from on top – had not yet been conceived of. A Portuguese map of Europe from the late fifteenth century used rows of tiny brown mounds, arranged in neatly geometric patterns, to represent mountainous areas: it looks as though a well-drilled and industrious team of moles has been at work on the continent. Odder still is the representation of the Alps on the Canepa Portolan map of 1489, where the mountains are slung upside down and luridly coloured. They resemble bunches of red and green grapes.

During the sixteenth and seventeenth centuries, cartographic techniques became more nuanced and more standardized, and greater attention began to be paid to differentiating between landscape features. In 1681 Thomas Burnet observed critically that 'The Geographers are not very careful to describe or note in their Charts, the multitude or situation of Mountains.' He proposed that all 'Princes' should have 'draughts of their own Country and Dominions' which properly depicted 'how the Mountains stand', and 'how the Heaths, and how the Marches are plac'd'. Burnet justified his suggestion on the mildly erotic grounds that ''tis very useful to imagine the Earth in this manner, and to look often upon such bare draughts as shew us Nature undrest; for then we are best able to judge what her true shapes and proportions are.'

Under the pressure of expectation of the Renaissance, cartographers devised ways of suggesting three-dimensionality. The ubiquitous molehill was adapted to create cone-shaped, flattened or craggy mountains. Shadowing was introduced to suggest relief from the ground around, and hachures – short lines of shading – began to be used to provide information about slope and steepness: the steeper the slope, the denser and darker the hachures. Frederick the Great instructed his Prussian military topographers that 'Wherever I can't go, let there be a blot.' Contour lines were an invention of the sixteenth century, but they could not properly be used until advances in survey techniques provided the detail required for them.

The charm and the pleasure of a map lie in its reticence, its incompleteness, in the gap it leaves for the imagination to fill. As the traveller Rosita Forbes noted, a map holds 'the magic of anticipation without the toil and sweat of realisation'. In my family, the maps would always be bought well in advance of the next trip to the mountains. New maps are noisy and ill-behaved. When you open them, they put up resistance, try to spring back into their folded form. They clack and crack as folds are reversed, and stiff panels of paper pop in and out of shape. We would wrestle our maps flat on to a floor, weight their four corners with books and then kneel down to plot possible routes across them. Early on, my father taught me to read contour lines, so that the whole map rose magically out of itself.

Maps give you seven-league boots – allow you to cover miles in seconds. Using the point of a pencil to trace the line of an intended walk or climb, you can soar over crevasses, leap tall cliff-faces at a single bound and effortlessly ford rivers. On a map the weather is always good, the visibility always perfect. A map offers you the power of perspective over a landscape: reading one is like flying over a country in an aeroplane – a deodorized, pressurized, temperature-controlled survey.

But a map can never replicate the ground itself. Often our mapping sessions would induce us to bite off more than we could chew. At home we would plot a route over terrain that would, in reality, turn out to be sucking bog, or knee-high heather, or a wide boulder-field thick with snow. Sometimes a landscape would caution us of the limits of our map's power. I have had a map snatched from my hand by the wind and whirled over a cliff edge. I have had a map pulped into illegibility by rain. And I have stood in a white-out on a mountain-top and been able to put my finger on a map and say 'I am here', but still have had to take shelter in a snow-hole until the storm passed.

Maps do not take account of time, only of space. They do not acknowledge how a landscape is constantly on the move – is constantly revising itself. Watercourses are always transporting earth and stone. Gravity tugs rocks off hillsides and rolls them lower down. Grouse swallow quartz chips to use in their craw, and excrete them elsewhere. There is a continual trafficking of objects, of stones. Other changes occur. A sudden rain-shower can transform a tiny tributary stream into an uncrossable torrent. The meltwater outflow from the mouth of a glacier will sculpt silt into ceaselessly changing patterns of abstract beauty. These are the dimensions of a landscape which go unindicated by a map.

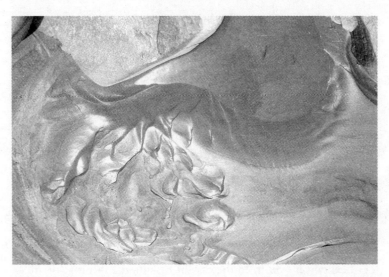

Patterns formed in glacial silt.

Francis Galton (1822–1911) is now best known as the man who fathered and christened eugenics, but like many Victorians he was many things. Explorer, climber, mystic, meteorologist, criminologist and advocate of fingerprinting, Galton was also an innovative cartographer. One of his most enduring coups was to combine symbols for weather systems with maps, thereby creating the prototype of the TV weather map. Galton believed that maps should convey more than just spatial information about terrain. He wanted to give travellers a phenomenal impression of the lands they visited. Maps, he felt, should somehow duplicate the smells, scents and sounds of a place:

> that of the seaweed, the fish and the tar of a village on the coast, the peat-smoke smell of the Highlands, or the gross, coarse and fetid atmosphere of an English town . . . the incessant and dinning notes of grasshoppers: the harsh grating cry of tropical birds, the hum, and accent of a foreign tongue.

Galton's multi-media map was ill-conceived, for what he was proposing was nothing less than a facsimile of the world itself. But a map is
an abbreviation: this is its definition, its strength and its limitation.
To know a landscape properly, you must go into it in person. You
need to see how in winter a tree gathers warmth to itself, and melts
the snow it stands in. You need to hear the rifle-crack of a crow's call
snapping over icy ground. You need to feel the remoteness of a huge
grey pre-dawn Alpine sky, with the lights of the nearest town blink-
ing thousands of feet beneath you.

Most of the world's mountainous areas were mapped in the nineteenth century, the imperial century. Mapping has always marched in
the vanguard of the imperial project, for to map a country is to
know it strategically as well as geographically, and therefore to gain
logistical power over it. In the case of Britain, the intuitive desire of
the British to purge the globe of its unknown spaces fitted the political ambitions of the imperium.

When, from the early 1800s onwards, the expanding British and
Russian empires began to chafe against one another in Central Asia,
detailed cartographic knowledge of the trans-Himalayan region
became vital. In 1800 Robert Colebrooke, then Surveyor-General of
Bengal, extended a mandate to all British infantry officers to enter
and map any country they chose. At this point, the Andes were still
thought to be the highest range in the world, and when these illicit
surveyors began returning even greater heights for the Himalayan
peaks – Lieutenant W. S. Webb, for example, observed Dhaulagiri
from four survey stations in the plains, and calculated its height to be
26,862 feet – they were ridiculed by professional cartographers and
accused of fumbling their figures (the currently accepted height for
Dhaulagiri is *circa* 26,800 feet).

The information these maverick map-makers gleaned often came
at a price. Beyond the objective dangers of the terrain they moved
through, the surveyors risked being attacked by bandits or punished

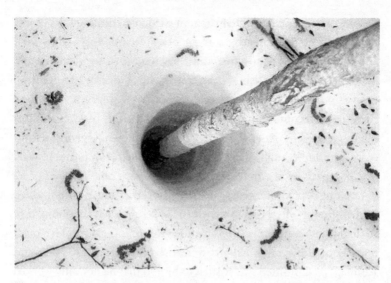

Tree trunk in old snow.

Rock citadels at dawn.

as spies. The Emirs of Afghanistan, in particular, did not take kindly
to the officers of a nearby foreign power wandering round their
country. After losing too many of their own men to accidents and
assassination, the British – characteristically – decided to train up
native Indian cartographers, disguise them as pilgrims, and send
them in to reconnoitre and map the parts British officers couldn't
safely reach. The *pandits*, as they became known – giving us our
word 'pundit' – taught themselves to count their own paces, to walk
at 2,000 paces to the mile, and to mark off each one hundred paces
by moving a bead on their rosaries. They carried their notes hidden
in their prayer wheels, and in their staffs were stashed thermometers,
so that they could measure altitude by boiling-point. The most
famous of these early *pandits* were the Singh cousins, Nain and
Kishen. So committed was Kishen to his job that he not only worked
out his own pacings, but also those of a galloping horse; when a
bandit attack forced him to escape on horseback, he was therefore
able to continue mapping the terrain through which he fled.

In 1817 the Great Trigonometrical Survey (GTS) of India had got
under way on the baking plains of Southern India, under the super-
intendence of the soldier-surveyor William Lambdon. The aim of the
GTS was to create a so-called 'grid-iron system' for the whole of
British India: a pattern of interlocking cartographic triangles which
would permit the estimation of the relative distances and heights of
any two points on the subcontinent. The GTS caravan moved northwards up the country from Cape Comorin, creating their triangles
and gathering demographic and topographic information as it went.
By the early 1830s the vanguard of the GTS was within sight of the
Himalaya. Twenty-yard-high towers of stone were built from which
the survey's theodolites could be trained on the pale distant summits
of the Himalaya, peering deep even into forbidden Nepal and Tibet.
Allowances were made for the illusory clarity of the air and for the
lateral pull exerted on plumb lines by the gravity of the Himalayan

range, and seventy-nine of the Himalaya's highest peaks were 'fixed'. These were the key to the whole Himalayan puzzle: 'The peaks,' wrote one superintendent of the survey, 'can be made the basis of subsequent surveys; the courses of the rivers and the positions of lakes can be laid down with regard to them; the trends and forms and magnitudes of the ranges can be inferred from the distribution of the peaks.' Overseeing it all until his death in 1866 was George Everest, the surveyor who would – rather unwillingly – leave his name attached to the world's most famous geological feature.*

For with mapping came naming. The nineteenth century, more than any other, saw the wild places of the world being franked and hallmarked. As each blank on the map – down in the Antarctic, up in the Arctic and throughout the mountainous areas of the world – was first penetrated and then accounted for, it had imprinted on it the tiny, cursive names of its discoverers. Many mountains, of course, had been named long before – the Jungfrau and the Eiger were christened in the eleventh and twelfth centuries respectively, for instance – but it was during the 1800s that the micro-naming properly began. Niches, notches, shoulders, cols, ridges, glaciers, routes: all began to bear the names of climbers and explorers. Look at a large-scale map of the Alps now, and you will see the names still jostling for space, radiating out of geological features like small black spokes.

This obsessive naming was a form of commemoration. It was also, unmistakably, one of colonization: a thwarted expression of the Victorian drive to bring the Empire home. That acquisitive instinct – which reached its fullest expression in Britain with the Great Exhibition of 1851 – didn't work as well with mountains as it did

---

* To the Tibetans and Nepalis it was (and still is) unfathomable why a mountain as magnificent as Chomolungma (the Tibetan name for Everest, meaning Mother Goddess of the World) or Sagarmatha (the Nepali name for Everest, meaning Forehead of the Ocean, or Goddess of the Sky) should be named after a human being.

The Nojli Surveying Tower, North India. Photograph probably taken in the 1890s.

with, say, flora and fauna. The Victorians transported their mountains symbolically, of course, in the form of rock samples. But properly to prove where they had been, they left their names behind. It was a form of imperial graffiti.

The Victorian explorers' habit of place-naming was not only a function of their imperial instinct, however. It was also a more fundamental mechanism for making sense of landscapes that, by virtue of their extreme difference from home, might otherwise have been unknowable. The urge to mark places in a landscape with names – to attempt to fix a presence or an event within time and space – is a way of allowing stories to be told about that landscape. Here, at this place which I shall name *x*, we ate food, or we fell ill, or we saw an astonishing sight, and then we moved onwards to the place I have named *y*. For the explorers, names gave meaning and structure to a landscape which might otherwise have been repetitively meaningless. They shaped space, allowed points to be held in relation to one another. They provided a stability – the stability of language, of narrative, of *plot* – to the perpetually changing upper world of ice and storm and rock through which they moved. Naming was and remains a way to place space within a wider matrix of significance: a way, essentially, to make the unknown known.

Once in the desert in Egypt I climbed a little hillock, only a few hundred feet high, of golden rock and sand. It was noon, and the desert rang with a metallic white light. Near the top of the hill, but low down on an exposed pillar of sandstone, I caught sight of some lettering. I squatted down to look at it, and put a hand up to my forehead to shield my eyes from the glare: *Lt Carter 1828*. The sandstone around the letters was dark brown, deeply sun-tanned by hundreds of thousands of desert days. But the lettering was still pale and bright: only nearly 180 years old, it had not had time enough to darken.

I tried to imagine Lieutenant Carter there, crouched down, scratching away with his bayonet tip, etching himself in time. I could understand his behaviour: a person far from home, wanting to write himself in some way into this frighteningly indifferent landscape. I left Carter's graffito behind and walked on up for the ten minutes it took me to reach the top of the hill. I looked out at the dunes for a while, then heaped together three or four loose lumps of sandstone to form a makeshift cairn, and turned to head back down the path.

The Victorians were in many ways the unknown's most implacable foes. Yet even as they worked so energetically to eradicate it, they began also to feel the need for the continued existence of inaccessible places – places of great imaginative potency. There emerged an impulse to preserve the unknown for its power of resonance, for its quality of nullity.

George Eliot, always so attuned to the national mood, sensed this feeling early on in its development. There is a moment in *Middlemarch* when the young Will Ladislaw declares that 'he should prefer not to know the sources of the Nile, and that there should be some unknown regions preserved as hunting-grounds for the poetic imagination'. To many in the closing decades of the nineteenth century, Ladislaw's sentiment seemed an increasingly just one. The century had been spent trying to enlarge the frontiers of knowledge, and that effort had now evoked a claustrophobia at the diminishing limits of the unfamiliar. The age of realism had discovered that it yearned for mysteries.

This claustrophobia was in no small part a consequence of technological modernity – telegraph lines tying the world up in a cat's cradle of communication, train tracks and steamships criss-crossing it faster and more frequently – which was exercising its distinctive trick of compressing time and space, of bringing the distant nearer faster. In 1900, on the cusp of full-blown modernity, Joseph Conrad's Lord Jim had to go as far as Borneo to find somewhere 'beyond the end of telegraph cables and mail-boat lines'. Towards the end of the 1800s in both Britain and North America, calls were made (as one writer put it) 'rigidly to economize the regions of dream' – to conserve the world's remaining wildernesses from the intrusions of industrial modernity. 'The case for the safeguarding of natural beauty,' wrote the mountaineer F. W. Bourdillon,

> is recognized by all Englishmen and most Europeans as the mainspring of moral life . . . Already it is more difficult to find sustenance for our imaginations than in the days when Herodotus or Ulysses roamed in worlds all romantic and unknown, more difficult even than in the spacious times of great Elizabeth.

By the end of the First World War, the two polar blanks on the map had been filled in, or at least the two poles had been 'touched'. The geographical mysteries which had so attracted the young Joseph Conrad to Africa had all been solved. The only region which apparently remained pristine was the Tibetan plateau, on the southern edge of which was Mount Everest: the so-called 'Third Pole', the last fastness of the unknown. It wasn't unknown to the Tibetans and the Nepalis, of course, who had worshipped the mountain for centuries without feeling the slightest inclination to climb it.* But as so often

---

* Tellingly, the Sherpa people – who inhabit the Khumbu region of Nepal, near Everest, and whose name is now synonymous with excellence in high-altitude mountaineering – do not have a word in their language for the 'top' of a mountain: only for 'pass' and 'flank'. Both the Nepali and Tibetan cultures practise a pantheistic religion, in which gods are thought to inhabit landscape features. Prior to the growth of Himalayan mountaineering in the twentieth century, a very Western import, to the Nepalis and the Tibetans the notion of climbing the summit of a high snow mountain existed somewhere between downright lunacy and outright blasphemy.

in the history of exploration, the existence of indigenous people did not in any way diminish the Western explorers' sense that they were the first into the area.

In 1920, when it was first made public that an expedition would be launched to climb Everest, there was an outcry at the prospect that the entire surface of the globe was to be filled in. 'It will be a proud moment for the man who first stands on the top of the earth,' lamented an editorial in the *Daily News*, 'but he will have the painful thought that he had queered the pitch for posterity. For my part, I should like to think that some corner of the globe would be preserved for ever inviolate. Men will never lose the sense of wonder, but they will always try to do so, and such a sanctuary would have a world wide effect.' The *Evening News* took a much stronger line, declaring that 'Some of the last mystery of the world will pass when the last secret place in it, the naked peak of Everest, shall be trodden by those trespassers.'

Precisely the same worry at the dwindling of the unknown has dogged our own era. 'The surface of the globe,' wrote the explorer Wilfred Thesiger in his autobiography, *The Life of My Choice*, 'having now, thanks to the internal combustion engine, been thoroughly explored, no longer affords scope for the adventurous individual in search of the unknown.' It is not only the movement of individuals which destroys the unknown, of course, but the movement of information. The global information networks which have been established during the past century – the internet foremost among them – mean that almost nothing remains unrepresented in some medium or other. At the click of a mouse we can summon up images, verbal or visual, of almost anything we wish for. There seems barely any room left for the unknown or the original. So we, like the Victorians before us, have taken steps to relocate the unknown. We have displaced our concept of it upwards and outwards, on to space – that notoriously final frontier – and inwards and downwards, to the innermost chambers of atom and gene, or the recesses of the human psyche: what George Eliot called 'the unmapped country within us'.

In a way, though, there is no such thing as the unknown. Because wherever we go, we carry our worlds with us. Consider, for instance, the gentleman mountaineer Douglas Freshfield, who in 1868 explored the then little-known Caucasus range, navigating only by the vague indications and blue smears of an old Russian map. In his journal, Freshfield comforted himself over and over again by seeing the alien landscape in terms of Victorian Britain. A pair of unclimbed peaks is 'of steep writing desk form', a glaciated cirque is 'as flat as a cricket ground'. A 'day of rainstorms and gleams' is 'like English Lake weather', a rich Caucasian dessert he finds 'rather like Devonshire cream'. So many of the nineteenth-century exploration accounts do the same: the jungle pool carpeted with iridescent algae appears 'as smooth as billiard baize', the lustrous water of a distant ocean glitters 'like the Serpentine on a bright day'.

We don't come fresh to even the most inaccessible of landscapes. 'History,' as the American writer Susan Solnit has observed, 'which is itself an act of imagination, is carried in the mind to the remotest places to determine what one's acts mean even there.' So traversing even the most uncharted landscape, we are also traversing the terrain of the known. We carry expectations within us and to an extent we make what we meet conform to those expectations, as Freshfield did. A raft of largely undetectable assumptions and pre-conceptions affects the way we perceive and behave in a place. Our cultural baggage – our memory – is weightless, but impossible to leave behind.

So perhaps the unknown exists most perfectly in anticipation, in the imagination. The journey, the climb, the expedition, the discovery, are most purely experienced in the future tense, before the feet are set, before the comparisons are made. Had I gone into that unexplored valley in the Tian Shan, I would almost certainly have found it very like other snowy valleys I have visited. I would have been disappointed by its familiarity.

Yet we *are* still capable of being surprised by strangeness, of being shocked by the new. In the right frame of mind, to walk from one room in a house to another can be exploration of the highest order. To a child a back garden can be an unknown country. The best writers of children's books have understood this. Richard Jefferies's overlooked *Bevis, the Story of a Boy* (1882) follows the adventures of two boys, Mark and Bevis. They first 'discover' a lake near their home, which they imagine to be an uncharted inland sea surrounded on all sides by impenetrable jungle. They then build a boat, and set out to explore the reaches of the sea. On their journey they discover and name a New Formosa, a New Nile, Central Africa, the Antarctic, the Unknown Island and many more territories besides.

Jefferies described the book as a celebration of the wondrousness of childhood, a time 'where there was magic in everything, blades of grass and stars, the sun and the stones upon the ground'. Arthur Ransome would use the same idea to more acclaim several decades later in his *Swallows and Amazons*, where Roger, Titty, John and Susan set sail across Windermere – which they know just as 'the lake' – on a voyage of exploration. The northern and southern tips of the lake are to the children the *terrae incognitae* of the Arctic and Antarctic, and it is surrounded to the east and west by the unexplored High Hills, and to the north-east by the Great Mountains. What Jefferies and Ransome both realized, and explored, was how the alchemy of the imagination can turn a lake into an entire world; can turn the thoroughly known into the thoroughly unknown. No

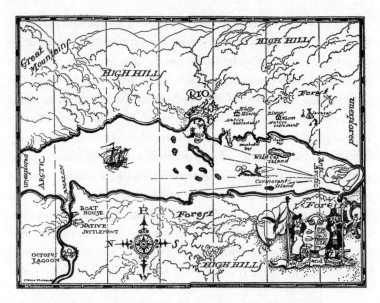

The map, drawn by Steven Spurrier, which accompanied the first edition of
Swallows and Amazons (1930). Note the High Hills, the Great Mountains, and
the unexplored antipodes of the Arctic and Antarctic. Reproduced by permission
of the Spurrier family.

matter that Windermere – the lake on which Roger, Titty and the
others sailed – was thick with yachts and houseboats; to the children
they were its explorers, its pioneers, the first to sail across it.

Snow is the ideal surface for would-be explorers. It has the appealing quality of refreshing itself, of obliterating the traces of those who
have been before. To walk across a fresh snow-field is to be in a very
real sense the first person to have trod that path. J. B. Priestley caught
some of the quality of novelty and of exploration that snow brings in
a brilliant passage from his *Apes and Angels*: 'The first fall of snow is
not only an event, but it is a magical event. You go to bed in one kind
of world and wake up to find yourself in another quite different, and
if this is not enchantment, then where is it to be found?'

One New Year's Day I got up at dawn, and walked out to Parker's Piece, the grassy common in the centre of Cambridge. There was no one else around. Snow had fallen early that morning, and then stopped. The sun was emerging from behind the rooftops. Only two chalky plane trails, slashed over each other like a gigantic teacher's cross, blemished the blueness of the sky. I stood for a few minutes and watched as the plane trails disappeared, depleting themselves from the ends inwards. Then I started walking across the open ground. The surface of the snow had frozen into a crust. It was not solid enough to hold my weight, and with each pace I crunched through into its downy, stuffed interior. When I reached the far side, I looked back. My line of footprints bisected the field of snow like the perforations on the white backs of postage stamps. I could have been the first person ever to cross the land, and that morning I was.

7

A New Heaven and
a New Earth

Suppose a Man was carried asleep out of a plain Country
amongst the Alps and left there upon the Top of one of the
highest Mountains, when he wak'd and look'd about him, he
wou'd think himself in an inchanted Country, or carried into
another world; every Thing wou'd appear to him so different to
what he had ever seen or imagin'd before.

THOMAS BURNET, 1684

It was a winter afternoon and I had walked up into a high valley in
the Canadian Rockies, following a river whose banks were formed of
round boulders. The water of the lake at the head of the valley, on
whose shoreline I stood, was frozen – the red reed beds at its periphery locked into place by the ice. A big storm was on its way,
according to the radio weather report I had listened to back at the
road. Away to the east, I could see thunderheads congregating, and
the valley was flooded with storm-light. It was a fixing light, which
cast the scene – stilled it, held it. But it was also a light which made
the most ordinary objects seem marvellous: the individual rocks
around the shore, the slopes of snow lying between the firs, the

pine-needles, like pairs of dividers, which had blown on to the lake ice.

A strong wind was blowing, and increasing in strength by the minute as the storm neared, herding the turbulent air before it. I had walked up here – a good three hours' graft – because I wanted to catch the wildlife, but there was nothing to be seen. Prints in the snow showed that considerable natural traffic had passed through since the last snowfall: rabbits and hares, certainly – their black droppings punctuated the whiteness like a scatter of full stops – and deer, which had left their prints crisply, like pastry cut-outs. Birds, too, pressing their cuneiforms into the snow.

Across the valley, to the west, where the mountains which formed the headwall of the valley shelved into the lake, scores of middle-sized waterfalls should have been pummelling down into the water. That day, though, most of them were frozen into stiff shining curtains of ice. Although some of the bigger waterfalls remained unfrozen, the lake water near the shore was undisturbed.

But there was something even more strange about the waterfalls, and it took a few seconds before I realized what it was, and began to smile. All the waterfalls which were unfrozen were falling *up* the cliff-face. It felt briefly as if I had been turned on my head, or the whole cliff face flipped upside-down. But no; it was the wind. The storm-wind which was blowing against the rock face was so strong that it was bullying the waterfalls back up the cliff. Where the water spilled over a lip of granite, it was plummeting upwards into the sky. These weren't waterfalls, they were waterrises.

I looked along the mountains on the far side of the lake, and I could see dozens of silver waterfalls doing the same. They looked like a row of chimneys, bellowing silver smoke into the air. I stayed and watched them for an hour or so as the storm approached.

During the sixteenth century a group of ground-breaking naturalists which became known as the Zurich School was formed. It is remembered nowadays for its attentiveness to the diversity and detail of nature. The most important member of the Zurich School was Conrad Gesner (1516–65), a man with little tolerance for the superstitions of his age.

Gesner's most famous act of rationalism took place on Mount Pilatus, the peak which rises above Lucerne. The citizens of that city lived in fear of the malignant ghost of Pontius Pilate which was reputed to inhabit Lake Pilatus. On 21 August 1555, Gesner and a friend climbed Mount Pilatus and cast stones down into the grey waters of the lake, in deliberate provocation of any supernatural entities which might have been lurking there. The waters didn't erupt, the ghost of Pilate was not seen abroad, and no cataclysm immediately overtook Lucerne. Gesner's symbolic exorcism of the citizens' fears is now often taken to mark the beginning of the banishment of superstition from Western imagining of the mountains.

Gesner was a lover of the mountain world in a century when such a love was considered lunatic. In 1541 he wrote a letter to his friend James Vogel on the subject of mountain-going. It began stridently: 'Men dull in mind find no cause for wonder anywhere; they idly sit at home instead of going to see what is on view in the great theatre of the world.' And it continued in a similarly uncompromising tone:

> Therefore I declare that man to be an enemy of nature who does not esteem high mountains worthy of long study. Of a truth the highest parts of the loftiest peaks seem to be above the laws that rule our world below, as if they belonged to another sphere. Up there the action of the all-powerful sun is not the same, nor is that of the air or winds. There the snow is everlasting and this softest of substances that melts between our fingers cares nothing for the fierceness of the sun and its burning rays. So far is it from disappearing with the lapse of

time that it passes into hardest ice and crystals that nothing can dissolve.

Gesner was one of the first thinkers to propose the idea that the world of mountains was a world entirely apart: an upper realm in which physical laws operated differently and where conventional, lowland ideas of time and space were turned topsy-turvy. 'Up there', Nature was not like herself at all. The elements metamorphosed into one another, disregarding their natural states and interactions, and complicating the human relationship with matter. The hierarchy of the elements was reordered – the hot sun had no purchase on the ice, which remained defiantly solid before it. 'Up there', the transparent wind became visible: once filled with ice crystals or snow flakes, its billows and contours were given dramatic visual expression. The air, too, was clearer, and thinner; and the blue of the sky an entirely different hue and texture, more like tinted porcelain, from the overcast serge of a lowland sky. And 'up there' waterfalls could flow upwards, in disobedience of gravity.

As I gazed across the valley at the light flattening the scene, and at the rows of waterfalls, I thought of Gesner's letter. *Of a truth the highest parts of the loftiest peaks seem to be above the laws that rule our world below, as if they belonged to another sphere.* He was right. The mountains are another world. In the mountains, I have felt my body tingle from toes to skull with the aerial charge of imminent lightning. I have struck grape-green phosphorescent sparks from the snow with my boots while tacking up a slope in the pre-dawn light. I have seen exquisite flowers of snow fall from the sky, and watched the collapse of rock towers which have stood for millennia. I have sat on a tightrope-ridge of rock with one leg in one country, the other in another. I have dropped into a crevasse, and been bathed in turquoise ice light.

Literature and religion are littered with stories of other worlds – uncharted oceans, secret realms, imaginary deserts, unclimbable peaks, unvisited islands and lost cities. The curiosity and attraction we instinctively feel towards the locked room, the garden over the wall, the landscape just beyond the horizon, the imagined country on the other side of the world; these are all expressions of the same desire in us to know somewhere apart, somewhere hidden. When Gesner called the mountains *another sphere*, he was locking into or launching an idea of huge imaginative power. Those early travellers who did penetrate what Thomas Burnet in 1684 called 'the inchanted country' came back with astonishing reports of eternal snows, dizzying geological structures and awesome catastrophes of rock and ice – scarcely believable, let alone conceivable, to those who had never seen such an environment.

To my mind, the finest of all other-world stories occurs in C. S. Lewis's Narnia chronicles. Peter, Susan, Edmund and Lucy, those four very ordinary English children, are evacuated to a house in the countryside to escape the Blitz. While they are exploring the house, Lucy pushes through some fur coats at the back of a big wardrobe – the sort that has a looking-glass in the door – and steps out into a world of eternal winter, where fauns carry umbrellas and the White Witch drives her sleigh across the snows. What makes Lewis's story so potent is how close that other world is to real life. The extraordinary is there, hidden behind a rack of old coats, tucked away in a nook of the everyday. You just need to know where to look, and have the curiosity to do so.

Going to the mountains – into what one nineteenth-century poet called 'that weird white realm' – is like pushing through the fur coats into Narnia. In the mountainous world things behave in odd and unexpected ways. Time, too, bends and alters. In the face of the geological time-scales on display, your mind releases its normal grip on time. Your interest and awareness of the world beyond the mountains falls away and is replaced with a much more immediate hierarchy of needs: warmth, food, direction, shelter, survival. And if something goes wrong in the mountains, then time shivers and reconfigures itself about that moment, that incident. Everything leads up to it, or spirals out of it. Temporarily you have a new centre of existence.

Returning to earth after being in the mountains – stepping back out of the wardrobe – can be a disorienting experience. Like Peter, Edmund, Susan and Lucy returning from Narnia, you expect everything to have changed. You half-expect the first people you see to grip you by the elbow and ask you if you are all right, to say *You've been away for years*. But usually no one notices you've been gone at all. And the experiences you have had are largely incommunicable to those who were not there. Returning to daily life after a trip to the mountains, I have often felt as though I were a stranger re-entering my country after years abroad, not yet adjusted to my return, and bearing experiences beyond speech.

The upper world of the mountains has not always been regarded as a wonderland, however. In the early history of the West, mountains provided an obvious residence for the supernatural. Just as the uncharted Poles became the repositories for myths either of Arcadia (the land of zephyrs and eternal daylight which lay beyond the barriers of ice) or of evil (the northern armies led by Gog and Magog which hung above the innocent southern races), so the upper realm of mountains, abstracted above the normal world by the simple fact of altitude, was regarded as the dwelling-place of both gods and monsters. Giant chamois, trolls, imps, dragons, banshees and other fabulously sinister beings were reputed to patrol the higher slopes of mountains, and divinities to dwell on their summits. John Mandeville described mountains of gold in Ceylon mined by ants as big as dogs. The Franciscan writer Salimbene of Parma recounted how Peter of Aragon climbed to the summit of a mountain to be met with '*tonitrua horribilia et terribilia valdè*' – thunderbolts and lightning – and a '*draco horribilis*' which flapped away in surprise, its leathern wings blacking out the sun.

Local myths and legends gathered around each hill, and the phenomena of the high mountains – their shape, their storms, their glaciers, their light – were interpreted according to the pattern of these legends. Between 1580 and 1630, for instance, at the height of the European witch crazes, mountains were considered the retreat of witches; storms and blizzards were assumed to be the meteorological spin-offs of their saturnalia. In the early 1600s the Swiss scientist Jacob Scheuchzer drew up a famous compendium of the different species of dragons which he knew to exist in the Alps. To those who have seen how, with the sun above it, a bird can send a silhouette many times its own size slipping across the rocks below, Scheuchzer's dracopoeia will not seem like quite such a flight of fantasy.

This superstitious attitude towards mountains survived in Europe well into the eighteenth century. When Windham and Pococke arrived in Chamonix in 1741 they were warned off ascending Mont Blanc by the villagers who told them – Windham jotted down scornfully in his diary – 'many strange Stories of Witches &c. who came to play their Pranks upon the Glaciers and dance to the Sound of Instruments'. In Windham's scoffing tones can be heard the growing cultural cynicism of the Enlightenment towards such credulousness. It was the spread of rationalism in Europe which routed the imaginary dragons from the mountains.

There is also the belief in the upper world as the home of gods. In the Judaeo-Christian tradition, it has habitually been up mountains that prophets and seers have gone to receive divine counsel. Moses, for example, saw into the promised land from the summit of Mount Pisgah, and ascended Sinai to receive the ten commandments. Holy men and anchorites have long found in the upper world of the mountains an environment more conducive to contemplation than the secular bustle of the lowlands. My favourite mountain eremite is the eighteenth-century Disentian monk Placidus a Spescha, who would regularly climb to the summit of one of the mountains near his monastery in the Swiss Alps, and sleep there, wrapped in cowl and habit, to spend the night closer to his God.

Spescha has had many recent counterparts, who have been drawn like him to the mountain tops by a faith in the simple geometry of enlightenment, according to which 'up' means towards heaven. One such was Maurice Wilson. Wilson was a Yorkshireman by birth, a salesman by trade, and insane by the age of thirty. As a young man, he became obsessed with the idea that he could ascend mountains through a combination of fasting and prayer, thus coming closer to God. In the early 1930s Wilson decided that Mount Everest would be his ultimate target. In 1934, after flying an open biplane called *Ever Wrest* 5,000 miles from London to Purnea (quite against the wishes of the English, Nepali and Indian authorities), Wilson began his illegal ascent of the mountain, which had not at the time been climbed. Despite being under surveillance by the Indian police, he managed to slip out of Darjeeling in the early hours of a cold April morning disguised as a pilgrim – draped in a thick woollen mantle of royal blue, billowed about with a twelve-foot red silk sash, the whole outfit constellated with brocade and golden buttons – and started his approach of the mountain on foot and mule across the wind-scoured Tibetan plateau.

Given his emaciation, and lack of climbing experience, Wilson got remarkably high on the mountain. The Sherpas he had hired abandoned him – wisely, though not without reluctance – at 21,000 feet, in the upper basin of the Rongbuk glacier. Wilson climbed on up into the teeth of desperate weather and impassable obstacles (bergschrunds, yawning crevasses) and died of malnutrition and exposure. A British reconnaissance party ascending by the same route a year later discovered his corpse lying on a small beach of shale. They interred him in a crevasse, and sat down under a rock overhang to read his diary: a small book bound in green leather, with coarse pages. Wilson's firm handwriting became more spidery towards the end, his syntax less assured. But the final entry, for 31 May, was written clearly: 'Off again, gorgeous day.'

What deflected the imaginative perception of the upper world away from gods and monsters, and towards the feast of natural phenomena which Gesner found so delighting, was natural theology – an influential doctrine which spread across Europe between the 1690s and the 1730s.

The founding premise of natural theology was that the world in all its aspects was an image given by God to man. It was, in the words of Thomas Browne, a 'universal and public manuscript' in which could be read God's grandeur. To scrutinize nature, to discern its patterns and its idiosyncrasies, was thus a form of worship. The mountains were among the finest of God's texts; the best seats in what Gesner had called 'the great theatre of the world'. 'Providence,' declared the Abbé Pluche, one of the principal theorists of natural theology, 'has made the air invisible in order to allow us to witness the spectacle of nature.'

Therefore, to visit the upper world and contemplate its marvels was to be elevated spiritually as well as physically. If you looked hard enough, and if you bore God firmly enough in mind, it was possible to overmaster the automatic sensations of fear and horror which the mountainous environment was still felt by many to inspire. The natural theology movement was crucial in revoking the reputation of mountains as aesthetically displeasing, for it forced intellectual Europeans into a more specific experiencing of the physical world. A new way of looking at wild landscape established itself, which combined sweeping experiences with a close attention to the micro-phenomena – the tiny special effects – of the mountains.

It was under the pressure of natural theology, as well as science's new inquisitiveness concerning the physical matter of the universe, that towards the end of the eighteenth century the idea of the 'upper world' of the mountains became common imaginative currency. Wherever we look in landscape writing of that period, the same image is being used. Horace-Bénédict de Saussure called the mountains 'a sort of terrestrial paradise'. The French explorer Jean de Luc, who in September 1777 discovered the Glacier du Buet, described how he felt himself levitated into 'the pure upper atmosphere'. Marc Bourrit wrote in his *Journey to the Glaciers of the Duchy of Savoy* (1774) of how in the 'other world' of the mountains the traveller finds his 'mind voluptuously employed in the contemplation of so many wonders'. The most influential of these accounts of the upper world was Jean-Jacques Rousseau's *Nouvelle Héloïse* (1761), the book which is now widely credited with having created secular mountain-worship. 'It seems as if, being lifted above all human society,' Rousseau wrote of the Alps:

> we had left every low terrestrial sentiment behind: and that as we approach the aethereal regions, the soul imbibes something of their eternal purity. Imagine to yourself all these united impressions; the amazing variety, grandeur and beauty, of a thousand astonishing sights; the pleasure of seeing only totally new things, strange birds, odd and unknown plants, to observe what is in some sense another nature, and finding yourself in a new world . . . one isolated in the higher spheres of the earth. In short, there is a kind of supernatural beauty in these mountainous prospects which charms both the senses and the minds into a forgetfulness of oneself and of everything in the world.

Here was a manifesto – couched in Rousseau's winningly ebullient prose – for the 'aethereal regions' of the mountains as a new and enchanting world which teemed with astonishing sights.

As the cult of the upper world spread, and more people were attracted to the mountains, so too the casualties began to occur. In 1800 a young Frenchman fell into a crevasse on the Glacier du Buet. When his maimed body was retrieved – 'the unfortunate young man', wrote a witness, 'had experienced the most sudden and violent compression' – his rescuers turned out his pockets in an effort to identify him. They found seventy-eight *livres* in money, a notebook, and a well-thumbed edition of the third volume of de Saussure's *Voyages dans les Alpes*. Tucked between the pages of his notebook for safe-keeping, they also found an uncompleted letter written to his father. It began, heartbreakingly: 'You see, my dear father, that I have undertaken a journey: you see also that this journey is one of the most interesting and beautiful that can be wished . . .' The death of the young man was a stern reminder as the nineteenth century chimed in that the mountains and their environs could be fatally punitive, as well as wondrous.

During the 1800s John Ruskin in England, and the intellectual dynasty of Ralph Waldo Emerson, Henry David Thoreau and John Muir in North America, penned rapturous essays in praise of the mountains, which paid especial attention to the exquisite minutiae of the high hills – the glaciers 'like moving pavements of marble', or the miraculously unique architecture of each snowflake. Ruskin wrote of how he had watched inky storm clouds breaking like 'troublous seas against the crags', and concluded that of such spectacles 'there can be as little imagination or understanding in an inhabitant of the plains as of the scenery of another planet than his own'. When the first volume of *Peaks, Passes and Glaciers* was published in London in 1859, it was littered with impassioned references to 'the upper ice-world'. From the middle of the century, too, the new-born medium of photography enhanced the status of the mountains. 'It must be set down to the credit of photography,' wrote one Himalayan photographer modestly of his own plates, 'that it teaches the mind to see the beauty and power of such scenes as these, and renders it more susceptible of their sweet and elevating impressions.'

A community of wilderness connoisseurs specializing in the precise observation of nature and the controlled play of the imagination emerged during the nineteenth century. Ways of calibrating the attractiveness of different mountains were proposed and argued over: this one had a ridge whose curve imitated the contours of the sail of an Egyptian felucca, that one evolved a delicate lattice-work of ice in the winter months. The appreciation of mountain beauty no longer took the form of generalized awe, but was a much more specific responsiveness to the phenomena of the hills. Accounts of mountain-goers from the 1800s tend to be exuberant with detail, written by travellers whose eyes have become newly sensitive to the particular beauties of the mountains. Particularly striking is a love of stone and rock. Again and again in travel journals, attention is drawn to curious geological outcrops: arches, caves, stalactites and pinnacles, or rocks that resembled lions, bishops, 'Moors' Heads', cannon, camels . . . Explorers returned from the Atlas mountains in Morocco, the Mountains of the Moon, the Rik range of South Africa, and the Mei-Ling Ridge in China, bringing back with them stories of the gigantic beauties of these mountains – the 'rugged precipices', the 'innumerable rocks', the 'immensely high cliffs' – but also of their minute lithic splendours: mica chasms a few inches wide, or boulders plugged with crystals of smoky quartz or clothed with emerald moss.

A complementary fascination emerged for the transient beauties of the mountains: those fugitive effects – winds, blizzards, storms, snow-devils, technicoloured parahelia, Brocken Spectres, coronae, fog-bows – which hovered on the verge of the intangible and the invisible. This fascination was fostered in part by the Sublime, and in part by the fondness for the Rococo style which characterized art and architecture of the later 1700s. The Rococo aesthetic cherished immateriality, evanescence and fragility, qualities supplied in abundance by the filmy effects of light or cloud, by the fleeting blue and green tints of ice, by mist, clouds, snow, spume, spindrift, and by all the other phantasmagoria on display in the high mountains. Painters squared up to the challenge of how to paint sunsets, cloud formations, fog and the other miasmic aerial effects of mountains. Writers lavished long descriptions on how clouds formed around the summit of peaks like white Elizabethan ruffs, or on top of them like floury wigs. Goethe, during his winter trip to the Savoy Alps, wrote a

detailed analysis of the behaviour of freezing fog, and also tried to puzzle out how altitude affected the blueness of the sky. A few years later Shelley lounged on sun-warmed boulders on the lower slopes of the Alps and let his imagination model the passing clouds into animals and scenes from the Bible. There was an exciting sense of volatility to the upper world, which contrasted so pleasingly with the solidity of its rocky substructure.

Reading about these natural historical miracles away from the cold, thousands of people were drawn to seek out the splendours of the upper world. A tyro mountaineer writing in 1859 spoke for many when he declared that he had been lured to the Alps by the rumours of its beauties and its solitude. 'The praises I had always heard bestowed upon the great beauty and grandeur of the scenery,' he said, 'had long excited my curiosity and given me a strong desire to explore this wild and unfrequented region . . . these trackless wastes of ice and snow.' Climbing upwards came to represent – as it still does – the search for an entirely new way of being. Experience was unpredictable, more immediate and more authentic in the mountains. The upper world was an environment which affected both the mind and the body in ways the cities or the plains never did – in the mountains, you were a different you.

It is the light of the mountains which has always attracted more comment than any other aspect of their beauty. Early travellers wrote, amazed, of the billion tiny 'flashes of fire' which a sunlit slope of snow radiates, or how when the sun shines upon icy rocks 'there are a thousand suns reflected instead of one'. Many were staggered by the magnificent effects of alpenglow. Alpenglow – which is caused by the reflection of the rising or setting sun off snowfields – makes the sky appear underlit by powerful pink or red lights of massive wattage, and steeps the mountains in mauve, carmine, cochineal. For a long time it wasn't known what caused alpenglow. In the Eastern Alps it was rumoured to be the reflection of sunlight off a trove of bright treasure buried beneath the ice. Some of those who saw the alpenglow at its fiercest and most lurid thought that a conflagration must have taken place beyond the rim of the horizon; a colossal inferno.

Nowhere but in the mountains do you become so aware of the incorrigible plurality of light, of its ability to alter its texture rapidly and completely. Even the light of the desert doesn't rival mountain light for velocity of change. Light in the mountains can be harsh and volatile: the dazzle and flicker of a snowstorm in sunshine, for instance, like a flutter of blades; or the ostentatious splendour – the extravagant *son et lumière* show – of a thunderstorm. On a bright day snow and ice-fields glow with a magnesium intensity, a white light so concentrated that you cannot look directly at it for long without the risk of searing your cornea. At dusk, light can take on a matt, atomized quality, as though it were composed of vast and visible photons.

Mountain light can also be architectural: the spires and pillars of luminescence which certain cloud configurations build, or the fan-vaulting effect created when the sun shines from below and behind a jagged rock ridge. It can be visionary, as when you climb above the clouds and the light strikes off the fields of ice beneath you, and it seems as though there are brilliant white kingdoms stretching as far as the eye can see. There is the Midas light, the rich yellow light which spills lengthways across the mountains, turning everything it touches to gold. And there is the light which falls at the end of a mountain day, and unifies the landscape with a single texture. This light possesses a gentle clarity, and brings with it implications of tranquillity, integrity, immanence.

Trekking through Tibet en route to Everest in 1921, George Mallory experienced this light. By day he found Tibet to be an unsightly country of rough gravel plains and abrupt, jagged hillsides. For Mallory, the angles and textures of the landscape were all wrong; its appearance grated on his eye. But, 'in the evening light', he wrote back to his wife, Ruth, 'this country can be beautiful, snow mountains and all: the harshness becomes subdued, shadows soften the hillsides; there is a blending of lines and folds until the last light, so that one comes to bless the absolute bareness, feeling that here is a pure beauty of form, a kind of ultimate harmony'.

Moonlight, as well as sunlight, can impart the oddest qualities to the mountains. Travelling into Chamonix for the first time on a

night coach, Goethe saw the moonlight reflected off the silver roof of Mont Blanc and briefly mistook it for another planet: 'A broad radiant body,' he wrote amazedly, 'belonging to a higher sphere; it was difficult to believe that it had its roots in earth.' On a clear night, moonlight can perform a more mundane electrolysis, turning the mountains silver. I remember early one summer, camped high in the Alps and unable to sleep out of nervousness for the next day's climb, creeping outside in the small hours and watching these silent shapes about me, all silvered by the moon. They looked strangely temporary – like a great caravanserai of tents, pitched by happenstance and ready to be bundled up and rolled away the next day in preparation for the march.

Mountain light is spectacular. It can also, in conspiracy with the other elements at play in the mountains, be deceptive: producing mirages, tricks of the light. On snowfields or glaciers your normal spatial perspectives are warped by the whiteness and the uniformity of the landscape's texture. Distances become hard to judge. Wandering the snow plains of the Alps in the 1830s and 1840s, the

Scottish scientist and mountaineer James Forbes found himself
unable to focus on anything at all, astonished by the 'effect of inter-
minable vastness with which icy plains outspread for miles,
terminated by a perspective of almost shadowless snowy slopes'. On
the Glacier du Buet, the combination of sunshine and high snow
produced a mirage of smoothness so persuasive that Jean de Luc
became convinced he was 'suspended in the air on one of these
clouds'.

Some travellers had more bizarre and more specific hallucina-
tions – an English climber on Everest in the 1930s reported giant
teapots pulsating in the sky above the summit – and others more
macabre ones. When Edward Whymper was lowering himself gin-
gerly down the Matterhorn in 1865, only a few hours after three of
his companions had plummeted to their deaths, he saw three crosses
floating in the foggy air, one higher than the other two: a misty
Golgotha marking the death of his three friends. The explanation for
Whymper's vision is now thought to be either embroidery on his

part – he was known to have an elastic sense of truth – or to have been a peculiarly complex form of the so-called Brocken Spectre. The Brocken Spectre, which was first seen and described by Bouguer in Peru in 1737, is a trick of the light which occurs on bright days, when the observer is standing between the sun and a bank of mist or cloud. The observer's shadow is cast on to the mist, and the sun is refracted by the water suspended in the air to produce halos of colour around the shadow. I have seen a Brocken Spectre only once, on the Isle of Skye. I was walking up the spine of a long, elegant ridge running north–south. The morning sun was shining on me from the east, and I suddenly noticed my shadow projected on to the damp mist below me, with a colourful nimbus. It looked like an attentive genie, scudding along on his magic carpet of mist, always preserving the same distance from me.

In the mountains, the early travellers discovered, nature was given another medium with which to sculpt: the snow. To read through the journals and letters of mountain-goers from the eighteenth and nineteenth centuries is to watch the evolution of a new aesthetic towards snow and ice – a new responsiveness towards the precise beauties of winter. At first glance snow seems to simplify a landscape, to smooth out its complexities. Stones are turned to spheres, trees to spires, mountain-tops to cones. The landscape gains a simple Euclidean beauty, and a unity.

Cold also brings intricacy and variety with it. 'Who would have thought that snow could meld itself so many ways?' asked one astonished traveller in the 1820s. Snow is the disguise artist of the mountains. It can rock benignly down through the air in flakes as big and soft as duck down, or be fired from the clouds in shotgun-pellets of hail. It can lie in neat windrows, or in irregular waves. Spindrift is one of the most charismatic features of snowy mountains. Climbing a lee-slope in a big wind, you can look up to see sheets of spindrift flaring out over the ridge, or it can undulate over the surface of hard

snow like a supple second skin. As ice, it can coat objects in glisten-
ing shellac, or form a tracery of icicles which stretches out across a
rock face. Once, ascending a glacier 15,000 feet up in the Himalaya,
I glanced up from my plodding feet to see acres of frozen ice slopes
stretching away from me on either side, as smooth, hard and bright
as china.

Snow is not always white, either. Old snow looks thick and
creamy, like sallow butter. A fresh fall of snow, frozen overnight, glitters a hard blue. Lumps of ice reflect light like a glitter-ball, shooting
different coloured squares of light in every direction. Then there are

the odd algal blooms which tinge snowfields the colour of water-melon, or mint, or lemon. In certain areas of the Himalaya, northerly winds sweep up tons of mustard-coloured sand from the Punjab and dump them on snowfields, turning them gritty and yellow.

One of the most fragile and beautiful effects of cold is rime ice. Rime ice is formed when super-cooled air (air whose temperature is below 0°C) carrying liquid water-droplets is blown on to a surface suitable for the droplets to freeze on: a rock, for example, or more dangerously, the leading edge of an aircraft's wing. Rime ice tends to form into delicate feather-like structures. What is curious about it is that it grows *into* the wind. As each new layer of rime ice is formed, it becomes the surface on which the next layer will crystallize. So by the alignment of rime ice on a rock you can tell which way the prevailing wind has been blowing: an example of how the land keeps its own meteorological archives. One winter I came across a pair of the granite tors which protrude from the summits of the Cairngorm mountains. It had been cold for several days, and the dark stone of the tors was invisible beneath a thick layer of rime ice. Reaching out with a gloved hand, I touched a feather of ice and was shocked when it crumbled away into powder, like a structure of ash left behind by a fire.

Many mountain travellers recorded their wonder at the variety of shapes and structures into which ice forms itself. Take, for instance, the testimony of Marc Bourrit from 1774, marvelling at the 'ice-buildings' he stumbled upon among the Savoy glaciers:

we saw before us an enormous mass of ice, twenty times as large as the front of our cathedral of *St. Peter*, and so constructed, that we have only to change our situation, to make it resemble whatever we please. It is a magnificent palace, cased over with the purest crystal; a majestic temple, ornamented with a portico and columns of several shapes and colours: it has the appearance of a fortress, flanked with towers and bastions to the right and left, and at bottom is a grotto, terminating in a dome of bold construction. This fairy dwelling, this enchanted residence, or cave of Fancy . . . is so theatrically splendid, so compleatly picturesque, so beyond imagination great and beautiful, that I can easily believe the art of man has never yet produced nor ever will produce, a building so grand in its construction, or so varied in its ornaments.

Bourrit's unstable analogies – now it's a temple, now a fortress, now a fairy dwelling – were a function of the ice's own slipperiness; its resistance to firm description. Ice and snow have always been substances off which language slides and slithers, unable to get a good grip. But Bourrit, like many after him, found something attractive in this visual fickleness, because it meant that the ice's beauties were bespoke. Each traveller saw what he chose to see in this visually biddable world: 'We only have to change our situation to make it resemble whatever we please,' he wrote. Ice could be sculpted by the sun and by the perceiving mind into almost any conceivable shape: a pagoda, an elephant, a fortress. The process could work in reverse as well – other things could resemble the ice. When Wordsworth was in the Chamonix valley one Sabbath in 1820, he watched a procession of white-robed votaries winding in slow motion between the dark and spiry pine trees, and they looked to him like a cortège of pale glacier columns, marching slowly down the valley towards the church. It is the unpredictability and inconsistency of the play of light off ice which has made it such a difficult subject for artists. The Victorian artist Silvanus Thomson declared that he was 'never happier than when painting ice', but spent his life being disappointed with his inability to render properly its subtle luminosities. Ice is a substance more lustrous than water and, for all its solidity, more capricious. Only photography –

literally light-writing – comes close to recreating the contingent
brilliancies of ice, its millions of scintillas.

The ice edifices which so astonished Bourrit can be seen more
often in miniature. If, on the afternoon of a hot day, you kneel and
put your face close to the surface of a glacier or a frozen lake, you will
enter a new architectural world of tiny palaces, town halls and cathedrals. They are formed by the uneven melting power of the sun on
the ice's surface and are fruitlessly exquisite creations: destined to be
erased overnight and then recreated in further baroque variations
with each sunrise. I once spent a quarter of an hour on my knees in

the snow, examining a huddle of these tiny ice buildings, and then looked up to find the mountains there. I was shocked for several seconds by how startlingly large they were in the winter sky.

Travellers found that the coldness of the high mountains possessed another remarkable property beyond the beautiful visual effects it produced – the property of arresting time. Cold kills, but it also preserves; it slows down the organic processes of disintegration. I have come across butterflies laid out on the ice, each tessera of colour on their wings still in place, as though they had just been puffed with ether. Leading a train of cargo mules through a labyrinth of glacier columns on the Portillo snowfields in 1833, Charles Darwin looked up to see 'on one of these columns of ice a frozen horse was exposed, sticking as on a pedestal, but with its hind legs straight up in the air'. The horse had slipped into a crevasse and then, by dint of the glacier's strange machinations, had been lifted up and out of the body of the glacier. Its corpse was perfectly intact, as though it were still alive. The glacier had embalmed it expertly. On its icy pole it must have looked like a skewed merry-go-round pony.

Human bodies, too, are preserved by the cold, and the literature of the mountains contains many accounts of the discovery of corpses which look eerily alive. Unlike the ocean, from which bodies turned up bloated and nibbled, or the jungle, in which the best an explorer might hope to find would be a mouldering pith helmet on top of a pile of bones, in the mountains – as at the Poles – time was often halted by the cold. Charles Dickens was both horrified and fascinated by the cryogenics of altitude. There is a scene in *Little Dorrit* where a group of travellers cross the Great St Bernard Pass. Approaching the hostel, they are caught in a swirling snowstorm. As they make themselves thankfully warm in the hostel, they are unaware that:

silently assembled in a grated house half-a-dozen paces removed, with the same cloud enfolding them and the same snow flakes drifting in upon them, were the dead travellers found upon the mountain. The mother, storm-belated many winters ago, still standing in the corner with her baby at her breast; the man who had frozen with his arm raised to his mouth in fear or hunger, still pressing it with his dry lips after years and years. An awful company, mysteriously come together! A wild destiny for that mother to have foreseen!

Dickens's 'grated house', with its grim company of corpses, reminds me of the garden of the White Witch in Narnia, queen of the winter, who freezes those who disobey her in mid-gesture and arranges them as garden ornaments.

The sky and the air, too, were found to be magnificently different in the mountains. At altitude, on a clear day, the sky was no longer the flat ceiling of the lowlands, but an opulent cobalt ocean, so sensuously deep that some travellers felt themselves falling up into it. Looking at it, you could be bowled over by what one traveller – lost, like so many, for words – described as 'an inexpressible sensation of immensity'. On reaching an Alpine pass in 1782 the German Leonard Meister was overwhelmed by the new sense of space. 'Inspired, I raised my face to the sun; my eyes drank in the infinite space; I was shaken by a divine shudder; and in deep reverence I sank down.'

Night skies were also extraordinary in the mountains. Away from the smog and the light pollution of the cities the stars multiplied, and the universe seemed deeper, more limpid. Sleeping outside at 6,000 feet in the Alps in 1827, John Murray enjoyed 'a night gemmed with stars innumerable, sparkling with a light so vivid as to defy comparison with the scene witnessed on the level of the sea, or amid the dense and vapoury atmosphere of Britain'. It was indeed, wrote an ecstatic Murray, 'a new heaven and a new earth'.

8

Everest

Up where no overshadowing mountain stands,
Towards the great and the loftiest peak
A fiery longing draws me.

PETRARCH, *c.* 1345

If I try to imagine Everest in my mind's eye, it appears not as a single image but as three contrasting pictures.

There is the mountain itself, the physical structure of black rock which I first saw from the slopes of a peak forty miles distant. Streaming out from its summit is its *kata* or blessing-scarf – the white trail of ice crystals flung out by the jet-winds that scour the mountain for eight months of the year.

There is an image of the South Col of Everest now – the empty oxygen bottles stacked like bright bombs, the tent poles collapsed skeletally on top of each other, and the gaudy fabric of the tents shredded and flapping in the wind like prayer flags. It resembles a battlefield.

And thirdly there is George Mallory, who died on the summit slopes of Everest in June 1924. Mallory's memory is inextricable from the mountain on which he perished. The image of him I have in mind is from a photograph taken in Tibet during the approach march to Everest in 1922. Having undressed for a river crossing, Mallory is naked except for a dark felt hat and a rucksack. He is side-on to the camera, and his left leg is pushed chastely forward so that his thigh is concealing his groin. His skin is luminously pale and his body surprisingly curvaceous: there is a roundness to his buttocks and the bow of his stomach. His face is shadowed from the pure white Tibetan sunlight by the brim of his hat, and he is looking directly at the camera and giving a saucy, seaside smirk. He emanates warmth and good humour. Two years after the photograph was taken, the geologist and climber Noel Odell would watch two dark specks – one was Mallory, the other Andrew Irvine – making their way slowly up the final slopes of Everest, until the cloud swirled in and hid them for ever.

Everest is the greatest of all mountains of the mind. No mountain has exerted a stronger pull over more imaginations. And no one has been more attracted to Everest than George Mallory. It was an attraction which ripened quickly into obsession and then climaxed, three years later, in tragedy. Three times Mallory tried to climb the mountain – in 1921, 1922 and 1924 – and the third time he did not return. Mallory sensed the power the mountain had over him. 'I can't tell you how it possesses me,' he wrote to his wife, Ruth, in 1921. 'Geoffrey,' he wrote to his old climbing partner and mentor, Geoffrey Winthrop Young, 'at what point am I going to stop?'

Mallory was an exceptional individual, who climbed from the heart: of this there is no doubt. But he also climbed under the influence of 300 years of changing attitudes towards mountains. I have sat

in archives and read his letters home to Ruth, I have read his corre-
spondence with friends and family, and I have read his journals. All
of these documents brim with Mallory's love for height, for views, for
ice, for glaciers, for remoteness, for the unknown, for summits, and
for risk and fear. In Mallory, the ways of feeling about mountains
which earlier chapters of this book have tried to trace coincided
forcefully and lethally.

In a sense, almost everyone we have met in this book – Windham
and Pococke swigging wine from the bottle in celebration of that first
trip to the Savoy glaciers in 1741, Dr Johnson striding along the
Buller of Buchan in 1773, Caspar David Friedrich painting his
Traveller above a Sea of Clouds in 1818, Albert Smith booming out his
tales of valour on Mont Blanc to a rapt audience in 1853, and the
hundreds of other people who each made tiny adjustments to the
way mountains were imagined – is involved in Mallory's death. He
was the inheritor of a complex of emotions and attitudes towards
mountainous landscape, devised long before his birth, which largely
predetermined his responses to it – its dangers, its beauties, its meanings.

Mallory had been introduced to mountains while he was a pupil
at Winchester College, and had developed a profoundly Romantic
love of them. The company he kept while at university and afterwards amplified his passion for mountains; made him even more
susceptible to the mesmerism of high places. He eddied about on
the periphery of the Bloomsbury set – he was friends with Rupert
Brooke and Duncan Grant, among others – a milieu which celebrated idealism, adventure and the exceptional individual. With
Rupert Brooke, Mallory shared a love of the mountains. Brooke
once sent a postcard to Mallory declining regretfully the invitation
to come climbing in North Wales. The postcard was of Rodin's
Penseur. 'My soul yearns for mountains, which I adore from the
bottom,' wrote Brooke. 'But the pale gods have forbidden it.'

Mallory's mountain gods were less wan, more Thor-like, than Brooke's pallid divinities, but his sense of legend and myth was not different.

Eventually, and terribly, Mallory's yearning for mountains would prove stronger than his love for his wife and family. Three centuries earlier he would have been cast into Bedlam for his obsession with Everest. In 1924 his death on the mountain cast a nation into mourning, and Mallory into myth.

❄

The world's tallest mountain was once a sea-floor. One hundred and eighty million years ago, the outline of the earth's landmasses looked very different. Imagine, to begin with, the triangle of what is now India, separated from the main body of Asia by an ocean which no longer exists: the Tethys Sea. This India was moving northwards on its plate towards Asia at high speed (six inches a year or so), propelled by the same geological action – the convection currents of liquid rock pulsing away in the mantle – which had cut it so neatly out of the supercontinent of Pangaea 20 million years previously.

Where the leading edge of the Indian Plate met the immovable Tibetan Plate, a subduction zone formed. The landmass of India was still at this point separated from Eurasia and Tibet by the Tethys Sea. Thick layers of marine sediment accumulated on the floor of the Tethys Sea, formed from sand, coral debris and the innumerable corpses of aquatic creatures. Much of this sediment was laid down in the deep trench of the subduction zone.

Over the course of millions of years, the northern edge of the Indian landmass moved towards the southern edge of the Tibetan landmass. As the two edges closed together, the mass of sediment which had been laid down was squeezed together. Heat and pressure combined to petrify it. Some of this rock was forced downwards between the plates, and pushed into the mantle of the earth where it was melted to magma. But most of it – billions and billions of tons of it – was forced upwards.

In this way the Himalaya were created. India hurtled into Tibet, and the marine sedimentary material packed between the landmasses was coerced upwards to form the four curvilinear ridges of the Himalaya, the high point of which was Mount Everest. The shapes of these original mountains were far more smoothed and curved than the complex forms which we now see: their latter-day complexity has been brought about by the subsequent erosive power of earthquakes, monsoons and glaciers.

So what is now the highest point on the earth's surface was composed in one of the earth's deepest places. In the yellow rock-band which stripes Everest just below its summit, there are the fossilized bodies of creatures which lived in the Tethys Sea hundreds of millions of years ago. The rock up which so many people aspire to climb has itself climbed tens of thousands of metres vertically upwards, from the darkness of the Tethys trench to the sunlight of the Himalayan skies.

❄

It was the collision of India with Tibet which created the Himalaya geologically. And it was the collision in the nineteenth century of the northward-expanding British Empire with the eastward-expanding Russian Empire which created the Himalaya in the Western imagination.

Before that point, almost nothing had been known in the West about the uplands of the trans-Himalayan region. Until the 1600s, indeed, most Europeans were unaware that the Himalaya existed.

Herodotus described India but made no mention of mountains to its north. Ptolemy compressed the Himalaya and the Karakorum into a single range, and elided the Central Asian plateau entirely. In the mid-sixteenth century, cartographers had succeeded in fitting together the perimeters of the countries, but the interiors of continents other than Europe remained mysterious.

At the beginning of the 1800s, however, the incipient threat of Russian expansion made it imperative for the British to gain information about the trans-Himalayan region. Among the seventy-nine high Himalayan peaks fixed by the GTS in the 1840s and 1850s was a Peak H, soon renamed Peak XV. It was sighted by a surveyor called John Nicholson, in observations carried out from viewing-stations on the plains of Bihar, 176 miles away from the mountain itself. The information culled by the GTS in the field was passed for computation and double-checking to the regional survey headquarters. It took seven years to verify the calculations for Peak XV, and to factor in the variables of temperature, pressure, refraction, and the gravitational pull of the Himalayan chain itself.* Finally, in 1856, the surveyor general Andrew Waugh confirmed the altitude of Peak XV. It was, he felt confident to declare, at 29,002 feet 'higher than any [peak] hitherto measured in India, and most probably the highest in the world'. So the mountain which we now call Everest, but had for centuries been known to the indigenes of the high Himalaya, was 'discovered' by the West.

Discovered, but not approached, because Peak XV stood on the frontier between the forbidden kingdoms of Nepal and Tibet. It was visible to the long-sighted telescopes of the Grand Trigonometrical

---

* It is not only human imaginations over which Everest exerts a powerful pull. The mass of the Himalaya and the Tibetan plateau is strong enough gravitationally to attract all liquids in its vicinity towards it. Thus the surface of a puddle of water at the foot of the Himalaya will assume an irregular form.

'Thebet Mountains', in William Orme's *Twenty-Four Views in Hindostan* (1805).
The implausibly jagged and spirey mountains resemble a barrier, both to human
passage and to the imagination.

Survey, but for reasons both political and geographical it was practically unapproachable on foot. The British had long agreed to respect
the sovereignty of the kingdom of Nepal, and that had put the southern reaches of the mountain out of bounds to surveyors or explorers.
And Tibet was, after the Poles, the great unknown of the later nineteenth century. The novelist H. Rider Haggard spoke for many when
he described it yearningly as 'the untrodden land'. So few Westerners
had penetrated into Tibet that it remained largely a *tabula rasa*,
undefiled by fact or reportage – a blank sheet stretched tight over the
highest plateau on earth, upon which the Western imagination could
doodle its fantasies of the Orient.

Chief among these fantasies was that of Tibet's spiritual purity. To
many in the West the country seemed like an icy Eden: an elevated

sanctum in the heart of Asia. There the Tibetans led undisturbed lives, in harmony with the rhythms of the dramatic landscape around them, and morally purified by the beauty and the thin air. There what Ruskin called 'the storm cloud of the nineteenth century' – the three-fold miasma of industry, atheism and rationalism – had not gathered. A British traveller to Tibet in 1903 likened one of its mountains to 'a vast cathedral', and when at about the same time a French explorer finally reached the Tibetan uplands he described feeling as though he had ascended 'through layers of cloud, from hell to heaven, leaving behind and below me this scientifically technical world which has done so much to increase man's misery'. What Switzerland had been to the eighteenth century, Tibet was to the nineteenth: an upland Arcadia, enchantingly antipodean to the grimy cityscapes of Europe, Britain and America.

Clamped between Tibet and the forbidden kingdom of Nepal was Everest: the Third Pole, as Edward Whymper dubbed it in 1894. For seventy years – between the measuring of Everest, and the arrival of the reconnaissance expedition at its foot in 1921 – no Westerner got within forty miles of the mountain. There was a vacuum of information about Everest, and into this vacuum rushed hopes, fears and speculations. Undoubtedly, Everest's inaccessibility helped to enhance its imaginative allure. In 1899 Lord Curzon, then Viceroy of India, gazed up at the white ramparts of the Himalaya from the windows of his cool and shadowed palace at Simla. Everest enchanted him. 'As I sat daily in my room,' he wrote, 'and saw that range of snowy battlements uplifted against the sky, that huge palisade shutting off India from the rest of the world, I felt it should be the business of Englishmen, if of anybody, to reach the summit.'

❋

Five years after Curzon wrote those words, the mystery of Tibet was exploded for ever when Francis Younghusband led a British force into Tibet from India. The *casus belli* was allegedly territorial incursion – Tibetan 'troops' were reported to have crossed the frontier and carried off Nepali yaks – but in fact Curzon was worried about Russian influence in Tibet, and wanted to solidify British influence in the country. Younghusband, ever keen for action, recommended in the language of the day that 'the power of the monks should be so far broken as to prevent them any longer selfishly obstructing the prosperity both of Tibet and of the neighbouring British districts'.

The Tibetans did not let Younghusband and his army just walk in. The first stand-off came near the village of Gyantse. Two thousand Tibetans armed with matchlock guns, swords and spears faced a smaller British force carrying cannon and Maxim guns. The British fired, according to a Tibetan survivor, 'for the length of time it would take six successive cups of hot tea to cool'. When the guns stopped chattering, twelve British had been wounded, and 628 Tibetans killed. By the time Younghusband reached Lhasa, a further 2,000 Tibetans had died, compared to forty British soldiers.

The bloody fall of Lhasa meant that yet another unknown had been penetrated. John Buchan, commenting on the invasion of the city in his book *The Last Secrets*, wrote that 'it was impossible for the least sentimental to avoid a certain regret for the drawing back of the curtain which had meant so much to the imagination of mankind . . . With the unveiling of Lhasa fell the last stronghold of the older romance.'

The older romance may have fallen, but a new and perhaps more potent magic had been revealed within Tibet: that of Everest itself. And it had been revealed to a mountaineer, explorer, mystic, Romantic and patriot, a man perhaps more receptive than any other to the idea of surmounting that peerless mountain. From the barbed wire and sandbags of one of the British encampments, Francis Younghusband had seen Everest 'poised high in heaven as the spotless pinnacle of the world', and he had been entranced. That distant vision of Everest would take seed in Younghusband's imagination, and would flourish over time from a vision into an ambition.

It had time to flourish, because the 1904 Tibetan invasion led indirectly to the Anglo-Russian agreement of 1907 – a concord in which both sides agreed to prohibit further expeditions into Tibet. With Nepal still out of bounds, the 1907 agreement effectively made Everest unreachable. But in 1913 John Noel, a young British army officer, made an illicit sortie into Tibet disguised as an 'Indian Mohammedan' and got to within forty miles of Everest. He reported it as 'a glittering spire of rock fluted with snow'.*

Noel's account piqued the interest of many in Britain, not least the members of the Royal Geographical Society. Plans were made for an attempt on the mountain, but then the First World War intervened. Almost immediately after the Armistice, however, mechanisms were set in motion. And on 10 January 1921 the Royal Geographical Society – newly under the presidency of one Francis Younghusband – made public its plans to send an expedition to the mountain. In his book *Everest: the Challenge*, Younghusband recalled his determination 'to make this Everest venture the main feature of my three years' Presidency'. He had settled upon his Grail. All he needed was a knight-errant to lead his quest.

'Galahad' was what Geoffrey Winthrop Young used to call George Mallory. On 9 February 1921 Younghusband took Mallory out to lunch and asked him if he would join the first reconnaissance expedition to Everest, due to depart that April. Although he had already

---

* Noel's description is an example of the warping power of Everest not just upon gravity, but also upon the perception – from no aspect does it resemble anything like a spire. It is a big, burly, bulky mountain, not an elegant Gothic column.

been separated from his wife and three children for long periods, and although he had a job and a house to keep up, Mallory accepted quietly and quickly – 'without visible emotion', remembered Younghusband – over the snowy linen of the lunch table.

It was a career move of sorts. Had Mallory, then thirty-five years old, summitted Everest and returned successfully, the cachet of the achievement would certainly have made him financially secure for his lifetime. But there were other career paths open to him, less dangerous ones. He had a steady job as a schoolmaster at Charterhouse, he wanted to pursue his writing ambitions – journalism, fiction – and his left-wing interest in international politics. Above all, Mallory wanted to be with Ruth and his three young children, Clare (aged six), Beridge (aged four) and John (aged six months). After marrying in 1914, Mallory had been separated from Ruth for sixteen months during the second half of the war, fighting as an artillery officer on the Western Front. The separation was difficult for them both and when the Armistice came they both felt that their married life could now properly begin. Shortly before he returned to England from France, Mallory wrote ecstatically to Ruth of the 'wonderful life we will have together', and urged them both to realize 'what a lovely thing we *must* make of such a gift'.

It was not to be. Some force, some set of forces, deeply embedded in Mallory, meant that when he was given the chance to go to Everest, he accepted. And when twice he returned safely from the mountain, he twice chose to return again. To read Mallory's letters and journals from the three Everest expeditions, as I have done, is to eavesdrop on a burgeoning love affair – a love affair with a mountain. It was a deeply selfish love affair, which Mallory could and should have broken off, but which instead destroyed the lives of his wife and his children – as well as his own. We do not have Ruth's letters to Mallory during the Everest expeditions. Although she wrote regularly to him, only one of her letters has survived. So we cannot properly

George and Ruth Mallory in 1914. © Audrey Salkeld.

know how she felt about her husband's actions. Her voice in this three-way relationship – this love triangle – is practically inaudible. What we do know is that Mallory fell in love with Everest, and it eventually proved the death of him. What is hard to understand, and what this book has tried in part to explain, is how he could fall in love with a lump of rock and ice, when his own flesh and blood wife loved him so very much.

Concluding his public account of the first expedition, the 1921 reconnaissance trip, Mallory wrote that 'The highest of mountains is capable of severity, a severity so awful and so fatal that the wiser sort of men do well to think and tremble even on the threshold of their high endeavour.' It reads now like a warning to himself, which he failed to heed.

8 April 1921 – Mallory boards the SS *Sardinia* alone at Tilbury. The other members of the expedition have gone ahead, and he is to meet them at Darjeeling. The boat is small, his fellow passengers numbingly dull, and his cabin is claustrophobic, and noisy as a foundry. As soon as they have steamed far enough south for the air temperature to permit it, Mallory spends most mornings sitting in the bows, near where the ship's anchors are lashed by their chains. Only the dark figure of the watchman on the upper bow-lookout, seated behind a canvas windscreen, is visible. Otherwise the bows are devoid of humanity, and this suits Mallory well, because he cannot abide humanity as it is to be found on board the *Sardinia*. He likes, too, the feel of the wind in his face, and to watch the wide sea and the passing land.

They take the ordinary route, steaming straight down to Cape St Vincent, and then turning east from there through the Straits of

Gibraltar and into the warmer waters of the Mediterranean. Even at sea, Mallory's mind is with the mountains. Waking early one morning he sees the Rock of Gibraltar slipping by his porthole and rushes up on to deck. They glide past it, a grey mass in the blue light, and Mallory instinctively looks for the best climbing line up its sheerness. On 13 April, five days after leaving England, he looks through his field-glasses deep into Spain. He can see a range of clean and radiant mountains snow-covered to the waist: the Sierra Nevada. 'Blessings on them!' he writes to his diary. He gazes southwards, too, into Africa: its houses, churches and fortifications, its small cliffs and creeks, and the white sprawl of Algiers. It all passes him by smoothly to port and starboard, like a gorgeously slow news-reel, as the ship slides onwards over the guarded water of the Mediterranean, towards Port Said and the Suez Canal.

Mallory's mind often drifts homewards, to the family he has left behind, to the way the sunlight streams through the loggia at the front of his house, and the white lilacs which will be in bloom on the bank behind the cedar tree in the garden, spangling the lawn with their petals.

The Canal is far less impressive than he imagines it, and its twin coasts are depressingly strewn with the debris of war – disembowelled trucks and stripped tanks, and rust bleeding into the sand around them. Where the sides of the Canal are low, Mallory imagines that it must seem to watchers from the desert as though their vessel is passing through solid sand, ploughing a path through the dunes like an ice-breaker; a ship of the desert.

After the Canal, the Red Sea, and after the Red Sea the Indian Ocean. No coastlines to watch here, only the curve of the horizon, and the odd distant ship steaming past beneath a feather of smoke. The skies of this ocean are vaster than anything Mallory has ever seen before, far greater in acreage even than the fenland skies he has come from. Here the clouds do not scud along like a fleet of airships, keeping their formation, but pile up into thunderheads, made from the tangled wreckage of nimbus and cirrus: more a geological than a meteorological creation. Mallory wonders what it would be like to climb the clouds, to force a route up through their bosses, knolls and slopes, up to the rounded top of the topmost cloud. Then he realizes that the topmost cloud he can see is thousands of feet lower than the top of Everest. It reminds him of the audacity of what he is trying to do.

The sky elates him, but the sea puts him into an ominous mood. 'It is curious,' he writes, 'how much I have a sense of the nearness of disaster and danger . . . the sea is as deeply evil as it is attractive.' Briefly, on the bows of the ship, he yearns to shrug his coat off on to the deck and leap clear of the vessel and into the gun-metal water.

Then Ceylon appears, a smear of red and yellow surmounted by a luminous green stripe – which resolves itself, as they steam nearer, into clumps of painted houses set against the jungle. There is a welcome stop here for a day or two, and then the final sultry leg of the journey begins. Mallory sweats as he does his exercises on the fore-deck, as he lies in his cabin, and as he writes in the smoking-room. The air is rank with water – it is an amphibious substance, half-gas half-liquid. Sitting in the bows, willing Calcutta to appear on the horizon, it feels to Mallory as though his body is being pushed forward through something gelatinous. The Malayan for water, Mallory remembers, is *air*, and here in the tropics that apparent mix-up seems to make perfect sense.

They dock in Calcutta on 10 May, and after a night there Mallory takes the eighteen-hour mountain train across the plains, and then up to Darjeeling, the track cutting through hillsides stepped with tea-terraces, and steep-sided valleys whose vertical forests remind him of Chinese scroll paintings. It feels good to be in hill-country again after a month on the oceanic plains.

In Darjeeling he meets the other Everesters (as they have begun to call themselves) and it seems, finally, that the adventure might have begun. But no; before that the formalities must be observed. The first night there Mallory has to sit through a banquet arranged by the Governor of Bengal, their host in Darjeeling. It is a plumed and brocaded affair: lots of solemn pre-prandial hand-shaking, and then the many courses of the meal itself. Each diner has an attentive wallah standing disconcertingly behind their chair, like a ghost or a shadow. There is far too much pomp and circumstance for Mallory's taste, but then as this Everest trip is in so many ways an imperial mission, pomp must be tolerated. He gets to meet his fellow expedition members. That night, he sends quick, sharp judgments of them in a letter back to Ruth. There is Wheeler the Canadian ('you know my complex about Canadians. I shall have to swallow before I like him, I expect. God send me saliva.') And Howard-Bury, the leader of the expedition, whom Mallory instinctively dislikes. He reeks of Toryism, crassness, dogma. There is Bullock, who will be Mallory's partner on the mountain, and whom he knew at Winchester. Bullock has, bafflingly, brought a suitcase with him. Into it he has packed one coat and two sweaters to keep him warm, and a pink umbrella to protect him from snowstorms and sunlight, and to make him look 'picturesque' against the landscape. There is Morshead, the surveyor-mountaineer, who impresses Mallory: he looks tough. And there is Kellas, the Scottish doctor and mountaineer who has rushed back to Darjeeling after climbing a trio of high mountains in Central Tibet. Mallory takes to Kellas from the moment he arrives, ten minutes late for the Governor's dinner, dishevelled 'as an alchemist' and muttering insincere apologies in his thick Scotch accent.

From Darjeeling, after much delay, the expedition departs. Fifty mules and their muleteers, a throng of porters, cooks, translators and sirdars, and the Everesters themselves. For days they move through the greenhouse of the Sikkim jungle. It rains profusely, and this causes problems. Mallory has his black cycling cape and Bullock his pink umbrella, but nothing keeps you dry beneath such a prodigious downpour. Everything is wet, water slides and trickles off every leaf and stone. The mules they procured in Darjeeling are plump creatures, unused to the jungle paths. Nine fall sick, and one collapses and dies. After five days there is no choice: they decide to pack the mules and their muleteers back to Darjeeling, and extemporize with local transport – yaks, ponies – once they get into Tibet. The rain brings out the leeches, too. Both sorts – the string-thin, army-green leeches and the tuberous, ochre-striped tiger-leeches. They come from all directions, and in their hundreds: undulating over the ground at surprising speed, or standing erect on leaves and branches, waving like admonishing fingers in the air. The porters nip them off from their legs with a twist and a pull, leaving little rings of blood that bleed on for hours afterwards, and quickly the Westerners learn to do the same.

But there is also a beauty in the moist, riotous densities of the jungle. The rain glosses the thick leaves, and gathers in bulging silver puddles in flower heads. Dragonflies, like little neon bars, dart and hover over the ponds. Mallory is especially enchanted by the flowers: the roseate orchids, and the lemony flowers of the rhododendrons. And of course there is Bullock's umbrella, which upside down on the ground looks like an extravagant, unheard-of bloom.

Then, abruptly, the jungle ends. The party cross the watershed of Jelep La – all of them feeling the altitude a little at 14,500 feet – and from this high point they gaze north. The air here smells cleaner and colder; oxygen-flavoured, almost. For the first time the mountains are visible, the snow mountains which Mallory has come so far to see, leaping up above the rim of the horizon. In front of them lies Tibet, and somewhere inside that country, Everest itself. 'Goodbye beautiful wooded Sikkim,' writes an excited Mallory, '& welcome – God knows what!' The change in terrain is total. As they descend towards Phari, the air becomes much drier and the vegetation is transformed. Here there are tall silver fir trees, with dark rhododendrons at their feet.

Then on to the high gravel deserts of southern Tibet, which proceed for hundreds of glaring miles. It is six days' march from Phari to Kampa Dzong, the Tibetan hill-fort through which Younghusband's army passed en route to Lhasa. Six days over high sepia deserts. Like all deserts, these ones are cold and calm in the early mornings when they wake; by lunchtime the heat is rampant, shimmering up in waves ahead, glaring off the surfaces of rock rubble, creating a furnace hot enough to strip away the skin on one's cheeks. In the afternoon the wind stirs itself, and stirs too the tons and tons of dust which lie loosely on the ground. At night tailless rats scutter about unnervingly on the groundsheets of their tents, and the temperature hurtles downwards. The mountains which edge the deserts are bosomy in profile, cleaved by long-vanished glaciers and river gulches, shaley in texture, the higher ones striated horizontally with snow.

All the group are suffering from stomach problems now. Most afflicted, though, is Kellas, racked with dysentery and so weak that he has to be carried on a litter. He had started the expedition exhausted by his triple ascent, and has not been able to fortify himself since. He refuses to turn back, though. Just short of Kampa Dzong, on 5 June, not long after crossing a high pass, he dies in a splutter of blood and shit.

Suddenly this imperial progress has become a funeral cortège. It seems strange and wrong that death should have visited the expedition so early, so far from the mountain itself. Mallory writes to Ruth to reassure her of his own fitness, knowing that Kellas's death will make it into the despatches which Howard-Bury is sending back almost daily to *The Times*. Mallory's own letters take upwards of a month to reach England.

They put up a tent to house Kellas's body overnight. The next day they dig a grave in the friable earth of a stony hillside and bury Kellas so that he lies facing the three peaks that he climbed before the expedition began – and which indirectly killed him. Howard-Bury recites the standard passage from Corinthians into the empty air, and the four porters whom Kellas had come to know so well sit on top of a flat boulder near the grave, and listen to the Englishman speak. This done, they build a stone cairn over the grave, and march on.

Kampa Dzong is a Tibetan fort which guards the entrance to a narrow valley. Here, spirits improve. Bury shoots a gazelle and a fat-tailed sheep, and Bullock bags a goose and catches a dish of little fishes. Despite the death of Kellas and the asperities of the terrain, Mallory feels exhilarated by the prospect of getting closer to Everest, and of going where no one has gone before. 'We are now in a country which no European has previously visited,' he writes to Ruth. 'In another 2 days' march we shall be "off the map"; which was made at the time of the Lhasa expedition.' For Everest at this moment exists only in the imagination of the West. It is nothing more than a handful of distant sightings glimpsed over decades, a triangulated peak with a height and a set of coordinates to pin it down in space. It exists only in expectation.

The following morning, before breakfast, Mallory and Bullock climb the barren, scree-laden slopes – two steps up, one back – above the fort. They ascend for perhaps 1,000 feet, up into the golden sunlight, and then:

we stayed and turned, and saw what we came to see. There was no mistaking the two great peaks in the West: that to the left must be Makalu, grey, severe, and yet distinctly graceful, and the other away to the right – who could doubt its identity? It was a prodigious white fang excrescent from the jaw of the world. We saw Mount Everest not quite sharply defined on

account of a slight haze in that direction; this circumstance
added a touch of mystery and grandeur; we were satisfied that
the highest of mountains would not disappoint us.

He has seen it at last, the mountain which has drawn him so many
thousands of miles across the world. And, just for the time being, he
doesn't want to see Everest 'sharply defined', he wants it to retain its
mystery, to remain a conspiracy of imagination and geology, a half-
imagined, half-real hill. This is the Sublime at work inside Mallory,
stimulating his appetite for intimation, for haze, for mystery, con-
vincing him that what is half-seen is seen more intensely. Mallory is
attracted by what J. R. R. Tolkien would later call glamour – 'that
shimmer of suggestion that never becomes clear sight, but always
hints at something deeper further on'.

They leave Kampa Dzong after a few days' rest, and move on
westwards. Now they pass through the true badlands of Tibet, a
wilderness of sand dunes and mud-flats set in a bronze light. Here the
wind is almost a blessing, for it keeps squadrons of voracious sand-
flies pinned to the ground. The pack animals flounder in the mud,
and have to be coaxed up steep sand cliffs. To Bullock it seems the
most godforsaken, sterile region in the world. To Mallory's alert eyes,
however, it is not entirely bereft either of charm or colour. He notices
miniature blue irises blooming leaflessly from the gravel, and a few
vivid nasturtium-like plants with pink and yellow petals, and tiny
green leaves. It is as though there is a trove of colour buried just
beneath the desert surface, peeking through here and there.

One morning, as has become their custom, Mallory and Bullock
push on together ahead of the main group. On horseback now, they
ford a deep river and canter for miles along the bed of a gorge.
Suddenly the sides of the gorge peel back and they discover themselves out on a sandy plain. And there, before them, gleaming
through the cloud, beneath a cavernous sky, are the mountains they

have come so far to see. Again Mallory feels strongly the shiver and
thrill of going where no one has gone before:

> I felt somehow a traveller. It was not only that no European had
> ever been here before us; but we were penetrating a secret: we
> were looking behind the great barrier running North–South
> which had been a screen in front of us ever since we turned our
> eyes westwards from Kampa Dzong.

It is for moments like this that he has come on this 'great adventure',
as he has taken to calling it.

With time to kill while the others catch up, Mallory and Bullock
tether the ponies and scramble up a shaley small peak at the northern corner of the gorge. From its summit they turn westwards. The
clouds have come in and obscured the mountains since they emerged
from the gorge, and it seems that even with the field-glasses they will
be able to see nothing. But then

> suddenly our eyes caught glint of snow through the clouds; &
> gradually, very gradually in the course of 2 hrs or so visions of
> great mountainsides & glaciers and ridges now here now there,
> forms invisible for the most part to the naked eye or indistin-
> guishable from the clouds themselves appeared through the
> floating rifts and had meaning for us; – one whole clear mean-
> ing pieced from these fragments, for we had seen a whole
> mountain-range, little by little, the lesser to the greater until,
> incredibly higher in the sky than imagination had ventured to
> dream, the top of Everest appeared.

While they are at the summit a wind gets up and starts to blow the
sand of the plain, so that from above, while they are descending, the
plain seems like a basin of rippling silk.

Soon they pitch camp at Shekar Dzong – the White Glass Fort. The whitewashed walls of the buildings shine in the sun. To Mallory every detail of camp life – the fibrous guy-ropes, the tea chests which double as stools, the heavy canvas of the mess tent, the clinking cooking bowls – is made beautiful by the conscientious light of this place, which picks out each aspect and each grain of each object. Inquisitive Tibetans stroll among the Everesters: mothers with babies slung in their papooses, grimy toddlers, lean fathers.

They spend two nights at Shekar Dzong. The post arrives, and Mallory gets a sheaf of letters from Ruth. He replies straight away, and presses tiny Tibetan flowers between the pages of his letter. He tells her that this day – the day he saw Everest in snatches through the cloud – was 'somehow a great landmark'. Everest had now 'become something more than a fantastic vision'. To be sure, it is a landmark, or better perhaps to say a turning-point. For from this day forth Everest, more even than Ruth, becomes the focus of Mallory's letters. The mountain starts to intrude into his thoughts like a lover. The third point of the love triangle which will destroy both Mallory and Ruth is put in place. 'Where,' he asks Ruth in his letter to her, 'can one go for another view, to unveil a little more of the great mystery? – from this day that question has been always present.'

On 19 June, some four weeks after leaving Darjeeling, the expedition crosses a series of bridges slung like dilapidated train-tracks over churning rivers, and turns into the valley which leads up towards Tingri Dzong, a trading village on a hillock in the middle of a salt plain, forty miles distant from Everest. Here Howard-Bury sets up a permanent dark-room and mess tent. Tingri is to be HQ, the base of operations, the nerve centre of the expedition.

Mallory is keen to get on. After only a short break he and Bullock push up the Rongbuk valley to establish a more advanced base camp, some fifteen miles short of the mountain itself. Here Everest, 'amazing in its simplicity', looms over them. It is showcased by its surroundings. The long arms of the Rongbuk valley, its high walls perforated by caves in which Buddhist hermits live, extend downwards from the mountain like 'giant's limbs: simple, severe, superb'. And within them the Rongbuk glacier runs itself up into the cwm at the base of the mountain 'like the charge of the light brigade'.

It is from here that the work really begins. They are here, this year, to try to find the best way up Everest. To do this, they must unlock the mysteries of the mountain and its satellite peaks; must decipher its geography. Days and then weeks are spent mapping, probing, photographing, hurdling the ridges that radiate out from the hub of the massif. Each ounce of information about the mountain is gained through graft. On the good days they wake early – the sunlight at dawn moves across the campsite like a tide flowing in, inky on one side and gold on the other – and walk for ten or a dozen hours, often carrying heavy photographic equipment. It is not easy going. There is the altitude and the temperature, to begin with. And the Rongbuk glacier doesn't provide the walkway to the base of the mountain that it promised from afar. As Mallory quickly discovers, the glaciers in this part of the world – nearer the equator – are not as pedestrian-friendly as Alpine glaciers. Here, the ice has been wrought by the overhead sun into densely clustered forests of ice pinnacles, some of them fifty feet high, the ice beneath them fissured into a labyrinth of crevasses and pressure ridges. 'The White Rabbit himself would have been bewildered here,' writes Mallory. He soon realizes that progress is best to be made away from this weird scape of icy stalactites, up on the lateral moraines of the glaciers; though these routes have their own dangers, threatened as they are by rock- and ice-fall from the cliffs above.

Most of the time Mallory is enchanted by the landscape. On good evenings he watches red sunsets over Everest, and notes how twilight flattens the mountains to two dimensions, like cardboard cut-outs, and how the gleaming summit of Everest hangs over him 'like Keats's

An 'Everester' in front of the ice pinnacles of the Rongbuk glacier. Photographer John Noel. © Sandra R. C. Noel.

lone star'. In the mornings he watches almost lustfully as Everest divests herself of cloud:

> We watched again last morning that oft-repeated drama which seems always to be a first night, fresh and full of wonder whenever we are present to watch it. The clinging curtains were rent and swirled aside and closed again, lifted and lowered and flung wide at last; sunlight broke through with sharp shadows and clean edges revealed – and we were there to witness the amazing spectacle.

This is mountaineering as strip-tease. Mallory is smitten. He is possessed of a seemingly inexhaustible energy, a 'driving power' as he calls it. Everest has created for him, he writes to Ruth, 'an exhilarating life'.

Sometimes, though, very occasionally, Mallory is just sick of it all: the repetitive food, the bullying of the body by the altitude, the bad weather, the cramped little tents. By 12 July they have established a second advanced camp at 19,000 feet, at which altitude the Primus stoves won't work and the ice is as hard as stone. Pinned down by bad weather at this camp, listening to fine grains of snow falling incessantly on to the sides of the tent, Mallory writes to a friend:

> I sometimes think of this expedition as a fraud from beginning to end invented by the wild enthusiasm of one man – Younghusband . . . and imposed upon the faithful ardour of your humble servant. Certainly the reality must be strangely different from their dream. The long imagined snowslopes of this northern face of Everest with their gentle & inviting angle turn out to be the most appalling precipice nearly 10,000 ft high . . .

It is not entirely lost on Mallory that he is climbing a mountain of the mind, and by no means wholly of his own mind – more of Younghusband's. The talk back in Britain, at the Alpine Club and the 'Jog', had been of easy snow slopes. But of course no one before Mallory had been near enough to Everest to see its north face – these easy snow slopes, like so many aspects of so many mountains, had been imagined into being. The reality, as Mallory points out, is 'strangely different' – an 'appalling precipice nearly 10,000 ft high'.

From the beginning it has been clear that the North Col – the 'col of our desires' as Mallory calls it – holds the key to the mountain. It is the northern shoulder of the peak, from which an apparently climbable ice and rock ridge angles up to the summit. If a camp could just be pitched on the Col, then it seems likely the mountain will fall. The problem, though, is how to reach the Col itself. The first month is spent trying to force a way up from the main Rongbuk glacier. But it is too dangerous, and impossible for the porters. The route needs to be one up which supplies and equipment can be carried. So, in mid-July, Mallory and company decide to quit the main Rongbuk valley and walk round to the east of the mountain and see if there is a way up to the North Col from there.

There is. On 18 August they crack the geographical riddle. The answer involves coming at the North Col over a high pass known as the Lhapka La, and then up through the jumbled ice-falls of what they christen the East Rongbuk glacier. From there, apparently negotiable snow and ice slopes lead up to the North Col itself.

But, infuriatingly, just as they realize this the weather closes in. The monsoon has come to town. For almost a month they wait for a break in the weather. This is in many ways the hardest time of the whole expedition. As the men have worked the mountain, their bodies have begun to degenerate. Mallory, who has always been assured of his fitness, is slightly surprised by these signs that his body is vulnerable, that it can ever operate at anything other than optimum capacity. At night, they notice that their faces and hands take on a bluish tinge – from the oxygen deprivation – and Mallory is often woken by Bullock, who stops breathing for what seems like minutes. Bullock says Mallory does the same. The days are getting shorter as well, and the nights colder.

The enforced rest also gives Mallory too much time to think about Ruth. There are the wonderful moments when 'the mail comes and love flies in among us & nestles in every tent'. In the darkness he dreams that it is Ruth and not Bullock lying near to him. He dreams, too, of himself speeding back to her, the green sea creamed by the prow of the ship, headed for some sun-soaked Mediterranean port, where the gulls fill the air with their almost solid cries, and 'where I shall expect to see *you* smiling in the sunshine on the quayside'.

But he always wakes up next to Bullock. Bullock is one of those people who grow to fit their names: he has the power and diligence of a bullock, a bovine strength and dutifulness which Mallory quietly admires. He refers to him as his 'stable-companion'.

There is talk of calling it a day. But Mallory, more than anyone, feels a 'pull' to stay in the area and wait for his chance; 'the chance of a lifetime'. On 17 September the weather breaks. There is sunshine, and no snow. Quickly they move up to the upper camp, at 22,000 feet, reaching it on 23 September. And there the weather closes in again. During the night there is the sizzle of hard driving snow against the sides of the tent. Even in their eiderdown sleeping-bags the climbers shiver. The sardines they are meant to eat for supper freeze into little stone shoals which Mallory and Bullock have to thaw out by holding them in their hands. While they are melting snow for water, the two men take turns to lean over the pot so that the steam which tendrils off its surface warms their eyes. The wind rages continually at the tents, slapping the layers of canvas together, trying to rip the whole structure from the mountainside. Without the tent, without these few crucial millimetres of canvas, they wouldn't stand a chance.

Mallory awakes on the morning of the 24th, after one of the worst nights he has ever had, to find the roof of his tent bulging ominously inwards. Though the snow has stopped falling, the wind has barely dropped. It is hopeless, but they set off anyway, and try to force a way up the steep snow slopes towards the col. They clamber upwards over old avalanche debris. The wind whips the loose snow crystals and blinds the climbers. Miniature avalanches scutter softly down the slope behind them, triggered by their tread.

Seen from below, each climber has an aureole of spindrift, a frigid little halo. Hundreds of feet above them, like a fiery sheet of snow, spindrift is being rasped continually off the brink of the North Col. The wind down here, on the lee slopes, is almost impossible: up there it will be fatal. But Mallory, again, is keen 'to push the adventure a little further'. So he and Bullock and Wheeler cut steps gradually upwards to the edge of the col. There, just for the sake of it, they step out on to the col and for a few minutes bear the full brunt of the wind. They gaze upwards at the ridge, angling thousands of feet up to the summit. The wind is cyclonic, apocalyptic – a wind, Mallory remembers later, 'in which no man could live for an hour'. It is important that they have reached the col, though, because it means, as Mallory writes to Ruth afterwards, that the way to the summit has been established 'for anyone who cares to try the highest adventure . . .'

And that is it, over for the first time. There is the trek back to Darjeeling, and thence to Bombay, and then aboard the SS *Malwa* for the voyage home. Mallory feels deeply tired now. He is tired, he writes, of

far countries and uncouth people, trains and ships and shimmering mausoleums, foreign ports, dark-skinned faces and a garish sun. What I want to see is faces I know, and my own sweet home; afterwards, the solemn façades in Pall Mall and perhaps Bloomsbury in a fog; and then an English river, cattle grazing in western meadows.

From on board, as the ship nears Marseilles, he writes to his sister Avie: 'They've had thoughts of organising an expedition for next year . . . I wouldn't go again next year, as the saying is, for all the gold in Arabia.'

❄

2 March 1922 – The cry of gulls, wheeling on their wing-points around the quayside of the East India docks; Mallory striding up the railed gangplank of the SS *Caledonia*, bound for Bombay. The other Everesters are already on board. A new team, a new game. The *Caledonia* slips through the grey water and sea mists of the English Channel, skirts the Iberian peninsula, then rounds the Rock of Gibraltar into the Mediterranean. It threads the needle of the Suez Canal at night: the water so still and dark it seems more like a geological feature, a seam of graphite clamped between the layers of the desert. Then out into the hot air of the Red Sea, where the ocean is as calm as a reservoir and the ship moves across it leaving barely a wake on the water.

During the day the sky is flawless, like a cupola of glass, but each evening the greens and blues and yellows of a Middle Eastern sunset congregate in the air, and kaleidoscope together on the passing water. Flying fish scoot out of the sea, executing their stiff skimming little leaps and occasionally thunking into the ship's side. And dolphins chaperone the ship, leaping in and out of the water to port and starboard.

Life on board is pleasant enough. In the mornings Finch, a New Zealander, talks the team through the oxygen equipment they have brought, demonstrating valves, carrying-frames, flow rates. Mallory is sceptical of this ironmongery, all 900 lbs of it. To him it seems a way of cheating the mountain; like carrying your own atmosphere with you. But Finch is persuasive about its advantages, if a little monomaniacal. During the afternoons, when the heat lies heavy and still as a blanket upon them, there is deck-tennis and sometimes deck-cricket, and at 7 p.m. sharp a bugle signals dinner. After dark, from the stern, Mallory likes to watch the phosphorescent path left by the ship. He casts his mind back to Ruth, of course, but mostly he thinks forward, to the 'great work ahead'.

They dock at Bombay this time, and with their two tons of luggage – which includes cases of champagne, tins of quail in aspic, and hundreds of ginger nut biscuits – make a protracted, hot train journey across India to Calcutta. The track passes over baked khaki plains and through dark sycamore forests, the old trees rising on either side like the sides of a gorge. From Calcutta, the train chugs them up to Darjeeling, where there is an orgy of packing. The team is already pulling together well. It seems a much happier combination of people than last time. There is a new leader, General Bruce, always laughing at something and always wearing his bow-tie, tweed jacket and pith helmet, and carrying a field stick. Under the tweed are scars – bullet wounds from Gallipoli and elsewhere – and inside him rages malaria. Mallory likes Bruce much better than the insufferable Howard-Bury. There is Strutt, who, despite his polka-dotted socks and constant whingeing, is tolerable. There is John Noel, the photographer and cinematographer of the trip, and a handy climber to boot. And there is Somervell, Mallory's climbing partner and intellectual *confrère* on the trip, a man with a prodigious brain and strange jug ears.

They leave from Darjeeling in two parties, planning to unite at Phari and pool their 300 pack animals. It is earlier in the year this time round, and the Sikkim jungle is not as profuse or as beautiful as the last time Mallory ventured through it. There are fewer flowers, and 'the sense of bursting growth is absent'. Nevertheless, it feels good to be on the move, to feel the high air of the hills in the lungs, and to be getting closer to what Mallory now regularly calls just 'the mountain'.

Mallory, in the first group, reaches Phari on 6 April, and although there is an inch of snow on the ground and he has to sit huddled in his sleeping-bag after dark, he tells Ruth that he has experienced an unforeseen burst of excitement to be back in Tibet; an unexpected fondness for the bleak landscape. From Phari, they have a new route to Kampa Dzong – higher, but shorter by two days than the version of 1921. It takes them over the Donka La. As they approach the pass, the air becomes violently cold, and it begins to snow. It snows all night on 8 April. Mallory is concerned for the animals, and in the darkness he walks over the soft, sticky snow from his tent to where the yaks and mules are tethered. They are standing in untidy rows with snow lying like rugs on their backs. They shift unhappily from foot to foot, and from their nostrils snort out jets of wet white breath into the dark air. The mule-men are squatting in a circle behind a shelter of rocks. They seem happy enough despite the brutal cold, and not too concerned for their animals, so Mallory goes back to his tent, and falls asleep to the quiet carillon of yak bells.

The following day it is too cold to ride and everyone, even Mallory, who is suffering from enteritis, chooses to walk beside the animals in an effort to stay warm. It is an arduous day, with twenty-two miles of rough walking, all above 16,000 feet, and only a couple of short stops for tiffin. Just before nightfall they pitch a 'queer little camp' under an outcrop of rock. A gravel plain stretches away from them, and showing above its eastern rim are the three peaks Kellas climbed.

The following day is a rest day. Mallory sits outside and reads Balzac for the few hours it is warm enough to do so. Despite the hardihoods, he reflects, there is still a beauty to be found in the landscape: the shadows of clouds smudging the plains, the blueness of the far distance, and the subtle shades of red, yellow and brown on the nearer hillsides. But then the wind gets up, and he is forced back into the mess tent for warmth. There he tries to write to Ruth, though the ink in the pot keeps freezing. 'We have had a taste of the diabolical in Tibet,' he writes. 'I feel withered up by the absence of all the circumstances that lead to enjoyment.' He is wearing five layers of clothing and even so is 'just sufficiently warm except in the fingertips which touch the paper'. But the chill to his fingers is worth it, because the letter feels like a connection with Ruth: 'I am conscious of you at the other end; and very often dearest one I summon up your image & have your presence in some way near me.'

For days they follow the same rhythm; march and camp, march and camp. It is hard to drive tent pegs into this icy ground. At breakfast time, around the trestle table, they sit on upturned tea chests and wear herringbone tweed and fisherman's jumpers, hands thrust into armpits, hunched over against the cold with their heads tamped down into their bodies. On the wastelands near Kampa Dzong, a blizzard hustles in and softly overwhelms them, filling in their tracks as soon as they have been made, clearing up after them like a diligent housekeeper, abolishing all signs of their presence or progress. The plateau becomes a polar tundra. The snow clings to their stubble. Behind them for miles across the white plain are strung out the black battalions of the yaks and mules.

The cold is demoralizing and physically draining. For a while they forget about their ulterior purpose, and just concentrate on getting from camp in the morning to camp at night. But then, arriving finally at Shekar Dzong, the White Glass Fort, 'we had a clear view of Everest across the plain – it was more wonderful even than I remember & all the party were delighted by it – which of course appealed to my proprietary feelings'. In a way it *is* Mallory's mountain. He is the only member of the 1921 expedition who has come back for another try.

After Shekar Dzong they strike off south; a quicker route in to the East Rongbuk glacier and thence to the North Col. By the first day of May they have established a Base Camp on the terminal moraine of the glacier. From a distance the pale tents are indistinguishable from the jumble of pale tent-sized boulders which the glacier has bulldozed down the valley.

Bruce's plan is to lay siege to the mountain. His climbers will establish a series of ascending camps: Camp III will be just below the North Col – where Mallory had spent such an uncomfortable night – and Camp IV on the col itself. The hope is that this will provide the support network needed for a strike on the summit itself.

The weather doesn't get any warmer, but three camps are successfully pitched up the valley, and then on 13 May, Mallory helps to establish a route from Camp III up to the North Col itself. For long sections he has to cut steps into the steep blue glittering ice. Swing, crash, step, swing, crash, step. An exhausting rhythm at sea-level; shattering up here. Shards of ice fly dangerously with each blow of the axe, like shrapnel. After a while Mallory moves across to the left of the col, and discovers that there is thick, stable snow, which makes the going much easier. In a single day he manages to fix 400 feet of rope to help those coming up afterwards. He also reaches the North Col. The wind is not as bad as the year before, and he makes his way over the dangerously broken ground of the crevassed north ridge, through the broken cubes of blue ice, and reaches safe ground near where the ridge begins. The view south opens out with every step he takes, and he sits down to look at it in awe: 'the most amazing spectacle I have ever seen'. Camp IV is set at the North Col.

On 17 May Mallory sends a letter to Ruth 'on the eve of our departure for the highest we can reach', and the following day he, Morshead, Norton and Somervell set off from Base Camp to Camp IV. Their plan is to leave the North Col and move up the north-east ridge, bivouac, and then make a bid for the summit the following day.

After a cold night at Camp IV, they set off late up the ridge. They are delayed because they left their breakfast – tins of Heinz spaghetti – outside their sleeping-bags, and the spaghetti froze. They have to thaw them in water on the slow stoves and force the crystalline mush down before they can set off. Quickly it becomes clear that the wind is too strong and the air too cold. Nobody is properly clothed: the wool in their gloves and puttees stiffens to plywood in the cold; the fibres in their felt hats matt together and will not retain the heat. Slowly and painfully they move up the ridge, and are forced to bivouac far short of their intended goal, perched on a little ledge

of ice and rock on the lee side of the ridge at 25,000 feet. One of
Norton's ears and his feet have been frostbitten, and he cannot sleep.
Morshead, too, has been wrecked by the cold: the fingers on one of
his hands have gone an ominous raspberry-and-cream colour. All
night the men lie awake, two to a sleeping-bag, and listen to 'the
musical patter of fine, granular snow' on the tent. They bash the
sides of the tent with their flat hands when they begin to sag under
the weight of the snow, and send the snow hissing off on to the
ground.

When dawn lightens the tent canvas, they drag themselves outside,
except Morshead, who declares he can go no further. The summit is
beyond them, that much is obvious, but they struggle onwards and
upwards for a symbolic 2,000 feet before turning back. They pick up
Morshead at the camp, leave the tents where they are, and press on
back down to the North Col. It is a desperate retreat. Morshead can
barely walk, and keeps sitting down in the snow and asking to die.
Norton coaxes him on, an arm about his waist, whispering gentle
words in his ear. On a steep part of the ridge, Morshead slips and
tugs the other two climbers off. It is only Mallory's quick reactions –
driving his axe into the snow and throwing a loop of the rope about
it – which save all four of them from death. As they stumble back
into Camp IV Mallory notices apocalyptic weather away to the
west – a pile-up of black clouds, and distant flashes of lightning
brightening the sky, as though there were a war going on in a far
valley.

Mallory and the three others descend to Base Camp, and spend a
month recovering there. Four of Mallory's fingers have been injured
by the cold. While he is recuperating, Finch and the young Geoffrey
Bruce (cousin of Charles) take oxygen apparatus with them, and
make an assisted bid for the summit. They get higher than Mallory's
party, but they too are repelled by the cold. Bruce hobbles back into
Base Camp: his feet will take weeks to recover from their frostbite.

The season is getting on, and the monsoon snow has begun to fall. Once again there is talk of calling it a day. Two good attempts have been made, and both have failed. But again it is Mallory, more than anyone, who wants to have another 'whack'. His finger is not healed, he tells Ruth, 'and I risk getting a worse frostbite by going up again, but the game is worth a finger & I shall take every conceivable care of both fingers & toes. Once bit twice shy!' On 3 June he and two other climbers, along with a train of Sherpas, set off for the 'great battlements of ice on the North Col'. The snowfall has been heavy over the past forty-eight hours, and there is thick windslab lying on hard ice. It is classic avalanche territory. As he leads up the slope, Mallory tests the snow. It seems safe. He leads on.

Not far from the lip of the col, at 1.50 p.m., there is a cracking noise – like 'an explosion of untamped gunpowder' – and the snow Mallory is on begins to move. He loses his footing, and is swept a short way downhill before being spat out on to the surface of the snow. He pulls himself clear. There are cries from below him. Nine Sherpas have been swept by a faster torrent of snow over a sixty-foot ice cliff, and down into a crevasse. Two are rescued, amazingly unharmed. The other seven are never found, killed by the fall into the crevasse, or buried alive inside it by tons of snow.

A rough memorial cairn is built for the dead Sherpas at Camp III. Bruce is sanguine about the accident. Nobody's fault, he says. Nor do the families of the dead men seem interested in blaming anyone: their men died when they were meant to die. But Mallory won't be consoled. He considers their death his doing. 'It was not a desperate game, I thought,' he writes to Ruth, 'with the plans we made. Perhaps with the habit of dealing with certain kinds of danger one becomes accustomed to measuring some that are best left unmeasured and untried . . . the three of us were deceived; there wasn't an inkling of danger among us.' He is aware, too, of how close he came to dying. 'It was a wonderful escape for me & we may indeed be thankful for that together. Dear love when I think what your grief would have been I humbly thank God. I am alive . . .'

The expedition limps back through Tibet to Darjeeling, wounded and depleted, very much 'not the jolly company we were'. Morshead and Mallory are in pain from their fingers, Bruce's toes are not healed, and the soles of Norton's feet are grey and black with frost-bite. And yet the further Mallory gets from the murderous mountain, the more he falls back in love with it. By Darjeeling, the subject of the dead Sherpas has disappeared from his letters. His thoughts are only with Ruth. With Ruth, and with the possibility of the next trip.

29 February 1924 – Liverpool docks this time, and an inauspicious departure. Ruth has come to see Mallory off for what will be, surely, the last time. He stands on deck, leaning over the shining rail, wearing a dark trilby and a fur-collared coat. She is on the quayside waving as the SS *California* is cast off, and he waves back. For several minutes they carry on waving at each other, but the ship does not move. An announcement comes over the loudspeaker system. Out beyond the harbour wall, there is a westerly storm drumming up and the wind is keeping the ship pinned to its moorings. A couple of dirty little tug boats nose round the front and prepare to heave *California* out to sea. Ruth grows tired of waving at a stationary ship and Mallory at a stationary quayside. After a while she just walks away.

Why is he going again? There is now an element of helplessness to it all, an awareness of forces at work which are beyond her control, beyond his. Worse than this, Mallory has a bad feeling about this trip. One of the last things he does before he leaves for India is to pay a visit to Kathleen Scott, widow of the polar explorer Robert Scott, Britain's most heroic failure. There are mementos of Scott everywhere in the house: pictures in frames, letters. The absent husband, the fatherless children . . . It is all too suggestive of what might come to be. Mallory visits her in the company of Geoffrey Winthrop Young. In the taxi on the way back, Mallory tells Young that he believes this year on Everest it will be more like war than adventure, and that this time he does not think he will return alive.

The long voyage begins again. The ship is crowded with a Scottish tour group bound for Egypt and a group of soldiers and their wives. For the first two days they are strafed by the westerly wind, and make heavy weather over the steel-grey sea of the Bay of Biscay. Mallory works out in the gym on board, and admires Sandy Irvine's magnificent body. Andrew – Sandy – Irvine is a second-year undergraduate from Oxford who had impressed the Everest selectors with his resilience during a trip to Arctic Norway. He is a rowing Blue, but is missing the race this year to take part in the expedition. Mallory likes Irvine a lot; thinks he is 'one to depend on, for everything perhaps except conversation'. He writes the now habitual first letter back to Ruth, giving an account of the rhythm of life on board, and of his companions. He writes, too, about life after Everest, and assures her that things will get better for them once the mountain has been climbed. Everything seems to divide itself – as it has done for three years now – into before and after Everest.

> How are you feeling, you poor left-behind one? . . . Dear Love, I shall be thinking of you often & often. We have been very close together lately I think & I feel very close to you now. You are going to be outwardly cheerful I know and I hope you will also be inwardly happy while I am away. I love you always, dear one.

The voyage is largely unmemorable. Mallory, who has become a celebrity in Britain, is pestered by the Scottish tourists for photographs, signatures and *bons mots* about Everest. He escapes to the bows to read André Maurois's biography of Shelley, or keeps to his quarters. There is one moment, though – the sort of moment which sends excitement thrilling through him. They approach the Straits of Gibraltar one morning before sunrise and Mallory goes out on deck, as he did three years earlier, to watch them pass through the jaws of land:

> We were steaming due East and straight ahead was the orange glow spreading over the sky. Towards the centre of it the long thin lines of land on either side converged & left a gap – quite a small gap between little lumps of land, for the straits were 20 miles away or more. We were aiming straight for this little hole in the sky line where the light was brightest & I had the most irresistible feeling of a romantic world; we had only to pop through the hole like Alice through the garden door to reach a new scene or a whole kingdom of adventures.

That idea of crossing barriers, popping through holes, solving mysteries, in a word, of *exploration*: it exercises the profoundest fascination on Mallory. Everest is for him the greatest unknown, the deepest mystery.

At Port Said the other passengers leave the ship, which is a relief to Mallory. They sail on through the Canal and the Red Sea, and out on to the unusually smooth water of the Indian Ocean. Once more his thoughts turn to Ruth. He imagines the two of them in their silk dressing gowns, going up on deck to breathe the fresh morning air together: 'Dear girl we give up & miss a terrible lot by trying to do what is right, but we must see we don't miss too much.' What is right, Ruth might reply, is for Mallory to stay at home with his wife and children, and earn a less glamorous, but far safer, living as a lecturer and teacher. But there is a bigger 'right' at work here, sunk so deeply inside Mallory that it's invisible to him – his right to stand on the top of Everest, to be the first man up that matchless mountain.

The train journey across India is even hotter than before, and it is a relief to get up into the tepid air of Darjeeling. Bruce, who is leading the expedition again, joins them there, fresh from a successful tiger hunt near the border with Nepal. They are being put up this year in the Hotel Mount Everest; from his balcony Mallory can see the white and pink magnolias, 'startlingly bright against the dark hillside', he tells Ruth, writing a lengthy letter to her on the floridly headed notepaper of the hotel. He writes to her even more passionately and longingly than in previous years, repeating words for emphasis, as if grammar could somehow erase the fact of physical absence, the fact that he has gone away yet again:

> Dearest one, I often & often want you with me, to enjoy things with, & to talk over things & people quietly; and I want to take you in my arms & kiss your dear brown head . . . Would there were some way of bringing you nearer. I think the nearness depends very much upon the state of one's imagination. When it boils up, as it does sometimes at night, under the stars I could almost whisper in your ear, and even now dear I do feel near you . . . & I come very near to kissing you.

On 29 March they begin the trek through Sikkim. The weather is excellent this time, and Mallory feels full of 'valley-ease, warmth & languor, and the delights of the lotos-eater'. He bathes naked in rock-pools, and surprises 'a very fine jungle cat' in a glade – 'it is extraordinary how it makes the whole forest seem alive to see a beast like that'. The group are getting on famously, perhaps better even than the 1922 Everesters.

The trek to Base Camp on the East Rongbuk glacier takes five weeks this time. It is cold and the wind insistent, but the temperatures are not as low as in 1922. Indeed it is the sun and not the snow which is the chief peril this year. On the deserts near Kampa Dzong everyone's face gets burnished to the colour of chestnut. Fissures open in Mallory's lips and cheeks, and he keeps a pot of grease with him to rub into them. He walks with a shepherd's crook, and grows a goatee beard. Irvine wears his motorcycle helmet and goggles in an unsuccessful attempt to keep out the wind and the sun. Despite the sunburn, Mallory feels fitter than in any previous year, and his guts are holding firm for once. The sense keeps growing in him that there will be closure this time, one way or the other. To Ruth he writes that 'it is almost unthinkable that I shan't get to the top; I can't see myself coming down defeated'. To his friend Tom Longstaff he is even more adamant: 'We are going to sail to the top this time and God with us – or stamp to the top with our teeth in the wind.' There are other reasons for feeling good about it all: this year the quail are in *foie gras*, not aspic, and the champagne is vintage – 1915 Montebello.

But there are ominous moments, too. As when, one march short of Kampa, the team arrive at their destination well ahead of their pack animals. Unable to pitch their personal tents, they prop up the green mess tent and lie in its shade, waiting for the baggage to arrive. The white light refracted through the green canvas gives the tableau the glow of an aquarium. One by one they drop off to sleep, except Mallory, to whom, 'as they lay there snoozing with faces rendered ghastly by the green light', his team members looked exactly 'like a collection of corpses'.

The first blow to the expedition is struck on 11 April, when the group arrive at Kampa Dzong. General Bruce is so weakened by the approach march that, worried about his heart, he decides not to continue. Norton is promoted to commander of the expedition, and Mallory is made second-in-command and chief of the climbing

Crossing the high-altitude gravel deserts en route to Everest. The mountain in the background is Chomulhari. Photographer Bentley Beetham. © Royal Geographical Society.

team. It excites him to be in charge, and he quickly draws up what he thinks is a failsafe plan. There will be two summit bids made from Camp IV at the North Col. The first team of two will try without oxygen; the second team of two, which will set off after them, will use oxygen. Mallory puts himself in the oxygen party, and is confident that this will see him to the top.

As they draw nearer the mountain, Mallory starts to get excited. He is 'eager for the great events to begin'. They pitch camp at Rongbuk on 29 April, and almost immediately things start to go wrong. A blizzard – the blizzard they didn't meet in the badlands on the way in – tears into the Base Camp. The air is furious with snow. The temperature plunges to a depth almost too low for the thermometers to record. The plan this year is even more complex and multi-cogged than the effort of two years earlier. There are more camps, more porters, more equipment. This would have been fine in good weather, but the pitiless turn in the temperature – it drops as low as fifty degrees of frost at night – has made epic even the simplest segment of the operation, the ascent of the East Rongbuk glacier. The blue surface ice on the glacier is the texture of glass and the hardness of diamond. It is difficult to walk on in hob-nailed boots, and practically impossible for the porters in their slipshod shoes. But still the expedition battles on, everybody deteriorating by the day. Reaching Camp III, the camp below the North Col, Mallory finds the dud oxygen cylinders from 1922, piled against the rough cairn they had built to commemorate the seven dead Sherpas. The whole place has changed less than he can believe possible: the cold and the altitude have done their preservative work, stopping time in its tracks. Nothing ages up here; the snow just configures and reconfigures itself, drifts up against the cairn and melts away. There is nothing to tell the time by.

The weather at Camp III is unremittingly hostile, and for a day they are confined to their tiny tents. The snow gets in everywhere, whirled in by the wind, a fine powder which settles on every surface. As comfort and consolation Mallory, Irvine, Somervell and Odell – those four men up there in their tiny shelters, perched precariously on the shoulder of their mountain, enveloped in a blizzard, separated from the nearest sea by a desert and a jungle, and separated from Britain by four more seas – read poetry to each other from Robert Bridges's anthology *The Spirit of Man*. They find solace in Coleridge's *Kubla Khan* – with its 'sunny pleasure dome', its 'caves of ice' – in Thomas Gray's famous elegy, in Shelley's poem 'Mont Blanc', and in Emily Brontë's mournful lyrics ('I'll walk where my own nature would be leading – / Where the wild wind blows on the mountain-side'). On their mountainside the snow continues to fall, and it clumps on the outside of the tent, muffling the sounds they make. After a fitful night, Mallory wakes to find himself mired in two inches of snow. Twitching back the tent door, he can see cyclones of ice crystals, gyring and twisting in the air. And beyond them just whiteness: whiteness and the scream of the wild wind.

There is no option but to pull out. Every day spent up high, under such conditions, is at a cost to their bodies. The climbers and the porters retreat right back to Base Camp. Fifty porters have deserted, slipped away into the storm and back to their families and their farms at lower levels. A hospital is set up at Base Camp, and the injuries inflicted by the cold are treated. Frostbite, snow-blindness and hypothermia are ubiquitous. One Tibetan porter dies from a brain clot induced by the altitude. Another has to have his boots cut off because his legs are in so much pain, only to reveal that his feet are darkly purpled with frostbite up to his ankles, as though he has stood in ink. This porter dies too.

Mallory, miraculously, has remained fit, and he chafes at the delay. He wants to be up there, getting the job done. 'The retreat is only a temporary setback,' he declares in a letter. 'Action is only suspended. The issue must shortly be decided. The next time we walk up the Rongbuk Glacier will be the last.'

Around the pale boulders and among the stores boxes at Base Camp stride glossy ravens, opportunists who have come to try their luck while everything is in such disarray. They tilt their heads inquisitively, or hop about with both feet together, like long-jumpers, or sit in black-cloaked quorums. Fat pigeons, too, and the odd mountain sheep, come to investigate. Everest itself, when it is visible, is, as Mallory puts it, 'smoking hard': the plume of ice streams out from its summit, proving the force of the wind.

For a week they recoup and gather their strength at Base Camp. Then there is a break in the weather, and Mallory, Somervell and Norton push back up to the North Col. But the blizzards enfold them again, and the temperature drops to –24°F. They are driven back down once more to Camp II. More porters are injured by the cold, and the climbers are starting to suffer psychologically as well as physically. Even Mallory is no longer as optimistic. 'Dear Girl,' he writes to Ruth on 27 May, 'this has been a bad time altogether – I look back on tremendous efforts & exhaustions & dismal looking out of a tent door on to a world of snow and vanishing hopes – & yet, & yet, & yet there have been a good many things to set on the other side.'

And then, as if to reward his refusal to despair absolutely, there is a window in the weather. The wind drops, and there is sunshine. This is it. Mallory writes a penultimate letter to Ruth, telling her that they will make the bid. 'The candle is burning out & I must stop. Darling I wish you the best I can – that your anxiety will be at an end before you get this – with the best news, which will also be the quickest.'

The col is reached, and camps are set higher up the ridge. As arranged, the first proper attempt is made by the climbing pair of Somervell and Norton, without oxygen. They make good progress, keeping just off the brink of the ridge, where they are out of the wind, but where the terrain is more difficult. It is, writes Norton afterwards, like climbing up giant overlapping roof tiles. There is nothing to grip on to; everything is trying to shuck you off. Somervell has to stop, but Norton presses on to 28,000 feet before he realizes that he will die if he does not turn back. Precariously he descends the slabs, and meets Somervell. They descend together back towards the col, with Norton perhaps twenty yards ahead of Somervell. Suddenly Somervell coughs hard, agonizingly hard, and feels something from inside him, some object, detach itself and jam in his throat. He begins to choke to death. He cannot breathe, nor can he shout to Norton. Norton turns, but thinks that Somervell is hanging back to make a sketch of the mountain. No, he is hanging back to die. He sits down in the snow, and watches Norton walk on away from him. Then – a final effort – he hammers his chest and throat with his clenched fist, and simultaneously coughs as hard as he can. The thing dislodges itself and jumps into his mouth. He spits it out on to the snow. It is a chunk of his larynx, killed by frostbite.

Somervell and Norton descend to Base Camp, and Irvine and Mallory prepare to leave the North Col. On the morning of 6 June they have a last breakfast of sardines, biscuits and chocolate inside the sagging A-frame tents, and then get out on to the sterile, stamped-down snow of the col to make final preparations for the ascent. Each man has two big silver pods of oxygen strapped to a frame on his back: they look like early Jet-Pack Willys, as though they could just crank a lever and lift off vertically for the summit. They're wearing thick puttees, mitts and flying-ace goggles with silver rims to protect them from snow-blindness.

They proceed without incident up to Camps V and VI, and early on 8 June they depart for the summit. The air is clear when they begin to climb, but within hours a fine and oddly luminous mist has begun to gather about the mountain. Noel Odell, watching from a vantage point at 26,000 feet on the mountain, sees two black dots moving along the summit ridge. Then the mist closes around them.

Before they leave the mountain, the surviving climbers build a pyramidal cairn of stones. Embedded in it are slates, on which they scratch the names of the twelve men who have died for the mountain during the three expeditions. Nine of the bodies have not been recovered, but no one will forget their resting place, for it is marked by the biggest cenotaph in the world.

The trek back is a grim time. The Great War is only six years gone, and the empty chairs, the extra elbow-room at the dining table, the sense of ghosts – all of this has already been well practised by this generation. But practice makes it no less morbid. Everyone half-expects the hand on the tent flap in the middle of the night, the unexpected return from beyond the pale.

'The Last to Leave'. Note the memorial cairn in the middle of the foreground ridge. Everest rears up behind, 'smoking hard'. Photographer Bentley Beetham. © Royal Geographical Society.

At the Mallorys' home in Cambridge, on the evening of 19 June, a telegraph arrives, composed in the staccato heartlessness of telegraphese. 'Committee deeply regret receive bad news', it begins. Ruth gathers up her children and takes them into her bed, and tells them, and they all cry together. For weeks afterwards, Mallory's letters to her keep arriving – missives from the dead.

Almost as soon as he died, the process began of turning Mallory the man into Mallory the myth. Norman Collie, the Secretary of the Royal Geographical Society, sent a telegraph to Base Camp. 'Heroic

Achievements,' read his message, 'all deeply moved by glorious deaths.' *The Times* concurred, running an obituary for Mallory and Irvine which emphasized the fineness of their deaths and professed certainty that 'they themselves could hardly have chosen a better end'. For Arthur Hinks, the Secretary of the Mount Everest Committee, the deaths were mitigated by 'the knowledge that they died somewhere higher than any man had ever been before, and it is possible for their relatives to think of them as lying perhaps even at the summit'. Tom Longstaff, the climber who had been on the mountain with Mallory in 1922, picked up on the same idea. 'Now they'll never grow old,' he wrote, 'and I am very sure they would not change places with any one of us.'

The most astonishing response, however, came from Francis Younghusband. 'He knew the dangers before him and was prepared to meet them,' he wrote of Mallory:

But he was a man of wisdom and imagination as well as daring. He could see all that success meant. Everest was the embodi- ment of the physical forces of the world. Against it he had to pit the spirit of man . . . Perhaps he never exactly formulated it, yet in his mind must have been present the idea of 'all or nothing'. Of the two alternatives, to turn back a third time, or to die, the latter was for Mallory probably the easiest. The agony of the first would be more than he as a man, as a mountaineer, and as an artist, could endure . . .

It is an extraordinary idea; that Mallory should have chosen to die as an act of artistic formalism. To return thwarted but alive would, implies Younghusband, have been intolerable to him: far more artistic – far more aesthetically pleasing – to succeed, or to die up there. And, certainly, Mallory's story has a purity of form or plot about it, which has contributed to its survival in the imagination.

It is, structurally, a myth or a legend. Three times the beautiful
Mallory – brave Sir Galahad – ventures into the unknown at the
risk of his life, leaving behind the woman he loves. Twice he is
repelled, and the third time, returning despite his better judgement, he disappears into a cloud of unknowing.

So perhaps Younghusband, for all his brassy rhetoric, was right.
Perhaps the pressure felt by Mallory to conform to an archetype – to
push on until there was no turning back, to *either* death *or* glory, but
not failure – affected his decision-making on that day in June.
Everyone is susceptible to this pressure. In ways that are for the most
part imperceptible to us, we all bend our lives to fit the templates
with which myths and archetypes provide us. We all tell ourselves
stories, and bring our futures into line with those stories, however
much we cherish the sense of newness, of originality, about our lives.

The deaths of Mallory and Irvine seemed to almost nobody a
waste of life: a fruitless stealing away of a family man, and yet another
bright young boy from Oxford, for nothing more meaningful than
altitude. Nobody, except the families and friends of the men who had
died. The Irvines were devastated. Irvine's mother would not relin-
quish the belief that her son might one day arrive home, and for years
kept a light on in the porch of their house so he could see the way
back. And there was Ruth, of course, whose world had been
destroyed. She looked, Mallory's mother noticed through the haze of
her own grief, like 'a stately lily with its head broken and hanging
down'. To Geoffrey Winthrop Young, Ruth wrote despairingly: 'Oh
Geoffrey, if only it hadn't happened. It so easily might not have . . .'

In May of 1999, seventy-five years after he had disappeared,
Mallory's body was found by a search party. He was at an altitude of

nearly 27,000 feet, face down on the steep shelves of talus on Everest's north face, his arms flung up and out as though he had halted himself as he slid by digging his nails into the rock.

Mallory's clothes had been torn from his corpse by decades of wind and frost, and lay in rags. But the extreme cold had preserved his body. His back still undulated with muscle beneath skin that was bleached bright white. Up there, his body had not putrefied, it had petrified – his flesh looked like nothing so much as stone. When pictures of Mallory's corpse were released to the world's media, many commentators likened it to a white marble statue. In death as in life, for Mallory had been a man of unusual physical beauty whose appearance provoked ecstatic comparisons with classical sculpture from the men and women who fluttered around him. '*Mon Dieu!* George Mallory!' exclaimed Lytton Strachey famously after first seeing him in 1909. 'My hand trembles, my heart palpitates, my whole being swoons away at the words . . . he's six foot high, with the body of an athlete by Praxiteles, and a face – oh incredible.' Strachey's twittery comparison of Mallory with a Praxitelean sculpture in white marble would harden, ninety years later, into a macabre reality.

Mallory didn't know why he kept going back to Everest. Time and again, when he was asked, he rhetorically threw up his hands. To a questioner in a lecture in the United States in 1923: 'I suppose we go back to Everest . . . because in a word we can't help it.' In a letter to his friend Rupert Thompson: 'Perhaps you will be able to tell me why I embarked on an adventure such as this?' And, immortally, to a New York reporter in 1922 who asked about his reasons for return- ing to the mountain: 'Because it's there.' But then explorers, as Francis Spufford has observed, are notoriously bad at saying why.

In a way it doesn't matter why. Mallory went to Everest, and didn't come back, and that's that. We don't have a satisfactory or compre- hensive explanation for his behaviour, but that doesn't make the Mallory myth any less powerful. That's the way of myth. It acts, as

Roland Barthes put it, 'economically' – it 'abolishes the complexity of human acts, it gives them the simplicity of essences . . . it establishes a blissful clarity: things appear to mean something by themselves'.

In an important sense, however, it *is* possible to say why Mallory did what he did – and it is possibly we who are better placed than he was to answer the question he was asked so often, and failed to answer. We are better able than Mallory to notice the emotional traditions which he inherited and cultivated, and which made him so susceptible to possession by Everest. And that is in part what this book has tried to do – to understand why, historically, Mallory found so much more to cherish in the mountains than on the plains.

Since his death, Mallory has become a new and potent element of the mountain worship which cost him his life. He stands in history as a diffuser, dispersing and proliferating the spell of the mountains, casting it even wider. The fact that he, like so many before and after him, died out of love for high mountains has not weakened their strange attractive gravity; it has fortified it. Posthumously, Mallory has perpetuated the very feelings which killed him – he has made even more glorious the mountains of the mind.

9

The Snow Hare

Wonder is the first of all the passions

RENÉ DESCARTES, 1645

George Mallory was an extreme case, of course. He was someone who risked, and eventually lost, everything he held dear in his passion for a single mountain. Millions of people before and after Mallory, myself included, have found much to desire in such a hostile, unpredictable, elemental form of landscape as mountains. But for most of these millions of people, myself included, the attraction of mountains has had more to do with beauty and strangeness than with risk and loss.

Mountains seem to answer an increasing imaginative need in the West. More and more people are discovering a desire for them, and a powerful solace in them. At bottom, mountains, like all wildernesses, challenge our complacent conviction – so easy to lapse into – that the world has been made for humans by humans. Most of us exist for most of the time in worlds which are humanly arranged, themed and controlled. One forgets that there are environments which do not respond to the flick of a switch or the twist of a dial, and which have their own rhythms and orders of existence. Mountains correct this amnesia. By speaking of greater forces than we can possibly invoke, and by confronting us with greater spans of time than we can possibly envisage, mountains refute our excessive trust in the man-made. They pose profound questions about our durability and the importance of our schemes. They induce, I suppose, a modesty in us.

Mountains also reshape our understandings of ourselves, of our own interior landscapes. The remoteness of the mountain world – its harshnesses and its beauties – can provide us with a valuable perspective down on to the most familiar and best charted regions of our lives. It can subtly reorient us and readjust the points from which we take our bearings. In their vastness and in their intricacy, mountains stretch out the individual mind and compress it simultaneously: they make it aware of its own immeasurable acreage and reach and, at the same time, of its own smallness.

Ultimately and most importantly, mountains quicken our sense of wonder. The true blessing of mountains is not that they provide a challenge or a contest, something to be overcome and dominated (although this is how many people have approached them). It is that they offer something gentler and infinitely more powerful: they make us ready to credit marvels – whether it is the dark swirls which water makes beneath a plate of ice, or the feel of the soft pelts of moss which form on the lee sides of boulders and trees. Being in the mountains reignites our astonishment at the simplest transactions of the physical world: a snowflake a millionth of an ounce in weight falling on to one's outstretched palm, water patiently carving a runnel in a face of granite, the apparently motiveless shift of a stone in a scree-filled gully. To put a hand down and feel the ridges and scores in a rock where a glacier has passed, to hear how a hillside comes alive with moving water after a rain shower, to see late summer light filling miles of landscape like an inexhaustible liquid – none of these is a trivial experience. Mountains return to us the priceless capacity for wonder which can so insensibly be leached away by modern existence, and they urge us to apply that wonder to our own everyday lives.

❄

Late one January, three friends and I climbed Beinn a'Chaorainn, the Hill of the Rowan, near Loch Laggan in Scotland. The day began magnificently. Galleons of cloud were at full sail in the sky, racing slowly over the blueness. The sunshine was hard and bright, the snow tuning the light to its own white frequency. Despite the coldness of the air, or perhaps because of it, as the four of us walked into the mountain I could feel the blood pulsing warmly in my toes and fingers, and the sun burning on the edges of my cheeks.

From the roadside the Hill of the Rowan rises to three distinct tops. On its east flank, visible and forbidding, are two glacier-carved cirques which were gouged out of the mountain during the Pleistocene. That day the steep cliffs of the cirques were dense with ice, which flashed and glittered in the sunlight as we approached them. We passed first through a copse of pine trees, and then emerged on to open ground, where we crossed several wide swathes of sphagnum moss. In summer these would have been tremulous and brimming with rainfall, as wobbly as water-beds. But winter had hammered them into stasis and glazed them with ice. Looking down into the clear ice as I walked over it, I could see the moss, dense and colourful as a carpet, yellow-green stars of butterwort dotted here and there.

We began to ascend one of the east-facing ridges of the mountain, which separated the two icy cirques. As we climbed, the weather changed its mood. The clouds thickened and slowed in the sky. The light became unstable, flicking from silver to dirty grey. After an hour of climbing it began to snow heavily.

Approaching the top of the mountain, we were in near white-out conditions, and it was hard to separate the air and the land. It had become much colder. My gloves had frozen into rigid shells, which clunked hollowly when I knocked them together, and a thick scab of white ice had built up on my balaclava where my breath came through it, like a clumsy clown's mouth.

A few hundred yards from the summit the ridge flattened out, and we were able to unrope safely. The others stopped for something to eat, but I moved on ahead, wanting to enjoy the solitude of the white-out. The wind was blowing along the ridge towards me, and under its invisible pressure everything was on the move. Millions of particles of snow dust streamed just above the ground in a continuous flow. Rounded chunks of old hard snow were being blown reluctantly along, skidding over the surface of the ridge. And the big soft flakes which were falling from the sky were being driven into me by the wind. They walloped almost soundlessly against my clothing, and I built up a thin fur of snow on my windward side. It seemed as though I were wading upcurrent in a loose white river. I could see no more than five yards in any direction, and I felt utterly and excitingly alone. The world beyond the whirled snow became unimportant, almost unimaginable. I could have been the last person on the planet.

After several minutes' walking I reached the small summit plateau of the mountain and stopped. A few paces away, sitting and contemplating me, hunkered back on its huge hind legs, its tall ears twitching, was a snow hare. It seemed curious at this apparition on its mountain-top, but unalarmed. The hare was a clean white all over, except for its black tail, a small patch of grey on its chest and the two black rims of its ears. It moved on a few paces in its odd gait, its rear legs shunting its hindquarters slowly forward and up, almost over its head. Then it stopped again. For half a minute we stood there in the blowing snow, in the strange silence of the snowstorm. Me with my clown's mouth of ice, the hare with its lush white coat and polished black eyes.

And then my friends emerged like spectres from the white-out, their climbers' hardware clanking. Immediately the hare kicked away with a spurt of snow, swerving and zigzagging off into the blizzard, delicately but urgently, its black tail bobbing long after its body had disappeared.

I stayed on the top of the mountain for a while and let the others walk on ahead to begin the descent. I thought about the snow hare; about how for an animal like this to cross one's path was to be reminded that it had a path too – that I had crossed the snow hare's path as much as it had crossed mine. Then my mind moved away from the mountain-top. The solitude I had experienced in the white-out on the ridge had been replaced by a sense of the distance invisibly before me. I no longer felt cocooned by the falling snow, I felt accommodated by it, extended by it – part of the hundreds of miles of landscape over which the snow was falling. I thought east, to where the snow would be falling over the 1,000 million-year-old granite backs of the Cairngorm mountains. I thought north, to where snow would silently be covering the empty wilderness of the Monadhliaths, the Grey Hills. I thought west, to where snow would be falling on the great peaks of the Rough Bounds of Knoydart – Ladhar Bheinn, the Hill of the Claw; Meall Buidhe, the Yellow Hill; and Luinne Bheinn, the Hill of Anger. I thought of the snow falling across ridge on ridge of the invisible hills, and I thought too that there was nowhere at that moment I would rather be.

Acknowledgements

The history of mountains and mountaineering is by no means a trackless waste. More than once I have found myself wandering lost in a blizzard of information and ideas, and have only regained the path by following footprints not my own. Two books above all are to be thanked. The first is Simon Schama's *Landscape and Memory*, which expressed and extended with rigour and elegance my own rudimentary sense of landscape as a confection of imagination and geology. The second is Francis Spufford's magnificent cultural history, *I May Be Some Time*, about the imaginative history of polar exploration, a book which I encountered halfway through writing *Mountains of the Mind*.

I should like to thank those editors who have kept me supplied with review material, some of it mountainous and some of it not, throughout the writing of this book. I am very grateful for their trust and encouragement in allowing me word space: many of the images and ideas in this book were first tested out in newsprint. In particular I should like to thank Steve King at *The Economist*, James Francken at the *London Review of Books*, Stephanie Merritt, Robert McCrum and Jonathan Heawood at the *Observer*, Mark Amory at the *Spectator*, and Lindsay Duguid at the *Times Literary Supplement*. And thank you so much to Lucy Lethbridge for giving me a chance in the first place.

Gratitude is also extended for a variety of reasons to Richard Baggaley, John Brunner, Arthur Burns, Ben Butler-Cole, Guy Dennis, Dinny Gollop, Jo Griffiths, Peter Hansen, Robin Hodgkin, Thelma and Bill Lovell, George and Barbara Macfarlane, James Macfarlane, Garry Martin, Teddy Moynihan, Dan Neill, Robert Potts, David Quentin, Nick Seddon, Andy Shaw, John Stubbs, Captain Toby Till, Eammon Trollope, Simon Williams, Mark Wormald and Ed Young.

I should also like to thank: Robert Douglas-Fairhurst for his double-agency as my doctoral supervisor – both looking over my work and overlooking its absence; the Department of Physics, Heriot-Watt University; Mark Bolland for sending me unbidden his thesis, 'Nietzsche and Mountains' (University of Durham, 1996); and Ralph O'Connor for letting me see his forthcoming book on literary spectacle and nineteenth-century geology.

Santanu Das, Olie Hayes, Henry Hitchings, Julia Lovell, John and Rosamund Macfarlane, Ralph O'Connor, and Edward and Alison Peck all read the book in its draft stages. The perspicuity and respective expertises they brought to bear on it were invaluable.

I gratefully acknowledge Christina Hardyment and the other executors of the Arthur Ransome estate for permission to use a line from *Swallows and Amazons* as the epigraph to Chapter 6; John Macfarlane for permission to reproduce the illustrations on pp. 181 and 279; Rosamund Macfarlane for permission to reproduce the photographs on the endpapers, and on pp. 185, 212 and 221; the Master and Fellows of Magdalene College, Cambridge, and the Mallory family for permission to read and reproduce sections from George Mallory's letters; Sandra Noel for permission to reproduce the illustration on p. 247; the Royal Geographical Society for permission to reproduce the illustrations on pp. 264 and 269; Audrey Salkeld for permission to reproduce the illustration on p. 235; and the Spurrier family for permission to reproduce Steven Spurrier's map on p. 197. The illustrations on pp. 28, 30, 36, 46, 61, 118, 126, 130, 151 and 230 are reproduced by permission of the Syndics of Cambridge University Library. All other illustrations are copyright the author. I would like especially to thank: my agent Jessica Woollard, who plucked *Mountains of the Mind* from a prodigious slush pile, and told me to put an 'I' into it, and who has been a marvellous critic and enthusiast ever since; my editors, Sara Holloway at Granta and Dan Frank at Pantheon, for their brilliance at seeing what was wrong with the book and how to right it, and what was right with the book and how to keep it; my mother, Rosamund Macfarlane, for allowing me to use her magnificent photographs, and also for her ceaseless encouragement, enthusiasm and technical expertise with the illustrations; Julia for everything.

Above all I should like to thank my grandparents Edward and Alison Peck, for their enthusiasm, love and knowledge. *Mountains of the Mind* is dedicated to them.

Selected List of Sources

The literature on mountains is appropriately vast. The following is a selection of the books and articles which have contributed to *Mountains of the Mind*. Sources are arranged in alphabetical order per chapter. Each source is noted only once, in the first chapter in which it appeared. At the end is a list of the books which were of general use.

Chapter 1 Possession

Malcolm Andrews, *The Search for the Picturesque: Landscape Aesthetics and Tourism in Britain, 1760–1800* (Aldershot: Scolar, 1990)

John Ball, ed., *Peaks, Passes and Glaciers: a Series of Excursions by Members of the Alpine Club* (London: Longmans, Green & Co., 1859)

James Boswell, *The Journal of a Tour to the Hebrides, with Samuel Johnson* (London: C. Dilly, 1785)

Apsley Cherry-Garrard, *The Worst Journey in the World* (London: Penguin, 1922)

Bernard Comment, *The Panorama* (London: Reaktion, 1999)

G. R. De Beer, *Early Travellers in the Alps* (London: Sidgwick & Jackson, 1930)

——, *Alps and Men* (London: Edward Arnold, 1932)

Daniel Defoe, *A Tour through the Whole Island of Great Britain* (London: Dent; New York: Dutton, 1962, first published 1724–7)

Claire Eliane Engel, *A History of Mountaineering in the Alps* (London: George Allen & Unwin Ltd, 1950)

R. Fitzsimons, *The Baron of Piccadilly: the Travels and Entertainments of Albert Smith 1816–1860* (London: Geoffrey Bles, 1967)

Maurice Herzog, *Annapurna*, trans. Nea Morin and Janet Adam Smith, (London: Jonathan Cape, 1952)

John Hunt, *The Ascent of Everest* (London: Hodder and Stoughton, 1953)

U. C. Knoepflmacher and G. B. Tennyson, eds., *Nature and the Victorian Imagination* (Berkeley; London: University of California Press, 1977)

Arnold Lunn, *The Matterhorn Centenary* (London: George Allen & Unwin Ltd, 1965)

John Mandeville, *The Travels of Sir John Mandeville*, trans. C. W. R. D. Moseley (Harmondsworth: Penguin, 1983)

Alfred Mummery, *My Climbs in the Alps and the Caucasus* (London: Fisher Unwin, 1898)

John Murray, *A Glance at Some of the Beauties and Sublimities of Switzerland: with Excursive Remarks on the Various Objects of Interest, Presented during a Tour through Its Picturesque Scenery* (London: Longman, Rees, Orme, Brown and Green, 1829)

E. F. Norton et al., *The Fight for Everest: 1924* (London: Edwin Arnold, 1925)

John Ruskin, *Modern Painters*, 5 vols. (Volume IV, *Of Mountain Beauty*) (London: George Allen & Sons, 1910; first published 1843, 1846, 1856, 1860)

Horace-Bénédict de Saussure, *Voyages dans les Alpes, précédés d'un essai sur l'Histoire Naturelle des environs de Genève* (Neuchâtel: Samuel Fauche, 1779–96)

Ernest Shackleton, *South* (London: Heinemann, 1970, first published 1920)

Albert Smith, *The Story of Mont Blanc* (London: Bogue, 1853)

Leslie Stephen, *The Playground of Europe* (London: Longmans, Green & Co., 1871)

Edward Whymper, *Scrambles amongst the Alps in the Years 1860–69* (London: John Murray, 1871)

Frank Worsley, *Endurance: an Epic of Polar Adventure* (London: Philip Allan & Co., 1931)

Francis Younghusband, *The Epic of Mount Everest* (London: Edward Arnold, 1926)

Chapter 2 The Great Stone Book

Robert Bakewell, *An Introduction to Geology, illustrative of the general structure of the earth; comprising the elements of the science, and an outline of the geology and mineral geography of England* (London: J. Harding, 1813)

Georges Louis-Leclerc Buffon, *Natural History: Containing a Theory of the Earth*, trans. J. S. Barr, 10 vols. (London: J. S. Barr, 1797, first published 1749–88)

Thomas Burnet, *The Sacred Theory of the Earth*, ed. Basil Willey (London: Centaur Press, 1965, first published in Latin in 1681, and in English in 1684)

Georges Cuvier, *Essay on the Theory of the Earth*, trans. and ed. Robert Jameson, 5th edn (Edinburgh: William Blackwood, 1827, first published 1812)

Charles Darwin, *The Voyage of the Beagle* (London: Dent; New York; Dutton, 1967, first published 1839)

Isabella Duncan, *Pre-Adamite Man; or, the Story of Our Old Planet & Its Inhabitants, Told by Scripture & Science* (London: Saunders, Otley and Co., 1860)

Richard Fortey, *The Hidden Landscape* (London: Pimlico, 1994)

Douglas Freshfield, *The Life of Horace Bénédict de Saussure* (London: Edward Arnold, 1920)

Marjorie Hope Nicolson, *Mountain Gloom and Mountain Glory: the Development of the Aesthetics of the Infinite* (Ithaca: Cornell University Press, 1959)

James Hutton, *Theory of the Earth* (Weinheim: H. R. Engelman, 1959, first published 1785–99)

Charles Lyell, *The Principles of Geology: an Attempt to Explain the Former Changes of the Earth's Surface by Reference to Causes Now in Operation*, 3 vols. (London: John Murray, 1830–33)

John McPhee, *Basin and Range* (New York: Farrar, Straus and Giroux, 1981)

Hugh Miller, *The Testimony of the Rocks or Geology in Its Bearings on the Two Theologies Natural and Revealed* (Edinburgh: William P. Nimmo, 1878, first published 1857)

John Playfair, *Illustrations of the Huttonian Theory of the Earth* (London: Cadell and Davies, 1802)

Martin Rudwick, *Scenes from Deep Time: Early Pictorial Representations of the Prehistoric World* (Chicago: Chicago University Press, 1992)

Jonathan Smith, *Fact and Feeling: Baconian Science and the Nineteenth-Century Literary Imagination* (Madison, Wis.: University of Wisconsin Press, 1994)

Antonio Snider-Pelligrini, *Creation and Its Mysteries Revealed* (Paris: 1858)

Alfred Wegener, *The Origins of Continents and Oceans* (London: 1966, first published 1915)

Simon Winchester, *The Map That Changed the World* (London: Viking, 2001)

William Whiston, *A New Theory of the Earth*, 4th edn (London: Sam Tooke and Benjamin Motte, 1725)

John Woodward, *The Natural History of the Earth*, trans. Benjamin Holloway (London: Thomas Edlin, 1726)

Chapter 3 The Pursuit of Fear

Edmund Burke, *A Philosophical Enquiry into the Origin of Our Ideas of the Sublime and Beautiful*, ed. Adam Phillips (Oxford: World's Classics, 1990, first published 1757)

George Byron, *Letters and Journals*, ed. Leslie A. Marchand, 12 vols. (London: John Murray, 1973–81)

Charles Darwin, *The Origin of Species by Means of Natural Selection* (Oxford: Oxford University Press, 1998, first published 1859)

Elaine Freedgood, *Victorians Writing about Risk* (Cambridge: Cambridge University Press, 2000)

Yi Fu Tuan, *Landscapes of Fear* (Oxford: Blackwell, 1979)

Frances Ridley Havergal, *Poetical Works*, 2 vols. (London: James Nisbet & Co., 1884)

Samuel Johnson, *A Journey to the Western Islands of Scotland* (Oxford: Clarendon Press, 1985, first published 1775)

John Ruskin, *The Letters of John Ruskin*, ed. E. T. Cook and Alexander Wedderburn, 2 vols. (London: G. Allen, 1909)

Robert Service, *Collected Poems of Robert Service* (London: Benn, 1978)

Samuel Smiles, *Self-help* (London: John Murray, 1958, first published 1859)

Samuel Taylor Coleridge, *Collected Letters of Samuel Taylor Coleridge*, ed. E. L. Griggs, 6 vols. (London: 1956–71)

John Tyndall, *Mountaineering in 1861* (London: Longman, Green & Co., 1862)

Chapter 4 Glaciers and Ice: the Streams of Time

Louis Agassiz, *Études sur les glaciers* (Neuchâtel: Solothurn, 1840)

Henry Alford, 'Inscription for a Block of Granite on the Surface of the Mer de Glace', in *The Poetical Works of Henry Alford*, 4th edn (London: Strahan, 1865)

Karl Baedeker, *Handbook for Travellers to Switzerland and the Adjacent Portions of Italy, Savoy and the Tyrol*, 4th edn (London: John Murray, 1869)

Gillian Beer, *Open Fields* (Oxford: Clarendon Press, 1996)

Marc-Theodore Bourrit, *A Relation of a Journey to the Glaciers in the Duchy of Savoy*, trans. Charles and Frederick Davy (Norwich: Richard Beatniffe, 1779)

Samuel Butler, *Life and Habit* (London: Trübner, 1878)

Frank Cunningham, *James David Forbes, Pioneer Scottish Glaciologist* (Edinburgh: Scottish Academic Press, 1990)

James L. Dyson, *The World of Ice* (London: The Cresset Press, 1963)

James David Forbes, *Travels through the Alps of Savoy* (Edinburgh: Adam and Charles Black, 1843)

Edward Peck, 'The Search for Khan Tengri', *Alpine Journal*, vol. 101, no. 345 (1996), 131–9

Richard Pococke, *A Description of the East and Some Other Countries*, 2 vols. (London: J. & R. Knapton, 1743–5)

Robert Ker Porter, *Travels in Georgia, Persia, Armenia, Ancient Babylon, etc.*, 2 vols. (London: Longman, 1821–2)

John Ruskin, *The Collected Works*, ed. E. T. Cook and A. Wedderburn, 39 vols. (London: G. Allen, 1903–12)

Percy Bysshe Shelley, *Peacock's Memoirs of Shelley: with Shelley's Letters to Peacock*, ed. H. F. B. Brett-Smith (London: H. Frowde, 1909)

John Tyndall, *The Glaciers of the Alps* (London: John Murray, 1860)

Mark Twain, *A Tramp Abroad* (London: Chatto & Windus, 1901, first published 1880)

William Windham, *Account of the Glacieres or Ice Alps in Savoy* (London: 1744)

Chapter 5 Altitude: the Summit and the View

Richard D. Altick, *The Shows of London* (Cambridge, Mass.: The Belknap Press, 1978)

John Auldjo, *Narrative of an Ascent to the Summit of Mont Blanc* (London: Longmans, 1828)

Gaston Bachelard, *Air and Dreams*, trans. Edith R. Farrell and C. Frederick Farrell (Dallas: The Dallas Institute Publication, 1988, first published 1943)

Mick Conefrey and Tim Jordan, *Mountain Men* (London: Boxtree, 2001)

Alain Corbin, *The Lure of the Sea*, trans. Jocelyn Phelps (Paris, 1988, London: Penguin, 1990)

John Evelyn, *The Diary of John Evelyn*, ed. E. S. de Beer, 6 vols. (Oxford: Clarendon Press, 1955)

Bruce Haley, *The Healthy Body and Victorian Culture* (Cambridge, Mass.: Harvard University Press, 1978)

John Muir, *My First Summer in the Sierra* (Boston: Houghton Mifflin, 1911)

Jim Ring, *How the English Made the Alps* (London: John Murray, 2000)

Percy Bysshe Shelley, *The Poems of Shelley*, ed. Geoffrey Matthews and Kelvin Everest, 2 vols. (London: Longmans, 1989)

Joe Simpson, *The Beckoning Silence* (London: Jonathan Cape, 2002)

Andrew Wilson, *The Abode of Snow*, 2nd edn (Edinburgh: London: William Blackwood & Sons, 1876)

Geoffrey Winthrop Young, *The Influence of Mountains upon the Development of Human Intelligence* (London: Jackson, Son & Company, 1957)

Chapter 6 Walking off the Map

J. R. L. Anderson, *The Ulysses Factor* (London: Hodder & Stoughton, 1970)

Colonel S. G. Burrard and H. H. Hayden, *A Sketch of the Geography and Geology of the Himalaya Mountains and Tibet* (Calcutta: Government of India, Geological Survey of India, 1907–8)

Joseph Conrad, *Heart of Darkness* (London: Penguin, 1973, first published 1902 as a novella, 1899 as a serial)

——, *Lord Jim* (Edinburgh: Blackwoods, 1900)

George Eliot, *Middlemarch*, ed. W. J. Harvey (London: Penguin, 1985, first published 1871–2)

Douglas Freshfield, *The Exploration of the Caucasus*, 2 vols. (London: Edward Arnold, 1896)

R. L. G. Irving, *The Mountain Way* (London: J. M. Dent & Sons, 1938)

Richard Jefferies, *Bevis, the Story of a Boy* (London: Duckworth & Co., 1904)

Jon Krakauer, *Into the Wild* (London: Pan, 1999)

Barry Lopez, *Arctic Dreams: Imagination and Desire in a Northern Landscape* (New York: Charles Scribner's Sons, 1986)

Roderick Nash, *Wilderness and the American Mind* (New Haven; London: Yale University Press, 1973)

Colonel R. H. Phillimore, *Historical Records of the Survey of India*, 4 vols. (Dehra Dun: Survey of India, 1958)

J. B. Priestley, *Apes and Angels* (London: Methuen & Co., 1928)

Arthur Ransome, *Swallows and Amazons* (London: Jonathan Cape, 1930)

Eric Shipton, *Blank on the Map* (London: Hodder and Stoughton, 1936)

Susan Solnit, *Wanderlust: a History of Walking* (London: Penguin, 2000)

Wilfred Thesiger, *The Life of My Choice* (London: Collins, 1987)

Chapter 7   A New Heaven and a New Earth

Abbé Pluche, *Spectacle de la Nature . . . Being Discourses on Such PARTICULARS of Natural History as Were Thought Most Proper to Excite the Curiosity and Form the Minds of Youth*, trans. Mr Humphreys, 3rd edn (London: L. Davis, 1736)

Charles Dickens, *Little Dorrit*, ed. J. Holloway (London: Penguin Classics, 1985, first published 1855–7)

Conrad Gesner, *On the Admiration of Mountains*, trans. W. Dock (San Francisco: The Grabhorn Press, 1937)

C. S. Lewis, *The Lion, the Witch, and the Wardrobe: a story for children* (London: Geoffrey Bles, 1950)

Claude Reichler and Roland Ruffieux, *Le Voyage en Suisse* (Paris, Robert Laffont, 1998)

Jacob Scheuchzer, *Itinera per Helvetiae Alpinas Regiones* (London: Vander, 1723)

Barbara Maria Stafford, *Voyage into Substance: Art, Science, Nature, and the Illustrated Travel Account, 1760–1840* (Massachusetts: MIT Press, 1984)

John Tyndall, *Hours of Exercise in the Alps* (London: Longmans, 1871)

Chapter 8   Everest

Roland Barthes, *Mythologies*, trans. Annette Lavers (London: Paladin, 1973)

Peter Bishop, *The Myth of Shangri-La: Tibet, Travel Writing and the Western Creation of Sacred Landscape* (The Athlone Press: London, 1989)

Robert Bridges, ed., *The Spirit of Man* (London: Longmans & Co., 1916)

C. G. Bruce, *Twenty Years in the Himalaya* (London: Edward Arnold & Co., 1910)

——, *The Assault on Mount Everest, 1922* (London: Edward Arnold & Co., 1923)

John Buchan, *The Last Secrets* (London: Thomas Nelson, 1923)

Patrick French, *Younghusband* (London: HarperCollins, 1994)

Peter and Leni Gillman, *The Wildest Dream: Mallory, His Life and Conflicting Passions* (London: Headline, 2000). I publicly misjudged this fine biography when it appeared, a misjudgement for which I have apologized, but apologize again.

Michael Holroyd, *Lytton Strachey* (London: Vintage, 1995)

C. K. Howard-Bury and George Mallory, *Mount Everest: the Reconnaissance, 1921* (London: Edward Arnold & Co, 1922)

S. C. Joshi, ed., *Nepal Himalaya; Geo-ecological Perspectives* (Naini Tal: Himalayan Research Group, 1986)

John Keay, *When Men and Mountains Meet: the Explorers of the Western Himalaya* (London: John Murray, 1977)

Kenneth Mason, *Abode of Snow* (London: Diadem Books, 1987)

John Noel, *Through Tibet to Everest* (London: Edward Arnold, 1927)

David Pye, *George Leigh Mallory* (Oxford: Oxford University Press, 1927)

Cecil Godfrey Rawling, *The Great Plateau, Being an Account of Exploration in Central Tibet, 1903, and of the Gartok Expedition 1904–1905* (London: Edward Arnold, 1905)

David Robertson, *George Mallory* (London: Faber, 1969)

Royal Geographical Society and Mount Everest Foundation, *The Mountains of Central Asia* (London: Macmillan, 1987)

Audrey Salkeld and Tom Holzel, *The Mystery of Mallory and Irvine* (London: Pimlico, 1999)

J. R. Smith, *Everest: the Man and the Mountain* (London: Whittles, 1999)

Walt Unsworth, *Everest*, 3rd edn (Seattle: The Mountaineers, 2000)

C. J. Wessels, *Early Jesuit Travellers in Central Asia 1603–1721* (The Hague: Martinus Nijhoff, 1924)

Geoffrey Winthrop Young, *On High Hills* (London: Methuen, 1933)

Francis Younghusband, *Everest: the Challenge* (London: Nelson, 1936)

Chapter 9 The Snow Hare

James Joyce, *Dubliners* (London: Jonathan Cape, 1926, first published 1914)

General Sources

The *Alpine Journal*, a magnificent and venerable publication, has been an essential source of material, from its earliest avatar (as *Peaks, Passes and Glaciers*) through to the most recent issues. I have also drawn on, though not detailed, articles from *Blackwood's Edinburgh Magazine*, *Cornhill Magazine*, *Daily News*, *Philosophical Magazine*, *Philosophical Transactions of the Royal Society* and *The Times*.

Many books have been of general secondary use. Among the most valuable are Phil Bartlett, *The Undiscovered Country* (London: The Ernest Press, 1993); Ronald Clark, *The Victorian Mountaineers* (London: Batsford, 1953); Fergus Fleming, *Killing Dragons* (London: Granta, 2000); Wilfrid Noyce, *Scholar Mountaineers: Pioneers of Parnassus* (London: Dennis Dobson, 1950); Keith Thomas's superb *Man and the Natural World: Changing Attitudes in England 1500–1800* (London: Allen Lane, 1983); and Walt Unsworth, *Hold the Heights: the Foundations of Mountaineering* (London: Hodder and Stoughton, 1994). Jan Morris's *Pax Britannica* trilogy (London: Faber, 1968, 1973, 1978) provided me with an unequalled sense of what the British nineteenth century was *like*, as well as a trove of information.

The spelling of the names of Scottish mountains is a vexed business. I have adhered to the names as they are given in Donald Bennet, ed., *The Munros* (Edinburgh: The Scottish Mountaineering Trust, 1985).

Index

Keep in touch with
Granta Books:

Visit grantabooks.com to discover more.

GRANTA

LOVE OF COUNTRY
A Hebridean Journey

Madeleine Bunting

For centuries the remote beauty of the Hebrides has attracted saints and sinners, artists and writers. Journeying through these islands, Madeleine Bunting explores their magnetic pull, delving into meanings of home and belonging, and uncovers stories of tragedy, tenacious resistance, and immigration – stories that have shaped the identity of the British Isles.

'A magnificent book, a heroic journey that takes us as far into the heart as into the islands of the north-west'
Richard Holloway

'Excellent . . . I cannot think of a more intellectually challenging or rewarding travel book in recent years'
Mark Cocker, *New Statesman*

Also of interest and available from Granta Books
www.grantabooks.com

THE PHILSOPHER AND THE WOLF

Lessons from the Wild on Love, Death and Happiness

Mark Rowlands

When Mark Rowlands was twenty-seven and a young professor of philosophy, he bought a wolf cub. It was the beginning of a relationship that would come to define his life, and shape his thinking.

'Life-affirming, engrossing, thoughtful and moving'
Times Literary Supplement

'This year's most original and instructive work of popular philosophy . . . a remarkable portrait of the bond that can exist between a human being and a beast'
Financial Times

Also of interest and available from Granta Books
www.grantabooks.com

THE WILD PLACES

Robert Macfarlane

Are there any wild places left in Britain and Ireland? Or have we tarmacked, farmed and built ourselves out of wildness?

In his bewitching, inspiring and influential classic, Robert Macfarlane sets out in search of the wildness that remains.

'A wonderful evocation of Britain's natural beauty and a reminder of our need to connect with the wilderness'
The Times

'Bewitching . . . a formidable exploration by a naturalist who can unfurl a sentence – poetry really – with the breathless ease of a master angler, a writer whose ideas and reach far transcend the physical region he explores'
New York Times